W9-ADD-291

AN ECOLOGY OF COMMUNICATION

COMMUNICATION AND SOCIAL ORDER

An Aldine de Gruyter Series of Texts and Monographs

Series Editor

David R. Maines, Wayne State University

Advisory Editors

Bruce Gronbeck • Peter K. Manning • William K. Rawlins

David L. Altheide, **An Ecology of Communication: Cultural Formats of Control**

David L. Altheide and Robert Snow, **Media Worlds in the Postjournalism Era**

Joseph Bensman and Robert Lilienfeld, **Craft and Consciousness: Occupational Technique and the Development of World Images** (*Second Edition*)

Jörg R. Bergmann, **Discreet Indiscretions**

Herbert Blumer, **Industrialization as an Agent of Social Change: A Critical Analysis** (*Edited with an Introduction by David R. Maines and Thomas J. Morrione*)

Dennis Brissett and Charles Edgley (*editors*), **Life as Theater: A Dramaturgical Sourcebook** (*Second Edition*)

Richard Harvey Brown (*editor*), **Writing the Social Text: Poetics and Politics in Social Science Discourse**

Norman K. Denzin, **Hollywood Shot by Shot: Alcoholism in American Cinema**

Irwin Deutscher, Fred P. Pestello, and H. Frances G. Pestello, **Sentiments and Acts**

Pasquale Gagliardi (*editor*), **Symbols and Artifacts: Views of the Corporate Landscape** (paperback)

Bryan S. Green, **Gerontology and the Construction of Old Age: A Study in Discourse Analysis**

Jaber F. Gubrium, **Speaking of Life: Horizons of Meaning for Nursing Home Residents**

J. T. Hansen, A. Susan Owen, and Michael Patrick Madden, **Parallels: The Soldiers' Knowledge and the Oral History of Contemporary Warfare**

Emmanuel Lazega, **The Micropolitics of Knowledge: Communication and Indirect Control in Workgroups**

Niklas Luhmann, **Risk: A Sociological Theory**

David R. Maines (*editor*), **Social Organization and Social Process: Essays in Honor of Anselm Strauss**

Peter K. Manning, **Organizational Communication**

Stjepan G. Meštrović, **Durkheim and Postmodernist Culture**

R. S. Perinbanayagam, **Discursive Acts**

William K. Rawlins, **Friendship Matters: Communication, Dialectics, and the Life Course**

Dmitry Shlapentokh and Vladimir Shlapentokh, **Soviet Cinematography, 1918–1991: Ideological Conflict and Social Reality**

Anselm Strauss, **Continual Permutations of Action**

Jacqueline P. Wiseman, **The Other Half: Wives of Alcoholics and Their Social-Psychological Situation**

AN ECOLOGY OF COMMUNICATION
Cultural Formats of Control

DAVID L. ALTHEIDE

ALDINE DE GRUYTER
New York

About the Author _____

David L. Altheide is Regents Professor, School of Justice Studies, Arizona State University. A recipient of both the Premio Diego Fabbri and Charles Horton Cooley awards, Dr. Altheide was President of the Society for the Study of Symbolic Interaction in 1995–96.

Dr. Altheide is a frequent contributor to major journals, and is author of *Media Power; Creating Reality: How TV News Distorts Events;* and coauthor of *Media Logic; Bureaucracy and Freedom; Bureaucratic Propaganda;* and (with Robert P. Snow) *Media Worlds in the Postjournalism Era* (Aldine).

ALDINE DE GRUYTER
A division of Walter de Gruyter, Inc.
200 Saw Mill River Road
Hawthorne, New York 10532

This publication is printed on acid-free paper ∞

Library of Congress Cataloging-in-Publication Data

Altheide, David L.
    An ecology of communication : cultural formats of control / David
L. Altheide.
        p. cm. — (Communication and social order)
    Includes bibliographical references (p.   ) and index.
    ISBN 0-202-30532-5. — ISBN 0-202-30533-3 (pbk.)
    1. Communication and culture. I. Title. II. Series.
P94.6.A45   1995
302.2—dc20   94-44795
                                                          CIP

Manufactured in the United States of America

10 9 8 7 6 5 4 3 2 1

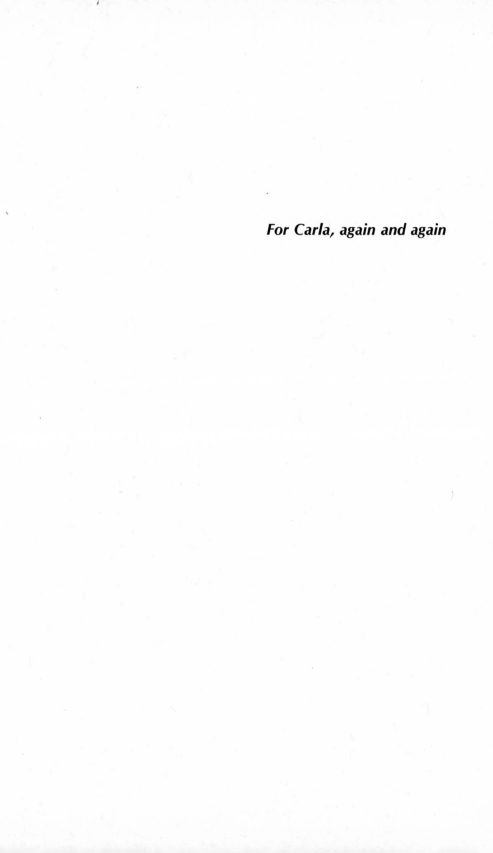

For Carla, again and again

Contents _____

Preface

This book is about social power and social control, how they are maintained, recognized, and challenged. The main interest is in some rituals, routines, and perspectives that have become commonplace in public and organizational life. There are some basic assumptions for this task. One is that social power is about controlling and enforcing the definition of a situation. Another is that those resources and particular elements that are used in defining and enforcing the definition of a situation are part of a symbolic and communicative process. Yet another major element is that the technologies and language (or discourse) of information technology and the mass media overwhelmingly are key elements of the process in our modern (and postmodern world). In short, social order is increasingly an electronically communicated and mediated order, and this has tremendous consequences for social life and especially for freedom and justice.

My focus is on the *ecology of communication*, or the structure, organization, and accessibility of various forums, media and channels of information. The challenge is to offer a perspective that joins information technology (IT) and communication (media) formats with the activities. The context of communication is addressed because the broader issue concerns social power. Social power resides less in individuals than it does in processes and communicative logics that inform how situations are defined, the sources of such definitions, and their consequences. Increasingly, such processes are involved with "records" and "procedures." It is records-as-life-and-event-documentation that haunt us more than particular individuals; it is processes and procedures-as-bureaucratic-rules-that-are-feared-and-reified that guide, yet limit, individual activity. It is, in brief, the "matrix" of information technology, formats, and activities that connects our past, present and futures in dot-to-dot-like patterns that are so taken for granted and even "believed in" that their range of implications has gone largely undetected. Indeed, for individuals to be authorized as an "appropriate person" for a position/job they must increasingly demonstrate their competence and skill in working with and through the formats and logics of information technology.

In our age, identity, biography, credibility, authority, and promise are all touched by information technology and formats of communication. Information technology has affected each of the following, and often disturbed previous distinctions and relations between each: working, eating, sleeping, loving, remembering, accounting, playing, fighting, learning, studying, and, of course, writing.

IT and the ecology of communication influence events by transforming and/or adding process to all activities: the nature, significance, and meaning of the activity may be changed; there is a "technology-trail" or trace left; it is recordable and retrievable; the trail can be treated as "objective"; activity performance is associated with the information processing (often mechanical/electronic) manipulations and processing. In our day, an increasing array of life is processed rather than lived, recorded rather than remembered and tracked rather than understood. One goal is to draw theoretical attention to the way in which activities have been changed and devised, as well as to "name" some elements of this process so that we can better understand them. A key consideration in this task is to see the connections, folding in, and integration of IT, formats, and activities. The complexity of the conceptual relationships set forth in the pages to follow challenged me to attempt to provide some spatial "models"; accordingly, a number of figures are presented, mainly in Chapter 1, in an attempt to assist those readers less familiar with a plethora of previous work on the nondeterministic but nevertheless significant contextual contributions of the mass media and information technology to cultural perspectives and social change.

Many people have contributed directly and indirectly to this work. For that reason, and when it is appropriate, I will refer to "us" or "we." Indeed, I use the term *we* more often than not, although I take full responsibility for errors and misinterpretations. My colleague and coauthor on a number of related projects, Bob Snow, can see his ideas throughout. As portions and earlier drafts of some of these materials appeared, I was fortunate to benefit from outstanding scholars. John Johnson, Carl Couch, David Maines, Norman Denzin, and Richard V. Ericson have contributed much in their patient reading of portions of this work, suggestions, and creative insights to help me move to the next "step" or "level" of analysis. My conversations with Dion Dennis have sensitized me to important issues about "cultural signs," especially that of the "market."

Portions and earlier drafts of several chapters appeared elsewhere:

Chapter 1, *The Sociological Quarterly*, 1994, 35 (4): Courtesy of JAI Press.

Chapter 2, from David Maines and Carl Couch (eds.), *Communication and Social Structure*, Springfield, IL: Charles C. Thomas, 1988: 215–30. Courtesy of Charles C. Thomas Publisher.

Chapter 5, *Symbolic Interaction*, 1992, 15(1):69–86. Courtesy of JAI Press.

Chapter 6, *The Sociological Quarterly*, 1993, 34(1). Courtesy of JAI Press.

Chapter 7, *The Sociological Quarterly*, 1987, 28(4):473–92. Courtesy of JAI Press.

The assistance on several projects by Noah Fritz (coauthor, Chapter 7) and Erdwin H. Pfuhl, Jr. (materials in Chapter 4), is gratefully acknowledged.

Support for most of the materials in Chapter 9 was partially provided by the Distinguished Research Award from the Graduate College of Arizona State University, 1990–1991, and an Invited Lecture at the Fulbright Colloquia, "Broadcast Media in Britain and the U.S.: Access and Control," University of Nottingham, September 18–20, 1992, provided an opportunity to synthesize a massive amount of data for an initial draft. The helpful assistance of journalists in the United States, United Kingdom, France, and Italy are also acknowledged. Numerous professors at the Universities of Florence, Lecce, Rome, Paris, Bradford, and Glasgow also contributed to this project. In particular, Professors Henri Peretz (Paris), Luigi Spedicato (Lecce), Greg Philo (Glasgow), Paul Rogers, James O'Connell, and Alan Bloomgarden (Bradford).

I would like to acknowledge my good fortune at living in Arizona where events like "Azscam" (an undercover operation to expose political corruption) seem to occur with regularity, and thereby provide a natural laboratory to develop further some of the key ideas in this work. Finally, I appreciate Richard Koffler's patience and encouragement for me to not miss yet another deadline as my analytic framework strained to incorporate the events of Operation Desert Storm, Operation Restore Hope, and what I refer to as "Whacko in Waco"; if, as one artist proclaimed, the song is never finished, it is also certainly true that the rapidly emerging array of events that display the impact of information technology and communication formats provides a challenging pace for any theoretical perspective. I have tried to recognize this challenge.

The Ecology of Communication and the Effective Environment

[The owner of the Boston Braves, James Gaffney] wanted a ballpark conducive to inside-the-park home runs, his favorite kind of baseball action, and that's just what he designed. The new park [Braves Field] was laid out so that the distance from home plate was 402 feet down each foul line and 550 feet to dead center. These wide-open spaces generated plenty of triples and inside-the-park homers, but the corollary was that hardly anyone could muscle the ball out of the park for a real honest-to-goodness Babe Ruth–type home run. . . .

Braves field succeeded admirably in producing inside-the-park homers. In 1921, for example, 34 out of 38 home runs hit there were of the inside-the-park variety. . . . Responding to fan demand, Braves management joined the parade and in 1928 pulled in the outfield fences by installing new bleachers in left and center fields. These shrank home-run distances to 320 feet down the left-field line, 330 feet to left center, 387 to center, and 364 feet down the right-field line. . . . [It is noted that many homeruns were hit.] Back to the drawing board. Hard to believe, but starting in 1928 the dimensions of Braves Field were altered almost annually.

—Lawrence S. Ritter, *Lost Ballparks: A Celebration of Baseball's Legendary Fields*

INTRODUCTION

Owners of baseball teams changed the playing fields to suit their teams and preferences, and changed the nature of the game. The playing fields of social life have also been altered by changes in information technology. While the fields are a spatial dimension, information technology has altered the temporal order of activities. This book examines how this is happening and what some of the consequences are for life in a postindustrial society.

Changes in communication media have altered social processes, relationships, and activities as information technology expands to mediate more social situations. While it is commonplace among social theorists that the message reflects the process by which it was constituted, they have paid much less attention to how social activities are joined interactively in a communication environment, and particularly how the techniques and

1

technology associated with certain communicative acts contribute to the action. Just as the dimensions of a baseball field contribute to the nature, style, and quality of play, so do the information technologies and organizing formats influence social activities. Seasoned fans are aware of a ballpark's contributions to a player's and team's success; they know that "playing" occurs in an important context, even if the context does not determine the outcomes. They know, for example, that one of the greatest plays of all time, Willie Mays's "over the shoulder" catch of Vic Wertz's 445-foot drive, would not be made today since no major league ball park has a field with these dimensions; Wertz's smash would be merely a home run today. These considerations form part of a fan's perspective and add immensely to the discourse of baseball, which serves to question and challenge cold "objective" facts, e.g., how many home runs a player hit in a given year or would hit today. One of the aims of this book is to contribute to the scholarly—and then "everyone's"—discourse about social activities by drawing out some crucial contextual features of contemporary social life. A related aim is to offer a perspective for examining social activities to see the relevance of information technology.

The notion that new media and technology can influence communication (cf. McLuhan 1962) can be contextualized by examining the impact of information technology in symbolic environments. Halloran's appeal for investigation into a wide range of information technologies is consistent with this book. Part of a comprehensive approach is:

> [t]o examine the introduction, application and development of the new electronic and communication technologies, the factors (for instance, finance, control and organization) which influence these processes, and related institutional changes at both national and international levels. (1986:57)

Following the insight by a host of symbolic interactionists that communication occurs in a context, as well as Barnlund's (1979) suggestion that the matrix of communication systems is most significant for understanding meaning, we examine the connections between some key elements of the social matrix involved in the definition, construction, and use of action-meaning systems in modern life. This book (1) offers a sensitizing concept (cf. Blumer 1969), *ecology of communication,* (2) to help grasp how social activities are joined with information technology, (3) to offer a perspective for reconceptualizing how communication frameworks can inform social participation, and (4) how activities can be investigated to clarify the significance of the communicative dimensions.

In its broadest terms, the ecology of communication refers to the structure, organization, and accessibility of information technology, various forums, media, and channels of information. It is incontestable that media and technology can make a difference in social life, although the nature and extent of this difference remains an issue. In order to promote this debate, the chapters that follow provide a conceptualization and perspective that joins information technology and communication (media) formats with the time and place of activities. This study is quite focused and does not address the entire range of questions about the effects of information technology on a global scale, although the pieces discussed in the following chapters would certainly be relevant for such a study. The research focus, then, is on specific activities and events as cases of the ecology of communication. But just as the emphasis is not on all societies, the emphasis is not on individuals (cf. Poster 1990) or on comparative study of diverse societies (cf. Traber 1986). Students of postmodernism and those operating with perspectives ranging from neo-Marxism to poststructuralism to critical theory offer erudite views of the role of communication technologies on subjects or individuals, including, for example, the impact of TV ads on viewers—even though actual viewers are seldom studied (cf. Poster 1990:43)! One of the major differences of our approach is that social interaction and social context are stressed in understanding the social impact of new information technology. Specifically, social meanings are derived through a process of symbolic interaction, even between a TV viewer and a program; mass media interaction is not "monologic" as poststructuralists assert, but involves two-way (dialogic) and even three-way (trialogic) communication. Nevertheless, as we reiterate below, behavior is not totally situational, unique, or random; social actors do have to take into consideration aspects of their effective environment that are not of their own making, including electronic media and information technologies. Accordingly, despite certain important theoretical differences between students of "information culture," there is a common interest in the way the social context and field of social interaction incorporate communication and information technology. However, the main focus in this work is on select activities and emphases:

> [T]hat the configuration of communication in any given society is an analytically autonomous realm of experience, one that is worthy of study in its own right. Furthermore, in the twentieth century the rapid introduction of new communicational modes constitutes a pressing field for theoretical development and empirical investigation. (Poster 1990:8)

While Traber is certainly correct that innovations and changes "need to be examined within the wider social context, and in the light of current social trends" (1986:47), the following chapters focus on the intersection of communication and information technologies and the implications for certain organized and routine activities. With Meyrowitz (1985) and others who have addressed the relevance of information technology and communication formats for social interaction and a "sense of place," the challenge for this study has been to refine further a perspective for understanding the role of communication in the time, place, and manner of social conduct.

The activities presented in the following chapters are simply those which were theoretically relevant and accessible to obtain the relevant data. They include testing and surveillance (especially this chapter), computer data-bases and orientation (Chapter 2), public information and self-awareness (Chapter 3), dispute resolution (Chapter 4), informal and formal legal sanc-tioning (Chapters 5 and 6), claims-making and the construction of a "social problem" (Chapter 7), diplomacy and terrorism (Chapter 8), and modern warfare (Chapter 9).

Several points must be very explicit at the outset:

First, many of the ideas, concepts and metaphors in the following chapters have been developed by others, including McLuhan and Innis, as well as a host of cultural studies scholars like Fiske and Carey. Cogent readers will see the influence of many symbolic interactionists and that tradition (e.g., Couch), as well as ethnomethodology, phenomenology, and existential soci-ology. While I assume responsibility for errors of omission and commission, there is a sense of "collective guilt" as well.

Second, I am not a technological determinist and do not endorse this perspective; the arguments to follow treat information technology as a com-ponent/aspect/feature/contributor/etc. of a changing social environment, increasingly embedded in a context of technological/organizational/control that operates according to communicative guidelines and codes referred to as formats.

Third, this work is part of a two-decade project to explicate how television news, official information, and electronic technology have contributed to the process of defining the situation for people in everyday life and public officials through social interaction and continually emerging social institutions.

Fourth, while many of the examples in the chapters that follow refer to television materials, and particularly news items, the argument extends be-yond television and explicit communication media: indeed, the focus in this book is to expand the project beyond the discussions of mass media formats to other elements of an ecology of communication. The emphasis is on the role of information technology in shaping numerous social activities that are not directly related to mass media products.

Fifth, I do not regard all of the changes in activities as bad or undesirable, nor is there an implicit call to arms to ban, halt, legislate, or actively oppose them.

The intent is to clarify how some information technology can combine with organizational logic and frameworks to influence social activities. An-other useful metaphor to complement that of the playing field is Lind's "culture stream":

What is clearly needed for most societies over long time periods is a model of processes by which the content of the culture pool is itself transformed, such that we must speak of the culture stream. (1988:178)

As a student of information technology, Lind explores cultural continuities and change, reflecting on the mechanisms and institutional forms that permit the past to be remembered in the present and passed along and changed in the future. The focus sharpens how cultural processes that are discovered, tested, altered, instituted, and then reified become taken for granted (cf. Berger & Luckmann 1967; Schutz 1967). These social forms join generations, as history runs through the present into the future. As suggested in Figure 1.1, various technologies (cf. Couch 1984) of communication facilitate these transitions and their embeddedness as part of the culture.

As Figure 1.1 indicates, there are numerous possibilities for the direction of change and transformation. It is the transformation dimension that is most relevant to our focus in this work, because as activities either change or emerge due to encounters with human agents sporting certain technologies and techniques, then old activities are transformed into new, but familiar ones, which in turn come to be taken for granted:

This transmission system takes on new significance, however, as we see information which has been inserted into ordinary members of the society by specialist disseminators beginning to be transmitted via the mechanisms of the informal culture stream, i.e., via adult-child relations, friendship, and other nonspecialist modes of contact. The loops of the face-to-face transmission system grow in complexity as more and more material from the formal system is internalized and passed on informally. (Lind 1988:181)

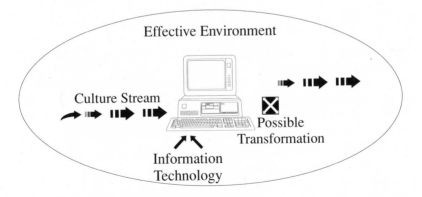

Figure 1.1.   The effective environment, culture stream, and information technology.

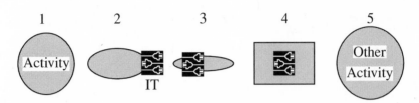

Figure 1.2. Moments in the change (shape) of activity due to information technology.

The process is how something new and different becomes internalized and eventually assumed and taught as something everyone knows. One's effective environment is contextualized by the culture stream and this encompasses the ecology of communication. When numerous activities are engaged in by human actors, and when these activities incorporate information technology and communication formats, then effective environments essentially become similar. One model is offered in Figure 1.2:

> The models developed here require reference to temporality: (1) the model of transformation requires a T1 and a T2, and (2) what is characterized here as the "culture stream" consists of cultural information transformed in an ongoing way over time. Cultural innovators are working on old elements already in the culture stream, metamorphosing them into new meanings—i.e., simultaneously effecting an input (new variant) and an old output (old variant). (Lind 1988:188)

It is the relevance of the effective environment and information technology to the culture stream that challenges the researcher. The use of case studies and constant comparative method of certain activities and events is a useful approach to articulate this interaction. One of Carey's provocative studies of the role of the telegraph in social life illustrates the relationship:

> I tried to show how that technology—the major invention of the mid–nineteenth century—was the driving force behind the creation of a mass press. I also tried to show how the telegraph produced a new series of social interactions, a new conceptual system, new forms of language, and a new structure of social relations. In brief, the telegraph extended the spatial boundaries of communication and opened the future as a zone of interaction. It also gave rise to a new conception of time as it created a futures market in agricultural commodities and permitted the development of standard time. It also eliminated a number of forms of journalism—for example, the hoax and tall tale— and brought other forms of writing into existence. . . . Finally, the telegraph brought a national, commercial middle class into existence by breaking up the pattern of city-state capitalism that dominated the first half of the nineteenth century. (1989:70)

Carey is not arguing that the telegraph caused these changes, but that many activities and approaches emerged as new applications for this technology were discovered. Similarly, what follows below should not be read as an argument that information technology, such as satellite relays, has caused world events to be handled differently, but rather that new applications and processes involving negotiation and news coverage have occurred with the nearly live coverage of events that is now possible.

The approach and emphasis in this book differs from Carey's because the focus is more on the process and relationship of information technology and communication formats to social activities. We want to address the way in which activities reflect some of the newer technologies and their attendant logics, and to suggest some of the ways social life is changing because of this.

COMMUNICATION AND THE EFFECTIVE ENVIRONMENT

Contemporary social life increasingly is conducted and evaluated on the basis of organizational and technological criteria that have contributed to the development of new communication formats, which modify existing activities as well as help shape new activities. Social life is a communicated experience, but the rules and logics of communication have changed drastically in recent decades with the maturation of magnetic recording devices, television broadcasting, and information-processing machines (e.g., computers). Many of these points are particularly applicable to postindustrial societies, where an increasing array of work and play involves symbols and symbolic manipulations. It is in this sense that our lives are increasingly mediated. More of our daily activities are symbolic, often requiring access to some electronic media, or working to comply with "document requirements" that will be electronically processed. As Carey (1989:123) and others note, the expansion of electronics into everyday life, or what they term the "electrical sublime," did not produce the utopia sought and predicted by many. Rather it has had consequences for adding machinery, formats, and "logic" for getting things done (e.g., for communicating in our age). One's competence is often judged by communicative performance, but this performance increasingly involves the direct or indirect manipulation of information technology and communication formats. Our aim is to develop further a perspective for understanding how information technology mediates and contributes to the nature, organization, and consequences of these activities (cf. Couch 1984; Carey 1989; Meyrowitz 1985; Altheide & Snow 1991).

Just as early explorers conceived of maps to harness cognitively terra firma, the symbolic dimensions of the culture stream, including numerous activities and events, must also be identified and charted. While some of these dimensions will include politics, culture, and various dimensions of power, a theoretical postulate of this work is that communicative dimensions are also significant.

The focus is on articulating a perspective for understanding more about the configuration of mediation in contemporary society. The emphasis is less on the "messaging" component of the meaning process described by Ong (1982), Gronbeck, Farrell, and Soukup (1991), and McLuhan (1962), but on the logic and principles of technologically informed communication that have become a more important part of our effective environment.

While being mindful of the significance of cultural context for the emergence of social activities (cf. Foucault 1977), the central query concerns how the communication process fundamental to social interaction is shaped by information technology, logic, and formats, which are implicated in everyday life, including the capacity for resistance to rational control guidelines (cf. de Certeau 1984).

A critical aspect of the social context in most industrial societies is formal bureaucratic organizations. A significant feature is rationality, which is operationalized as efficiency, based on data derived from monitoring and surveillance. In this sense, information technology and communication "chase each other." As suggested by Beniger (1986) and others, the "control revolution" and particularly the capacity to monitor and regulate the information loop was not only necessary for massive industrial technological change, but it has remained a guiding feature of modern society. The organizational society has been created as principles used in operating formal and bureaucratic organizations have been applied to more social activities. As Carey argues:

> Modern media of communication have . . . a common effect: they widen the range of reception while narrowing the range of distribution. . . . Consequently, modern media create the potential for the simultaneous administration and control of extraordinary spaces and populations. No amount of rhetoric will exorcise this effect. The bias of technology can be controlled only by politics, by curtailing the expansionist tendencies of technological societies and by creating avenues of democratic discussion and participation beyond the control of modern technology. (1989:136)

Notwithstanding the intents and purposes of those who apply the bureaucratic control model to social life, there remains a gap between potentiality and actuality; logics break, people resist, and sabotage is not uncommon. Consider the increased attention given to medical information databases, which were designed for medical assistance, but are used for legal, credit, and other surveillance purposes. When New York congresswoman Nydia Vasquez's medical records, which revealed an attempted suicide, were faxed to a New York newspaper and TV station, she responded: "I felt violated." There are more ways to be violated today—one is the social security identification number:

> Use of the Social Security number in medical records . . . would compound the risk. Notoriously easy to steal or forge, Social Security numbers are open to widespread abuse. Instead, privacy experts want everyone to get a new health identification number. (*Arizona Republic*, 21 February 1994)

Information technology and attendant logics are found increasingly at home, at work, and at play, e.g., keyboard appliances, tasks, and activities (cf. Altheide 1985). Thus, the discourse of social life has in many respects become less segmented and more uniform, particularly in terms of tasks, vocabularies of motive (e.g., responsibility, efficiency, violated), and, more broadly, conceptions of normality, order, and disorder (e.g., stress, deviance, and victim). The ecology of communication focuses on the contribution of such technologies to social activities, including underlying forms of interaction processes.

The following comments suggest a rationale for an ecology of communication, describe its elements, and illustrate its relevance for integrating information technology with media logic and formats, and the tendency toward control. We will use some examples from war, but the major emphasis will be on the convergence of the testing format and marketing via expanding information technology. In particular, we will examine how the bar code, born of computer technology and marketing logic, has altered some previous social activities, while adding a few new ones. Finally, we will suggest a research approach for expanding the conception we offer.

COMMUNICATION IN CONTEXT

The ecology of communication refers to the communication process in context. There are three dimensions to the ecology of communication: (1) an information technology, (2) a communication format, (3) a social activity (see Figure 1.3).

The ecology of communication can illuminate our *effective environments*, "referring to the social and physical environment as people define it and in terms of which it is experienced" (Pfuhl & Henry 1993:53). In short, attention is drawn to how the parameters of communication are influencing communication content in rather distinctive ways. Essentially, then, the ecology of communication is intended to help us understand how social activities are organized and the implications for social order. Very few rou-

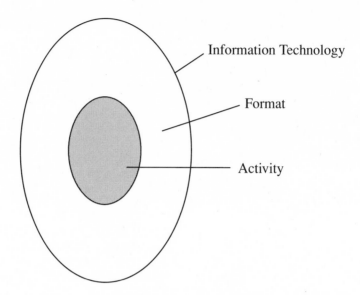

Figure. 1.3.   An ecology of communication.

tine activities remain unchanged in the face of drastic changes in information technology and communication. Partly because of the advent and use of a multitude of information technologies, it is increasingly common today for numerous human activities to involve or be mediated by the logics of these technologies. More than functional equivalents, the elements of the ecology of communication often do more than offer an alternative or faster way of doing the same thing; they contribute to different situational exigencies that must be taken into account when carrying out certain "old" courses of action, on the one hand, while adding new dimensions, on the other hand.

We prefer the *ecology* of communication rather than the *organization* of communication for several reasons. First, ecology implies relationships related through process and interaction. Second, ecology implies a spatial and relational basis for a subject matter. This means that the characteristics of a medium depend on a certain arrangement of elements. However, for our emphasis, spatial arrangements, which are usually implied by the concept of ecology, increasingly are replaced by temporal or sequential arrangements with information technology. It is primarily our language and penchant for analysis that leads us to focus on certain moments in a process and split them off for investigation. This approach often lacks the basic elements of ecology such as interdependence, mutuality, and coexistence. Third, the relations are not haphazard or wholly arbitrary; connections have emerged that are fundamental for the medium (technology) to exist and operate as it does. Fourth, there are developmental, contingent, and emergent features of ecology. The interdependence suggests that a change in any portion of the process is likely to influence another portion. In a sense, then, ecology does not exist as a thing, but is a fluid structure involving meaning, which we will treat as a kind of discourse or frame.

Communication involves the transfer of meaning. All distal communication involves a medium or some kind of a technology that shapes the message (cf. Maines & Couch 1988). This includes structuring the interaction of the audience or receivers of this information with the medium.

By *information technology* we simply mean those external devices and procedures that are used in helping create, organize, transmit, store, and retrieve information. All communication involves some form of technology, even oral traditions that do not rely on any mechanical devices external to the people engaged in a conversation. As Couch (1984) and others have shown , speech can involve tonal and rhythmic cadences for adding color or loudness and emphasis to statements. There are also a host of memory-enhancing or mnemonic procedures for helping people remember and re-call massive amounts of information. However, the present focus is primarily on the nature, role, significance, and impact of information technology external to the individual speaker or actor. Virtually all mass media qualify, but so do the range of electronic and print devices and products used in everyday life, e.g., microwave ovens, car stereos, and answering machines.

The way such technologies operate brings an added dimension to any activity that they are applied to and often reshapes the activity. This is because information technology operates according to a logic involving principles and assumptions that distinguish the technology from other means of preserving and transmitting information.

Format refers to the selection, organization, and presentation of experience and information (cf. Snow 1983) (see Figure 1.4).

Every medium of communication and the information technologies used to shape and transmit information does this through certain patterns, shapes, and looks and these we refer to as formats. Changes in the nature, impact, and preference of formats implicitly are an instance of social change. Indeed, even recent postmodern forays into dimensions of an ecology of knowing call our attention to "normal forms" by offering what are essentially alternative formats for reading, interpreting, and analysis (cf. Atkinson 1992:44ff.).

The relationship between information technology and format is not coincidental. Formats structure the purposes, so to speak, to which ITs apply. Moreover, IT formats provide the basic meaning pattern to an activity. For this reason there are always far more formats, or applications of IT, than there are types of IT, because the information technologies are utilized through various formats. (Figure 1.5).

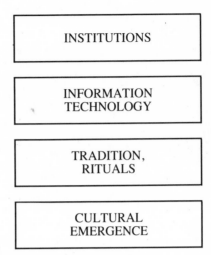

Figure 1.4. *Some sources of formats for activities.*

The combination of IT and format has altered some dimensions of our lives. While alterations may be only interesting, if social conduct is altered significantly in process, character, and meaning, then we get beyond "interesting" to social significance. Further, when the activity is changed significantly or a new activity created through the interactive process involving IT

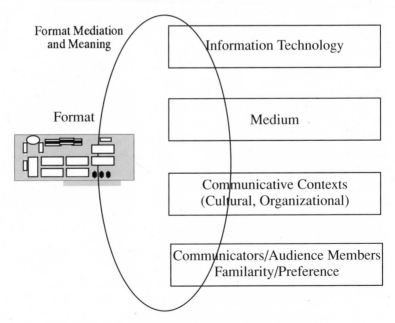

Figure 1.5. *Format mediation and meaning.*

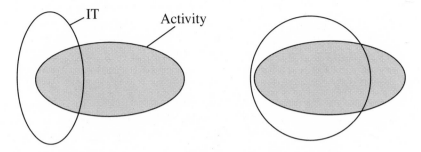

Figure 1.6.   Information technology and different activities.

and formats, then that activity is at least partially *controlled* by those IT formats (Figure 1.6).

From this perspective, little gets done today that is not communicated somehow with and through ITs and attendant formats. This is why the communication process and all that influences it is far more significant for a wide range of social activities than at any time in history. Figure 1.7 suggests the differential influences of IT for activities within a social environment. Our aim is to become more aware of this interaction between ITs, formats, and activities in order to recognize significant social processes that are transforming our lives. From this point of view, in our day of widespread adoption and integration of the ITs associated with the electronic and computer age, experiences and activities are increasingly looking like and

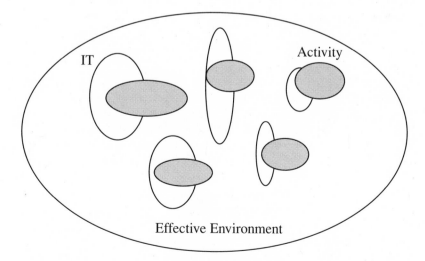

Figure 1.7.   The relevance of information technology for different activities.

operating in conjunction with the attendant ITs and formats. What some of these are, what they look like, how they might operate, and with what consequences are a few of the questions we hope to raise.

To summarize then, the concept of ecology of communication is grounded in the search for meaning, rather than causation or technological determinism. The combination of the key elements of communication provides a structure, logic, and competence for social action. We treat the interaction of information technology with social activities as part of the culture of information. The problematic is the way in which information technology has been integrated into some activities, while providing opportunities for the development of entirely different activities and perspectives. The technology and activity are joined or synthesized through the everyday life experiences of human actors. The key idea is that an increasing number of activities occur in a context of an ecology of communication.

Included in the questions a researcher might ask of activities and the events they make up in the effective environment are the following: How has the activity changed because of the introduction of information technology and new formats? In other words, how do social expectations about performing social activities imply information technology, and how have those expectations affected the human actors' awareness, skill, and competence in using such technology, logic, and formats in carrying out the activity, e.g., "talking on the telephone," or "getting in touch with me," or "letting me know your plans"? What temporal dimensions are involved, or do we assume that any competent actor knows about, in terms of realistic parameters of the activity: how much can be expected, and how many times? What about obligations as a feature of this technology? If, for example, we ask someone a question in the context of a formal bureaucratic organization, what can we expect them to do to answer the question? Simply give a spur-of-the-moment comment? Check into some "record"? Call someone else? Extending these mundane examples to "more serious concerns," what can we expect someone to do and with what limitations, if we want to know if an approaching aircraft is friendly or not? if we want to know if the enemy is building up troops? if we suspect that an elected official is corrupt? In short, activities can change and new ones can be added through information technology. A summary of these considerations is presented in model form in Figure 1.8, where any activity involves a format and an IT, which in turn inform the temporal and spatial focus and configuration of the resulting action.

Many activities can no longer be understood apart from the influence of ITs and their formats. An increasing number of activities must be understood in terms of how they are organized, interpreted, and used. IT now shapes more activities by molding them into formats of communication that guide our understandings than ever before. Social life is changing because of it. As

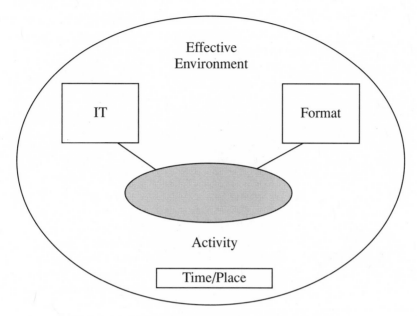

Figure 1.8. Model for an ecology of communication.

activities are adjusted and modified to stay current with ITs, the activities themselves change. One journalist's observation about the impact of new technologies on communication is correct, but still not expansive enough:

> The coming together of personal computers, TV sets, phones, and big databases into all-purpose units lies at the heart of "multimedia" and the new information highway. It's clear that technology is driving mass media, telecommunications, and computer hardware and software into one cohesive activity. (Glass 1994:49).

The significant point is that the IT-format-activity relationship is important in the definition of a situation (See Figure 1.9). Activity in the effective environment is a feature of complex interaction and negotiation between an individual and meaningful contexts of experience, including what is taken for granted, what is relevant to a task at hand (purpose), and of course, background information and expectations. The format of the ITs contributes to the structure of the connections of people to one another and to the activity. The issue then is one of locus of control and influence.

Since an increasing number of activities occur within an organizational context, it is appropriate to specifically address how IT and formats are contextualized by the situations and effective environments in which they

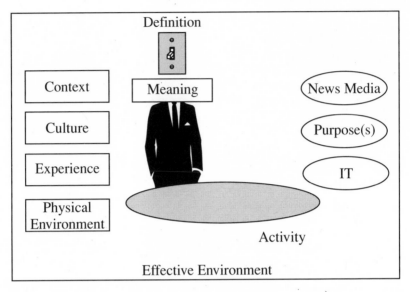

Figure 1.9.   Defining a situation in the effective environment.

are developed and used. Communication in many industrial societies is informed by a cultural context of rational bureaucratic coordination and efficiency. This requires extensive information work oriented to getting control of a domain of relevance, e.g., the market, while shaping the market through product development and selection to become more predictable and controllable. This requires expanded surveillance of the field(s), and attendant activities, e.g., shopping, working, watching, studying, and even researching. These activities increasingly are similar because of an ecology of communication bounded by common information technology and formats. Activities that share information technology and formats will have a similar social form, with shared typifications and recipes for engaging the particular phenomenon, albeit with varying degrees of success. We cook meals (microwave ovens), withdraw money (ATMs), record messages (answering machines), and tell time with the same operations. We also become eligible, qualified, employable, successful, and homeless by communicating experience (e.g., answers) via a mediating-logic machine, formatted for information surveillance, processing, retrieval, and dissemination. However, once they are used, activities and perspectives of the organizational workers and the tasks they pursue tend to incorporate or "fold in" the IT and formats (see Figure 1.10).

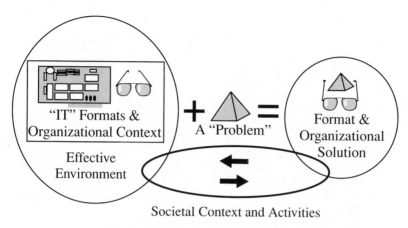

Figure 1.10.   The relevance of organizational IT and formats for societal activities.

International relations illustrate the new relationships that exist between information technologies, formats, and social action. Mass media, and especially television and the reach of satellite technology, make much of the globe seem relevant and manageable. New telecommunication technologies open a door to intervention and control (Altheide & Snow 1991).

Changes in the ecology of communication have altered many of the strategies, perspectives and activities of warfare. Application of game theory and strategies to computer-based simulations of war planning and combat has shifted the emphasis from model to reality. Nevertheless, the simulation of scenarios that one can experience hypertextually, or in pure simulation, such as anticipating an air attack on one's ship, can lead to reifying the model. Simulations may contain *ambiguities according to rule* (which are therefore no longer ambiguous). The problem is that actual situations that arise may be very ambiguous. As noted by Der Derian (1990) and others, in this day of discourses about simulation, surveillance, and speed in international relations, it is the hardware, software, and logic of the technology that shapes the images on the screen, our thinking about possible maneuvers, and our virtual disregard of problematics not easily included in these systems:

> [I]n the construction of a realm of meaning that has minimal contact with historically specific events or actors, simulations have demonstrated the power to displace the "reality" of international relations they purpose to represent. Simulations have created a new space in international relations where actors act, things happen, and the consequences have no origins except the artificial cyberspace of the simulations themselves. (Der Derian 1990:301)

In our day of hyperspeed missiles, high-tech death machines, and supporting logistics, the technological "intelligence" begins to lead the way; humans are asked to play supporting roles! Teaching with simulations becomes more convenient and appears to be realistic, especially with the array of images and instant feedback. The techniques and logics move from an appendage as a tool in one's box of aids to the foundation of the aid itself; more technical systems, albeit designed with human assumptions in interaction with the limits of the software (e.g., no contradictions allowed), can take precedence and serve as the basis for action.

A case in point is the mistaken downing of an Iranian civilian airliner by the USS *Vincennes* in 1988. The activities of identification and interdiction are products of IT and format. The simulation and reality look the same on the screen. Notwithstanding disclaimers by the navy and government officials that the error was human and due to stress, the outcomes can also be interpreted as a feature of training with "tapes that simulate battle situations, none of which included overflights by civilian airliners—a common occurrence in the Gulf" (Der Derian 1990:301).

In other cases, such as the Persian Gulf War in 1991 (see Chapter 9), we witnessed the same information technology that was helping define the possibilities and military options—now essentially playing a leading role in directing the war—also being used by television news operations worldwide for satellite feeds. Electronic communication is now as much a feature of weapons operations, targeting decisions, and logistical evaluation of impact as it is of broadcasting the message—better still, the image—to viewer-participants, who are now capable of experiencing these mediated features of the war in "real time!" One consequence of this immediacy of information is that there is less time to reflect on developing events and their relevance for issues, and what policy implications may be important. Journalist Daniel Schorr notes the implication of this in responding to Secretary of State Warren Christopher's remarks that "television images cannot be the North Star of America's foreign policy":

> Who says it can't, because I think it is. I think that our constant lurches in policy don't happen for no reason at all. I think that, long before we reach that thing called "the information highway," we are coming close to something called an interactive system of policy formulation. The instantancity (*sic*) of modern television makes it necessary to formulate policy on the run. (1993:19)

During the Gulf War in 1991, for example, William Webster, head of the CIA kept track of the war with the added assistance of CNN:

> I would push the button to (national-security adviser) Brent Scowcroft, and I'd say, "A Scud has just been launched from southern Iraq headed in the general

direction of Dhahran or Riyadh [Saudi Arabia], as the case might be. Turn on CNN." (*Arizona Republic* 27 September 1991).

Doing it and reporting it are bound together by the same information technology.

New ecologies of communication are bringing together what were previously distinct activities and perspectives. The operation of the CIA is particularly instructive. Its mission, rationale, and approach have been influenced by the effective communications environment. For example, the electronic information superhighway Internet provides an additional resource for the organization to use. According to Jayne Levin's (1993) analysis,

> Fourteen U.S. government intelligence agencies, led by the Central Intelligence Agency, are developing plans that would allow them to share unclassified information via the Internet.
>
> "Everyone is using it [the Internet]," said Paul Wallner, CIA Intelligence Community Open Source coordinator, in an exclusive interview with *The Internet Letter*. "Why not take advantage of it ourselves and use it."
>
> "The intelligence community will use the Internet to share information and ideas among themselves and the academic community," Wallner said. For example, if the CIA were asked about the nuclear waste problem in Russia, "a good way to find out would be to talk to the scientific community on the Internet," he said.

The effective environment for the CIA, university researchers, and others is becoming increasingly shared. Information technologies and their formats help structure activities. Peace groups and the CIA alike are on Internet; and now they can intentionally or inadvertently communicate with each other and, in a sense, "resist each other," albeit in a communication context.

Another example is the U.S. invasion of Somalia, Operation Restore Hope, in December 1992, when Pentagon press releases prepared dozens of journalists to be on a Somalian beach with lights ablaze to capture the U.S. "Seals" and marines who landed there at night. The planning of this military adventure and the communication of it were conducted in a common communications environment. The networks covered Somalia by a script written and produced by the Pentagon. Somalia is but the latest in a long line of events that have been planned and executed through media logic, including the use of formats for news presentation (cf. Altheide & Snow 1991). What has changed in recent years, however, is that "sources" such as the Pentagon and White House now routinely include this logic within their own planning (cf. Ericson et al. 1989). The role of visuals in the Somalia campaign has been noted by many observers, including journalist Daniel Schorr:

> Somalia is a classic case of pictures dictating policy. In Somalia, scenes of starvation pulled America into humanitarian, and then military, intervention.

Other scenes—of an American soldier's body being dragged through the streets—drove President Clinton to pull the troops out of Somalia. Going in and coming out—a function of reaction to the pictures that you see today on television. (1993:19)

Notwithstanding public outrage at the spectacle of Marines hitting the beach and finding themselves pinned down by camera lights, the media were no more irresponsible in this event than they were in the coverage of the Gulf War and its predecessors, Panama and Grenada. As Ed Turner, the VP for CNN, stated:

No one should have been surprised that there was a crowd of journalists on the beach because they were told what time and where, and encouraged to be there in briefings at the Pentagon and the State Department. . . . In effect, it was a photo op. (*Arizona Republic*, 10 December 1992).

Turner went on to say that he did not think viewers understood the situation, one that was defined by the ecology of communication as much as the Pentagon Briefing. What is very different is that the techniques involved in controlling certain activities increasingly are available to more participants, or potential controllers.

It is the widespread adaptation of and expertise with the ecology of communication that ironically makes it more difficult to achieve monolithic control. As some of the key elements essential to defining a situation become more widespread, including the acquisition of sufficient knowledge and other resources, these same elements can be used to resist others. Some citizens were outraged because they assumed that the mass media and the military had different objectives. As disparate as their activities may seem— the one waging war, the other (merely) reporting it—they work side by side in the effective environmental trenches of communication ecology.

WHACKO IN WACO

Another example of the nature and consequences of this "communicated doing" is the tragedy in Waco, Texas in April 1993. A well-established religious sect, the Branch Davidians, led by a controversial messiah, David Koresh, was suspected by federal agents of caching automatic weapons, molesting or abusing children, and other illegal acts. When they refused to come out of their compound and exchanged gunfire with law enforcement officials on several occasions, the American people—aided by a massive news force—entered into another conflictual standoff. During the negotiations between federal agents and cult members in the compound, a banner from a watchtower read, FBI Broke Negotiations, We Want Press. The previous week, a banner read God Help Us, We Need the Press. They got it, and also massive doses of media logic!

Throughout the fifty-one-day ordeal, hundreds of journalists were given daily briefings by government agents and sources, using a format remarkably similar to the one used during the Persian Gulf War in 1991. But the story dragged on, there was no end in sight, the agents were suffering fatigue, and it was getting expensive, even though local entrepreneurs were hawking wares at the perimeter, much like the 1951 movie classic, *The Big Carnival.* After weeks of failure by federal agents to get self-proclaimed messiah David Koresh and loyal followers to leave the well-armed compound—including an earlier assault that resulted in more than a dozen deaths of federal agents and Branch Davidian faithful—the FBI launched its deadly assault. (The next day NBC began work on a TV movie, but more about that later in this chapter.) The negotiations and intensive nightly TV news coverage continued. On Monday, April 19, 1993, government agents used tanks and other armored vehicles to ram and punch holes in the Branch Davidian compound in order to use tear gas to force out the people. A fire started and quickly consumed the structure and eighty-five of its inhabitants, including twenty-four children. The government immediately rallied forces and definitions to push the view that while the assault may have been ill-advised in retrospect, it was the leader, David Koresh, who bore responsibility for the deaths; officials even argued that the inhabitants torched themselves in a mass suicide attempt. This account was challenged during the next several days by six survivors, who claimed that the attack knocked over fuel stores that led to the conflagration. With language similar to that used against Saddam Hussein when the allies baked hundreds of Iraqi civilians in the Ameriva bunker during the Persian Gulf War, press reports were filled with official pronouncements and editorial statements. FBI official Jeffrey Jamar did his job well in yet another briefing when he stated, "Those children are dead because David Koresh had them killed. There's no question about that. He had those fires started" (*Tempe Daily News Tribune,* 21 April 1993). Immediate opinion polls indicated that 73 percent of those queried felt the FBI "acted responsibly" in pumping tear gas into the compound, with 93 percent blaming David Koresh for the deaths (*Tempe Daily News Tribune,* 21 April 1993). All that remained was for the TV movie to appear, which it did on May 24. The significance of NBC's production of a TV movie while the ordeal continued can be understood within the ecology of communication perspective.

FROM NEWS AS KNOWLEDGE TO NEWS AS ADVERTISING

It has long been recognized that TV news is entertainment oriented, but now there are indications that entertainment programs are becoming more like news programs as standard formats mold programming for a culture geared to a media logic that subtly folds TV criteria, discourse, and perspectives into everyday life. One indication is when surveys revealed that a majority of viewers, and especially younger ones, thought that the program "America's Most Wanted" is a news show! From the standpoint of media logic this is hardly surprising, since this show (and many like it) incorporates a number of standard TV news formats within its production formula. Another indication is the way in which extended news coverage of events foreshadows future TV movies and, in a sense, becomes a kind of preview or advertisement for coming attractions. The Waco debacle that ended in April 1993 is a good illustration of news as advertising.

The docudramas about Waco and other news events (e.g., Amy Fisher, Hurricane Andrew, and the World Trade Center bombing) indicate that this genre has been revised. As the docudrama formula has been learned and refined from the production end, the time period between the real event and its prime-time airing as a TV movie has been reduced to a matter of weeks, and in some cases days. Commenting on NBC's quick production of a TV movie while the Waco standoff was continuing, ABC senior vice president Judd Parkin stated, "Dramatizing such events before they're fully resolved can be irresponsible. In a way, it almost preempts the news" (Newsweek, 24 May 1993).

The key connection here is between evening newscasts' saturation coverage of events like the 51-day Waco standoff and audience familiarity with the topic. As TV networks continue to pursue lucrative ratings, they appear to have stumbled on a surefire way to attract audiences to their TV fare: Simply take news events, which are increasingly being cast in TV formats rich in entertainment value, and then follow up with a made-for-TV movie. After noting that ABC had its own Koresh docudrama in the works, a Newsweek reporter discussed what could be termed "advertising news":

> It isn't just their odor of exploitation or their penchant for selling fiction as fact: we've become all too accustomed to that. What's less obvious is the genre's habit, exacerbated by haste, of reducing a complex story to the simplest, most viewer-friendly terms. . . . Still, get ready for a lot more. In high-visibility disasters like Waco, the networks see a way to survival: instantly recognizable "concepts" with a presold market. . . . "We've reached the point," says ABC's Parkin, "where TV movies and news shows are competing for the very same stories." (Newsweek, 24 May 1993)

Since the audience familiarity and interest is subtly developed through extended reports about such events on regular evening news programs, and even documented with ratings, all that remains is to extend the news angle into prime time entertainment. As with any entertainment programs, audiences enjoy programs that resonate with feelings and issues with which they are familiar. This familiarity permits more audience anticipation, interaction, and participation, and therefore enjoyment. More than thirty million viewers—one third of the viewing audience—watched NBC's spectacle. Audience familiarity is nurtured as repeated news coverage of an event provides the familiarity of an event and its connection (often quite distorted) to dominant values and beliefs in order to make the report relevant. When a made-for-TV movie follows such coverage, less plot development is required to make the story credible—after all, it actually happened—and less advertising is required to move audience members to tune in. In brief, news becomes advertising. Thus, the distinction between news and TV movies becomes less clear, and indeed the broader context provided by such docudramas—albeit often inaccurate—can provide a gentler misunderstanding of the original event by inviting viewers to accept the grossly entertainmentized version in the movie. As my colleague Norman Denzin pointed out (personal communication), "news as advertising tidies up the real and reproduces the narrative cultural logics which give stories and lives sad and happy endings." *News as a form of knowledge* is transformed through *news as entertainment* into *news as advertising*, a preview of coming attractions on television, which in turn add to the context of experience, understanding, and perspective for future news events. The collapsing of several formats with the aid of innovative IT in the context of Waco would seem to reflect Carey's statement several years earlier:

> Modern media of communication have . . . a common effect: they widen the range of reception while narrowing the range of distribution. . . . Consequently, modern media create the potential for the simultaneous administration and control of extraordinary spaces and populations. No amount of rhetoric will exorcise this effect. The bias of technology can be controlled only by politics, by curtailing the expansionist tendencies of technological societies and by creating avenues of democratic discussion and participation beyond the control of modern technology. (1989:136)

From these brief examples, then, we have a framework for appreciating why ecology is a relevant metaphor for understanding our effective environment, much of social life, and communication.

COMMUNICATION AS SURVEILLANCE AND MONITORING

The combination of information technology and communication formats has altered the temporal and spatial order and social meanings of numerous activities. Organizational discourse and in particular surveillance and control are profoundly transforming, as new technologies and their formats infuse social structure. Our focus is on the relationship of the substance of knowledge and the way in which it is communicated.

The expanded role of the telephone in everyday life is an example of how social interaction has been influenced in numerous ways by ITs. New activities have accompanied the routine use of the telephone, cellular mobility, and fax machines to keep informed, stay current, and allow people to do several things at once that were previously separated. One can work at home via telephone modems and computer hookups, and one can talk and do business via a cellular telephone while at a ball game.

Surveillance and communication are intertwined (Marx 1988). Surveillance has increased with the convenience and affordability of telecommunications. It is increasingly easier to carry out what are quite different mundane, sociability, dramaturgical performances, e.g., to stay in touch, check in, and be accountable in time, across great distances. Individuals sentenced to home arrest by the criminal justice system can now be monitored with electronic bracelets. Workers are now more easily checked on as they are encouraged to keep in touch. One now needs an excuse to not be readily accessible, and while workers often bemoan this electronic tether, teenage youths have added the brightly colored beeper to their uniforms of the day to announce them as the kind of person who is in demand. And electronic devices to monitor children, e.g., Child-Guardian, Beeper Kid, Child Sentry, are advertised as one alternative to another time: "And remember when kids always could be found within shouting distance of their front door?" (Tribune Newspapers, "Tracking Kids a Must in Today's Society," 1994). In our media culture, the activity of getting informed and close to the action goes beyond watching TV news, to film of the latest military excursion into distant lands. It is this intersection of communication, information technology, and social conduct that is important for social order, particularly in formal organizations.

The organizational mandate of control and surveillance does not guarantee that it will be successful, but only that it will be relevant in how actors define situations. Safety and responsible parenting have become part of a marketing strategy to sell electronic tethers to parents, even though their impact is less certain. Of course, the context of crime and fear, particularly the social construction of the missing children problem in the 1980s (see Chapter 7), helped produce the audience awareness and sensitivity to such devices, for example, Childnet, a registration service in which metal labels with a twenty-four-hour 800 number are offered as a useful way to find a missing child, even though, according to a Scottsdale, Arizona, police department spokesman:

> We haven't had any incidents where a child has been recovered through Childnet. . . . But I can see where it would be very beneficial to us if we ran into a child that had been registered with Childnet (Tribune Newspapers, "Tracking Kids a Must in Today's Society," 1994).

As the ecology of communication pervades the effective environment with an expanding array of symbols of control and surveillance, more of social life is infused with information from afar, and control of that information is critical. It is the communication of control that is critical here for students of social control. As noted by de Certeau's advocacy for a "polemological" analysis of culture—to study the contradictions and constitutive patterns of resistance, "The imposed knowledge and symbolisms became objects manipulated by practitioners who have not produced them" (1984:xxvii, 32).

FORMATS OF CONTROL

It is the changing nature of formats and their more invasive and pervasive role in social order that attract our attention. However, these formats of control are significant because of the expanding relevance of information technology, and the way it has been incorporated into our everyday affairs. This change is perhaps best illustrated by the massive integration of a plethora of electronic devices, most of which are based on integrated circuitry that permits and indeed depends on extensive feedback and looping of signals as part of the process of making a particular production. This circuitry informs activities and interaction patterns that have become firmly established in consumer culture, as well as in organizational and work culture.

The electronic common denominator has emerged. Similar skills, perspectives, and basic competence for turning on, tuning, and turning off appliances, media, and even organizational processes (e.g., to get someone's attention to help us) have changed and incorporated many of the same formats. It is electronic circuitry, logic, speed, and processing that are the common face of our lives, as well as the global culture we are becoming. As futurists like Alvin Toffler (1990) and others have argued, it is the look of information and the circuitry process that increasingly defines the three historical faces of power: force, wealth, and knowledge. Weapons, currency, encyclopedias, databases, and educational innovations reflect information technology and the symbol system incorporating priorities about marketing contexts that have helped produce it. We have known this for some time. Testing and computerized merchandising/inventory—bar codes—provide another illustration of the ecology of communication that has emerged within the past few decades.

THE SIGN OF THE TIMES: THE TESTING FORMAT

The test frame has been hung on industrial society. Many of the examples discussed above illustrate how activities can change within and through their ecology of communication. Because the procedures, look, expectations and recipe knowledge gradually spread, we soon adjust and take for granted what are often quite distinctive ways of doing things, and the things themselves. When these logics become paramount in how we encounter old problems, adapt new activities, and anticipate certain outcomes, then these formats move beyond being merely regulative: they have become constitutive. The major societal impact on social change of changing communicative effective environments is the emergence of new *formats of control*. Formats of control derive their character from their meanings and use by human actors in their effective environments. When human actors rely on communication patterns and information technologies to set and accomplish certain objectives, then these logics are central to what the human actors will do, how they will do it, and how their action will be evaluated and interpreted. Formats of communication are consequential if they inform the process of defining, limiting, directing, and legitimizing human conduct. The testing format illustrates how new activities and logic have been modified to fit the discourse of control, efficiency, productivity, and predictability.

One prime example of the patterned relationship that has developed between a social objective, human meanings and goals, and subsequent conduct of action is testing, particularly of ability, performance, aptitude, attitude, and increasingly truth telling. Testing resonates control (Hanson 1993:19, 159). It both creates and is shaped by an effective environment of regulation, prediction, and control. Our focus is on the transformation of testing within an effective environment of the ecology of communication: "A test is a representational technique applied by an agency to an individual with the intention of gathering information" (p. 159).

Testing was about control before new information technologies were developed to make its impact even more onerous. Testing involves inclusion and exclusion on the basis of assumptions about criteria. For Hanson, there are two general kinds of tests: authenticity and qualifying tests. With the former, heroes were tested, or rather individuals became heroic as they rose to meet challenges or tests in specific circumstances. Historically, testing was cast in a cosmological and moral context, involving a significant event at a time and place, to demonstrate, for example, one's loyalty, truthfulness, or trustworthiness. These were what we will term *self-events*, in which one's character and true nature would shine through. Moreover, they were time and place specific so that another important element of testing could be maintained: a witnessing by an audience who shared the community's moral precepts and logic compatible with the cosmology. For example, persons suspected of evil, such as being witches or in league with the devil, were likewise subjected to torturous ordeals with convoluted logic, e.g., since water rejects impure things, if the accused were innocent, they would sink; if guilty they would float, and then would be retrieved and executed!

The modern approach in qualifying and achievement tests stresses achievement testing, with a rationale for testing somewhat different from its mythic antecedents as character displays. While our intent in this brief section on testing is not to give a definitive overview of its history, it is important to keep in mind that the context of its use was always significant, and an important part of this context was the nature and extent of power in society, the knowledge base, and the dominant mode of communication. In the example above about physical prowess to demonstrate one's loyalty or bravery, the significant event was the event itself; while the outcome would then be celebrated through an oral or, later, a written tradition, it was the physical outcome involving action of a body upon some object that was significant. The audience was the ultimate judge; the event was a kind of communal verification and celebration and revitalization of myth, past and present, which would then become part of the future via narrative accounts.

Centuries later, the idea of significant tests for emotional, spiritual, and even character challenges remains, but an element has been added: the meritocracy borne of several political revolutions, most notably the French Revolution, which posed an abrupt challenge to privilege. With the rejection of a deterministic or closed cosmology, individual will and ability were posited as a moral force for equality, liberty, and fraternity. If one's outcome in life was the result of something other than privilege, it would be merit or ability. Jobs, opportunities, and futures would turn on task performance at a specific time and place—the test. It would be constructed, delimited, administered, and evaluated by the tester or test official who had the key to the truth and signature of adequate performance. And many tests were given, but they were written, hardly compatible with mass testing. This changed over the next one hundred years as the positivistic dream was made scientific and quantitative by adjusting formats:

> Testing in America . . . flowered in the twentieth century, by which time the technology of testing had undergone significance changes. (Hanson 1993:195)
>
> Written examinations were extolled as superior to oral examinations in objectivity, quantification, impartiality, and economy for administration to large numbers of students. (p. 196)
>
> The major remaining obstacle to the fulfillment of this positivist dream had to do with the technology of testing. Intelligence tests such as the Stanford-Binet are conducted one on one by trained technicians. (p. 210)

World War I led to the quantitative standardized techniques developed by Robert Yerkes and others, which made it possible for psychology to contribute to the war effort through, e.g., efficiency and tests (Hanson 1993:210),

We have come a long way in testing. The test format operative in our day is reflexive of the technology, process and logic that produces it:

> I suggest that an important reason for the ascendancy of intelligence as the premier candidate for meritocratic selection is because it became technologically practicable to test intelligence on a massive scale. (Hanson 1993:253)

Another important consideration is that testing has been applied to an expanding array of topics. Jobs, intelligence, ability, truthfulness, aptitude, attitude, predilections, inclinations, and preferences are now given over to testing. Testing has been reified (cf. Berger & Luckmann 1967).

A critical point about testing, then is that it has been adjusted to conform to information-processing technology. When information forms are adopted by particular organizations to help in their work, it is common for that work to change. Most tests involve standardization formats and scoring. In most cases, the method of answering is done according to the method of analysis or scoring. The machine-readable answer sheets, or *scantrons*, have become part of the modern world of education, job application, and a host of information-processing needs. Standardized educational test scores, now basic to high school and university students, are but one example (cf. Hall 1988). The speed with which certain kinds of numerical information can be processed, compared, and normed with state and national standards has promoted a kind of rhetoric about comparison groups that was not previously possible. Now, entire school curricula are being adjusted—and in some cases developed—to be consistent with these new capacities. What began as a legitimate search for achievement norms became immersed—and captured—by the testing and test-correcting machinery that contained its own logic of uniformity that transformed it into "bureaucratic propaganda" (Altheide & Johnson 1980).

MORALITY PERFORMANCE

In addition to the techniques of testing, there is the broader rationale for testing that has now expanded beyond the narrower educational confines of ability, to include a very broad range of other eligibility requirements. These include polygraphy (lie detector) tests for job applicants, drug testing (or screening), and more recently health screening. In many instances these tests are given in symbolic forms, with questionnaires being answered using scantrons. Increasingly, however, the test format is applied to bodily fluids and tissue to assess not only whether one has AIDS, or drug residues or traces in one's system, but also whether one has risk factors for certain illnesses, conditions, and diseases. Testing for tendency or potential projects the traditional testing logic to look for what one has done or learned in the past, or what one can do now in the present, with what one is likely to do (or happen) in the future.

One consequence is that people are broken into parts, attributes, and behaviors, rather than whole persons: "Testing has a tendency to fragment or decenter the subject, to characterize the person in terms of one or a very few dimensions rather than as a fully rounded, integrated human being" (Hanson 1993:55).

However, this surveillance can become more significant if information technology is applied to put the pieces together, so to speak, through artful retrieving of an expanding plethora of databases and tracking devices, adjustments that some observers have treated as a kind of prison without walls:

> Today's "circuits of communication" and the databases they generate constitute a Superpanopticon, a system of surveillance without walls, windows, towers or guards. The quantitative advances in the technologies of surveillance result in a qualitative change in the microphysics of power. . . . The populace has been disciplined to surveillance and to participating in the process [social security cars, drivers licenses, credit cards]. (Poster 1990:93)

It is the development of a new technology that is very friendly with electronic ITs that permits, with relative ease, diverse applications of the information obtained and stored.

FROM TESTING AS SURVEILLANCE
TO MARKETING AS SURVEILLANCE

The power of testing as surveillance is easily transformed into more explicit manipulation and control through artful programming to retrieve, recombine, and dispense to all qualified knowers (read, those who can afford it!). This is the arena of marketing as surveillance, wherein the appropriate information technology is developed and applied under what Dion Dennis (1992) terms the "sign of the market." When this happens, then the perspective about new complex forms of control envisioned by Foucault (1977), Toffler (1990), and others takes on special significance in social life, as the new information technology and a new format of communication interactively create new possibilities and social activities, which fundamentally alter prior temporal, spatial, and sequential relationships.

People as test-takers can be reflective, resist, and even cheat in an effort to exploit the same impersonal and official logic of the test for their own purpose. Urine tests can be faked, requiring elaborate procedures of monitoring and surveillance, while access to achievement tests may require various pieces of identification, which can also be faked. Little of this was appreciated by Hanson (1993:305).

Elements of an individual's character, truthfulness, trustworthiness, and so forth can be gleaned from how answers to certain queries are evaluated. The obtrusiveness of testing has delegitimated it for many citizens, and many test-givers and interpreters operate in bad faith: They assume that customers, employees, and students are not truthful or trustworthy, and need careful monitoring. A spiral of mistrust has been spawned as objective measures and indicators that can have great consequences for one's life are feared and commonly usurped. This battle over legitimacy has been partly defined by the changing ecology of communication and is being fought within its symbolic borders. It is now increasingly likely, for example, that answers on job applications can be checked against several data bases, including financial history, health history, educational and job history, and criminal and driving records (cf. Marx 1988). Loan companies now draw on 'official information' about one's record and history instead of one's communal character. Indeed, many large lucrative companies have been spawned by their product of providing background information to a host of businesses and agencies. To apply for a loan or a job is to take a test. This information and the format through which it is requested and presented is so common that an increasing number of Americans seek out their background records to check for errors. In fact, the same companies that now serve credit companies, e.g., TRW, offer their services on a monthly basis to regular consumers, in order to keep abreast of their records, and to minimize mistakes. All for a nominal fee, of course! The sign of the acceptable self is looking more like the sum of dollars plus the bar code.

DECODING CONTROL: BEHIND BAR CODES;
OR CHECKING OUT BY CHECKING IN

When one communication format essentially dominates several activities, then that format is significantly powerful in one's effective environment. The changing character of this information base is illustrated with the advent and use of Universal Product Codes (UPC) or bar codes, the computer-scanner-readable product markings on most consumer goods in the Western world. Computer technology, dependent on silicon chips, has provided miniaturization and very fast massive information storage and retrieval. The applications are legion in an increasingly information- and knowledge-based social order, but new formats had to be developed that were compatible with this technology. Bar codes are a prime example of the ecology of communication because they illustrate how an information technology has been combined with a communication format to produce several social activities:

> The Universal Product Code or UPC . . . developed in the 1970s, because of its efficiency and accuracy, quickly spread nationwide. . . . Items being purchased are passed before an optical scanner which reads the code number and transmits it to a central computer programmed with descriptions and prices of the product. This information is transmitted back to the register, which prints the descriptor and price on the customer's receipt. At the same time, the computer can capture other merchandise information for use in a wide variety of reports. Inventory control and financial information are immediately available. (*Arizona Republic* 16 November 1993)

With expanded applications, the UPC has become an ideal format for expansive surveillance of social order. Bar codes permit at least eight distinct functions, even though the information provider and control subject—the customer—may have perceived that this computer format was primarily for showing the price, while saving the checker time and effort, e.g., no keystrokes are necessary on a cash register. Stated differently, we will suggest that one format organizes and essentially defines eight different activities, with more on the horizon: (1) advertising, (2) recording a sale, (3) inventory, (4) personal history, (5) group or actuarial history, (6) organizational surveillance, (7) rational decision-making, (8) promoting autosurveillance (or self-monitoring). Common to most of these activities is an unobtrusive information record of past performances. Bar codes, like their testing counterpart, are distinctive formats of conduct with more than incidental relevance to social control.

MARKETING AND PROMOTING PRODUCTS

Scanners can read bar codes on one product and trigger a mechanism to provide a customer with a coupon for another product:

> To encourage consumers to switch from another cookie brand to, say, Nabisco's Chips Ahoy, Catalina's system spits out a discount coupon for Chips Ahoy each time the scanner reads the barcode for a rival brand. If Nabisco wants Chips Ahoy munchers to try other Nabisco products, Catalina can spit out a coupon for those. "The name of the game is to market directly to the right consumer," says Catalina President George W. Off. (*Business Week* 29 March 1993, p. 60)

When an item, e.g., a six-pack of beer, is purchased, the price can be quickly recorded for the customer by passing the bar code on the cans across a scanner, common in supermarkets across the United States. The customer is on his/her way, but with the intrusion of a coupon offering an even better deal for the next purchase:

> David King, non-executive chairman of Catalina Electronic Marketing, who has worked with Asda to bring the system from the United States, believes it can be applied to numerous incentive schemes. "The system has enormous potential," he says. "If a shopper has not been to the bakery section, it can issue a coupon discounting bakery goods. It can even target individual customers by offering them tailor made discounts, so if they buy Pounds 10 of goods they will get a Pounds 1 discount voucher if they spend Pounds 15 next time." (*Times* 24 October 1993)

If the customer pays for this beer with a check, which may also be scanned into a customer file, or with a credit or debit card, the transaction as well as the bill is stored and posted for the customer to pay. This storage is important since this information can also be read, stored, and even sold to other merchandisers as lists for direct mailing advertising of related products, e.g., potato chips.

A customer profile or personal history of consumption and many activities that are purchased with a credit card, can be accessed for information pertinent to marketing:

> Advanced Promotion Technologies Inc. has developed an electronic checkout device that dispenses coupons and plays short commercials on a video screen. In 34 stores now, but soon to be in 722, APT's Vision Value Network offers credit or debit cards that double as frequent-shopper cards. Users can log points redeemable for items such as VCRs. The card also provides manufacturers and retailers with demographic data to target specific buyers and bring in repeat customers. (*Business Week* 29 March 1993, p. 60)

But it can also be used to obtain information about life-style, health-related issues, and purchasing practices, and in the case of employment applications it can provide indications of honesty, whether the person told the truth about drinking behavior. Just as many individuals who may disregard the importance of a late mortgage payment may later find that it could disqualify them for a loan, a job applicant may find that purchasing alcohol (because he/she had a discount house card) for four different parties in a two-week period may be interpreted by a prospective employer as excessive drinking, poor health risk, all according to the profile of a reliable worker. Thus, a private matter of purchasing a six-pack of beer becomes a moment of surveillance, and the individual may not get the job. In short, a mundane purchasing decision becomes recast in the ecology of communication as a character attribute!

When individuals become aware of this process, or merely anticipate it, individual behavior can be self-monitored, as autosurveillance (a prerequisite for resistance) sets in; people as customers may anticipate how actions will be interpreted when scrutinized as people as employees, people as potential adoptive parents, and of course, people as future politicians. (Consider the decision to rent a pornographic video in this context, despite a federal law protecting video rental records.)

The upshot is that the bar code information format, when combined with computer information technology, renders routines problematic and can transform banality into a frame of virtue and risk. New possibilities emerge, as tracking people becomes potentially as easy as tracking the purchase of a six-pack of beer. For example, retail and library security procedures have incorporated the bar code format as an official feature of their effective environment. And several states, including Arizona, plan to place bar codes on drivers' licenses to expedite license renewals, although it was also suggested that in the future police officers could scan the licenses of anyone they stopped in order to check for outstanding warrants. Given the accessibility of database information, it is not unlikely that complete profiles of motorists could be accessible at the time of a traffic stop, perhaps providing police officers an opportunity to question the suspect about overdue bills, etc. In short, if our argument is sound, police and surveillance functions will expand beyond traffic and conventional crime definitions to other activities commensurate with the available technology. We must wait and see.

The notion of applying all relevant technology to control one's environment extends out the shop door, into the streets, and as Foucault (1977) and others suggested, into the everyday life domain of *all people*. Consider a report about England's premier John Major's plan to tackle crime:

> JOHN MAJOR was accused of acting like Big Brother yesterday over his scheme to introduce compulsory identity cards to tackle crime. Cards would initially be issued to social security claimants to help stamp out fraud which is costing pounds 1 billion a year. . . . Ultimately, all citizens over 16 could be asked to carry compulsory laminated ID passes bearing photographs and fingerprints.
>
> Tory MP Roger Gale said: "I do not believe that any honest person would have anything to fear from such a system." (*Daily Mail*, 25 October 1993)

Marketing as surveillance entails precise temporal/spatial/activity location of individuals. TV programs, for example, help marketers "time" their commercial messages to the viewing preferences of target audiences, e.g., toys for children during cartoons or automobile ads for the evening news. However, as remote-control technology has enabled audiences to escape the commercial message by channel surfing, it has become more difficult to know for certain whether the commercial message is being received, and if so, with what effect. Simply trying to gauge the impact of advertisements from a slight increase in sales following a TV campaign is fraught with problems. However, the bar code provides a very precise, time-specific resolution of the problem. Scanamerica, a TV ratings company, has devised a strategy built on their practical understanding of the ecology of communication: A sample of TV viewers agrees to use a bar code reader, e.g., a light pen, to scan the products they have bought, and to also keep a close record of their TV choices:

> In the kitchen, Mom and daughter put away the groceries, but not before scanning the computer coded bars—the Universal Product Code—on the packages, using a pen-sized wand. All of the information later that night is fed by telephone from an unobtrusive black box atop the TV set to a main computer in Cincinnati. . . .
> It is the first research service to track both the viewing and buying habits of the same household. . . . By identifying who is watching and who is buying, the service allows media buyers to target their audiences, spending their advertising dollars where the message has more appeal. Consumers benefit because they see only the commercials designed to match their buying habits. (*Rocky Mountain Business Journal* 21 July 1986, p. 15)

In effect, the viewers are tested to see if their product choices are consistent with those being advertised. If not, perhaps the commercials will be adjusted in order to better facilitate communication so that dog food buyers can improve their performance. While certain tests, e.g., a polygraph, can interrupt a dialogue between two persons and "bisect [a subject] Cartesian-like, into physical and mental substance, body and mind" (Hanson 1993:93), communication formats integrating information technology within a social activity can reintegrate and create new discourses and meaning. Not unlike the TV newscasts that have adapted entertainment formats, and similar to those schools that now "teach tests" in order to improve student test scores, expanded surveillance merges with teaching, learning, competence, and control as social activities are altered, created, and evaluated within the dominant formats of contemporary ecologies of communication.

SUMMARY

One way power is manifested is by influencing the definition of a situation. Cultural logics inform this process and are therefore powerful, but we are not controlled by them and certainly not determined, particularly when one's effective environment contains meanings to challenge the legitimacy, veracity, and relevance of certain procedures. Resistance can follow, but it is likely to be formatted by ecologies of communication. Indeed, the contribution of expanded discourses of control to the narrowing or expansion of resistance modes remains an intriguing area of inquiry:

> We must locate the modes in which believing, knowing, and their contents reciprocally define each other today, and in that way try to grasp a few of the ways believing and making people believe function in the *political formations* in which, within this system, the tactics made possible, by the exigencies of a position and the constraints of a history are displayed. (de Certeau 1984:xiv, 185)

Some of the most significant cultural logics can be conceptualized within the ecology of communication that is part of the effective environment that competent social actors must take into account as they forge definitions of the situations. Just as markets contain a leveling dimension, e.g., anyone with the price of admission can play, so too does the increasingly technical information technology, with its common key to a host of activities. And while the price of admission excludes many, so too does the activity built on formats not easily accessible to everyone. It is within these symbolic boundaries that freedom and constraint are routinized and dramaturgically played out through an expanding array of social definitions in the social construction of reality. Obviously, many of the dominant logics lack authority for numerous actors, but the freedom to reject is itself bounded by the constraints of meaning, discourse, and most recent style of "competent rejection" as set forth by ecologies of communication.

The cultural context of social life is reflexive. We do by watching, we watch by learning, we learn by testing, and we test by surveillance. The sensitizing concept, ecology of communication, is offered as a lens to see how the integrated parts can produce a fragmented whole. As Marshall McLuhan noted several decades ago, social actors forge ahead while looking through a rear-view mirror. It is the mirror metaphor that we are questioning in the above remarks. The mirror is itself constituted reflexively; we "do looking" into what looks like a mirror. The signifier and the signified have become blurred. Perhaps the concept of ecology of communication can help us focus on the blurring process. We are not merely looking to the past or through our collective memories; while actors have always been constituting activities through the communicative process, the rise of information technology owned and operated by organizations with their own political and economic priorities adds another dimension to our effective environment. The nature and specter of failure and test-type-competence and ability has been a major transformative format that promises to expand even further into the next century as communication, information, technology, and power become joined through formats of control.

The role of communication formats in a range of activities is illustrated in the following chapters which are organized around three general topics: computer information, style, and impact; legal and social justice dimensions; social problems, issues, and war.

Computer Formats and Bureaucratic Structures 2

INTRODUCTION

The reflexive character of symbolic communication joins the future with the past, and process with product. The media of communication we use in any situation are not a passive channel over which symbols flow, but are themselves a part of the communication process. It is the logic, look, and consequences of a certain form of communication—electronic, and particularly computer communication—that are important.

Computers and computer applications to social life have had an enormous impact on social life. Because of computer logic and formats, we do many things today that we did not do before. But we also do some things differently now. The ways computer technology is used in everyday life, and especially how the computer "signature" and look influence many daily practices, are our focus in this chapter. While we will address numerous aspects of computer logic as a significant feature of the social matrix of communication, we will focus a lot on the expanding role of the keyboard in our lives. The emphasis is on the use and utility of a basic element of all computer applications, the keyboard, in numerous information situations. The latter part of the chapter focuses on the use and utility of keyboards to communicate the ordinariness, orderliness, and bureaucratic reality of our world, even as it extends to toys and play.

The aim is to understand further the ways in which basic communication processes influence and are influenced by technology and their social settings, as well as how they contribute to and shape them. A challenge is to treat *media* and *mediation* as a topic in their own right, rather than as a resource to be taken for granted (cf. Altheide 1985). It is the look, sense, and logic of a form of communication that is the foundation of social behavior. By mediation I mean the process involved in the definition, selection, organization, interpretation, and presentation of meaning. If these are routinized and taken for granted, then we have formats. Following a brief discussion about communication formats, I will turn to an appraisal of computer formats and their relevance for bureaucracy.

COMMUNICATION FORMATS

We tend to recognize and "know" changes in information technology by distinctive formats, especially when we first encounter them. Analytically, communication formats are the pregivens that set the temporal and spatial parameters for the configuration and meaningfulness of *all* forms of communication. These parameters may involve grammar, semantics, syntax, rhythm, and style (cf. Altheide & Snow 1979, 1991; Snow 1983). Different from *frame*, which refers to the way *experience* is organized, or the "principles of organization which govern events . . . and our subjective involvement in them" (Goffman 1974:10–11), format refers to the way *communication* is organized. Both are operative in a particular instance, but an awareness of the rules and logic of mediation precede and underlie meaningful communication. Giddens (1984) has referred to the process through which rules reflect the order they produce as *structuration*. In this sense, formats are metacommunication statements, or rules for the recognition, organization, and presentation of information and experience. Their power resides in employing a logic that joins the manner of specific acts to a temporal and spatial order.

Theoretically, formats can be regarded as central structural properties to "knowledgeable activities of situated actors who draw upon rules and resources in the diversity of action contexts, [which] are produced and reproduced in interaction" (Giddens 1984:25). In this sense, social order and social control turn on communication forms and processes. While major steps have already been taken to integrate mass communication within a general theory of communication (cf. Altheide 1985; Meyrowitz 1985), the role of computer formats in social life, and particularly in bureaucratic structures, remains to be explicated. The empirical task, then, is to illustrate and demonstrate how electronic formats articulate temporal and spatial dimensions in particular, and shape the communication process in general.

COMPUTER FORMATS

While formats are essential for all forms of communication, only recently have electronic communication formats come to dominate and essentially differentiate large segments of everyday life (cf. McLuhan 1960, 1962; Altheide & Snow 1991; Giddens 1984; Altheide 1985). As information technologies have been adjusted to organizational uses, e.g., more efficient record-keeping, the work has also changed. With easier retrievability, virtually all computerized record keeping systems can now be used for surveillance. Stated differently, it is not just the computers per se that are important, but rather the effects on the logic-in-use by bureaucratic personnel, who increasingly adapt features of computer formats into definitions of situations.

Computers exemplify pure work, or the unreflexive pursuit of tasks. However, since all human work—even in a bureaucracy—is reflexive, contextualized, and therefore somewhat ambiguous, major translations are necessary to bring people back into it. Basic features of computer logic-in-use include (1) determinate connectedness of procedures, (2) serial progression, and (3) constant form. Determinate connectedness of procedures refers to the integration of steps that must be followed to achieve an outcome. Shortcuts are not easily arranged within computer logic. Moreover, what is done at one point in the procedure will have implications for what is to follow. Serial progression means that Step 7 cannot be achieved without first passing Steps 1–6. Constant form refers to the orderly execution of procedures and the objective appearance of displays and output; combinations of bivariate switches are set in motion.

The way these procedures are defined, controlled, implemented, and institutionalized in an organizational setting is itself a key effect, including what they supplement, supplant, and alter. To paraphrase Bittner (1965), these affect action by providing modes for communicative compliance, stylistic unity, and corroborative reference. Stated differently, when things are to be done according to this format, some things will no longer be done, others will be done more efficiently, and still others will coexist, albeit with a new definition (e.g., unsophisticated, not up to speed). Thus, it is the context and general goal of efficiency, which separates the value of work from its product, that provides the symbolic passage of a format for pure work into a bureaucratic setting.

Perhaps the most significant feature of computers is the symbolic value they have been accorded. While this is less a direct derivation of their communication formats per se, it is nevertheless relevant to people's assumptions, use, and progressive imputations of legitimacy. It hardly needs to be stressed that computers have great symbolic worth. Gerth and Mills's description of "master symbols" seems to apply:

> By lending meaning to the enactment of given roles, these master symbols sanction the person in re-acting the roles. When internalized they form unquestioned categories which channel and delimit new activities . . . those symbols that justify the institutional arrangement of the order are its master symbols. (1953:276ff.)

While Gerth and Mills were referring to symbolic legitimation of social institutions, the form and appearance of rationality is accomplished prior to its institutional application:

The inventors of new communication systems, record keeping procedures, and production methods are offering the possibility of all human transactions taking the form of mediated contact. One talks with his friends via the telephone or radio, conducts economic exchanges through electronic media, and works in complete isolation. Automated production, mediated communication, and mediated economic exchanges are offering a world wherein no one becomes implicated with another. More and more coordinated action is action that is subordinated to machines. All are becoming machine like. *Rationality is equated with subordination of human activity to machines.* Newton equated cosmic movement with the tick-tock of clocks. Some modern intellectuals have developed theories of human life that equate human action, thought, and emotion with the electronic impulses of the computer. (Couch 1984:369; emphasis added)

Computers are increasingly being thrown at a myriad of problems, largely because decision-makers presume that virtually all problems of human agency can be reduced to speed and efficiency. Thus, while it is not directly a feature of computer formats, providing funds to purchase computers can be symbolically defined as a strong effort to solve the problem. For example, Bruce Babbitt, Arizona's former governor and secretary of the interior during the Clinton administration, was reported to have been

stung by two critical reports involving the administrative problems within the state's Child Support Enforcement Administration, [and] has wasted little time in an effort to solve the problem of delinquent child-support payments. . . . Babbitt sent a top Department of Economic Security official to Washington, D.C., to seek emergency approval for a new computer system . . . to eliminate problems encountered by the state Child Support Enforcement Administration in keeping *track of paper work.* (*Arizona Republic*, "State Hustles to Boost Child- Aid Collection," 7 April 1986; emphasis added)

Symbolically, the problem was defined as an inability to keep "track of paper work." The governor was able to show that something is being done, and that the onus was on the federal agency to provide the funds. More importantly, is that the problem is defined as "paper work" rather than a host of other problems, including inadequate personnel, a breach of good faith, low employment opportunities for many of the absent fathers, inadequate support for mothers on AFDC, and a virtual impossibility of tracking down errant payers and enforcing payment. In short, the speed and efficiency of information processing is always contingent on clear-cut directives, applications, and practical implementation.

Computers "Frame" the Work of Bureaucracy

When bureaucracies accept this equipment, they are also accepting the definition of the situation and, by implication, assume responsibility to solve the problem within this frame. Because it is a dominant frame, with its own communicative logic, other definitions will not easily be accepted. Within the logic of computer formats, this means that "software" will be developed to analyze "data" input, which in turn will provide a "database" for "accessing" errant payers, or whatever the problem at hand happens to be. Of course, the logic is never totally unique to the situation at hand, but must conform to the broader format, which generally involves more than mere software and machine language. For example, in the case noted, the idea was to be able to make the state's computer system compatible with those of its counties. Ultimately it is expected that a computer system will far exceed the efficiency of a manual system in solving the problem.

The operation of the computer system still depends on a manual system of a different kind. Supplementing stacks of paper and handwritten notes from files, computer formats necessitate using keyboards to interact with the machine. The rules and logic of such interaction, along with the temporal and spatial parameters of this interface, have added yet another specialization to the bureaucracy.

DIVISION OF LABOR

A bureaucracy easily incorporates features of computer formats within its own procedures, but it is not overwhelmed by them. With regard to the definition of the situation, computer equipment and procedures now enjoy great symbolic value. Providing scarce resources, especially those qualifying as master symbols, symbolically bestows authority upon leadership; delivering the goods, in computer terms, means getting goodies that other would-be leaders cannot acquire or, at a minimum, getting them first. Consequently, there is competition for these resources, a stockpiling of reserves, and end sweeps to undercut others' claims; bureaucratic workers fight over computers. One apparent winner is the expert who signals the institutionalization of computer formats.

The computer expert has been around bureaucracies for decades, although the implications of this status have not been fully explored. Primarily distinguished by technical knowledge and what other members call "computerese," the computer expert is defined as an extension of the machine and the keyboard; novitiates usually pass through this person(s) for instruction and, occasionally, physical access to the computer. Disproportionate symbolic and financial rewards often flow to this position, signaling to other workers about the merits of the skills. Not surprisingly, even though such information is often an official or unofficial credential for an expert's hiring, seldom is that the sole job description. Consequently, the requests by others for help and consultation to successfully engage in computer interaction may be met with rebuffs, but perhaps more commonly are seen as a resource to use in exacting additional organizational favors, including relief from certain duties.

The status and skill of the computer expert may spark resentment from colleagues, but they also suggest a paradox: The computer expert loves the interaction via computer formats, and especially the challenge of learning, developing, and, indeed, playing with new derivations and techniques, but often dislikes the mundane tasks of helping novices become literate, novices who do not share the same fascination and love of the activity per se. For the expert, the work with a computer is its own reward and, unlike for his or her colleagues, is fun beyond its crass utility of merely aiding a piece of work. Thus, the computer expert may resent requests for help, grudgingly give it, and ultimately disdain the very skills that partially justified that position. One solution is to provide this individual(s) with assistants to help in the task, but this may appear to add another piece to the bureaucratic infrastructure, and may be seen by many workers as a threat.

There is another matter that must not be overlooked. Organizations abhor obvious redundancy because it smacks of waste and inefficiency, which symbolizes poor leadership. If there is one thing a bureaucracy is not, it's efficient; but if there is one thing a bureaucracy hides best, it's inefficiency. Therein lies a dilemma for many workers. For example, within a university setting, it may be decided to throw computers at the faculty and staff so that efficiency will be increased. But that is also tied into a long-term cost-saving rationale: Other jobs can be eliminated or combined; people who only type in the computer age are expendable, and they are being expended. Moreover, it is assumed that eligible workers will become computer literate, but as we shall see below, this is not only an untenable assumption—it carries with it a threat of illegitimacy.

As master symbols, computers invest their keepers with legitimacy. Computer performance is increasingly associated with competence. Indeed, persons with high-tech, viz., electronic gadgets of all kinds, are now a distinctive target group, known as technologically advanced families (TAF), and their numbers have risen (over 10 percent of American families). The lure of distinctiveness membership is enticing. More than a few owners of small businesses have taken the advertisements to heart and purchased computer systems without understanding format, interactional, and socialization requirements. Bosses often realize too late that secretaries cannot simply operate sophisticated spread sheets to keep track of payroll, inventory, and a host of other concerns it would be nice to know about. As with the many parents who have rushed to buy their children computers, these entrepreneurs may wind up with the computer on display but unused or underused.

Workers in a bureaucratic setting have a special problem with computer competence: Those who have it tend to have higher status than those who don't, but they usually don't get it until they acquire the computer gear. However, once they get it, they are expected to use it, but what if they don't? Failure may be symbolically invested upon such persons. One alternative is secrecy, whereby an individual attempts to conceal from his/her colleagues that he/she is unaware of the format, procedures, equipment, and technique. However, the pressure is immense since more and more organizational products are expected to pass through the computer format. Moreover, as the logic of the format pervades the everyday routines and conversations of the workplace, the terminology, metaphors and imagery of format permeate language and human and idle time; the time, place and manner of the workplace can itself be sucked into the vortex of format. For example, it is increasingly common for people to speak computer languages such as DOS (e.g., "file not found") when conversing with family members and colleagues. In such a context of activity and meaning, the deviant is artfully produced by technical fallout; a point is reached where it becomes apparent that an individual does not use the equipment, the symbolic stuff of organizational and optimal efficiency. Rumors may circulate about withdrawing the support, and ultimately, what began as—and was assumed to be—a source of help can easily become a symbolic noose. Moreover, status and perks may be noted by "who's getting upgrades", e.g., a laser printer!

THE COMPUTER AND OFFICIAL INFORMATION

A major impact of computer formats on bureaucracy is the way solutions define the problems. As master symbols, computers and the personnel who use them tend to translate questions into computer solutions. A key part of the process of defining the situation involves the perception, construction, and use of databases, or information compiled into computer formats for electronic retrieval and analysis. Involving use of a standardized series of codes or categories, a phenomenon is dissected for atheoretical imperatives in order to address theoretical issues. This general direction has been lucidly described by Jack Douglas:

> In the beginning bureaucracies of official morality made use of roughly the same common-sense categories to construct more specific, concrete descriptions for their own use. But over the centuries these bureaucracies have moved steadily toward fewer and more isolated categories, rather than combining categories to construct more concrete descriptions. . . . Few social scientists would make claim to having developed specialized knowledge to the point where they *know* which categories actually constitute the scientists *fundamentum divisionis.* (1971:53ff.; emphasis in original)

One result has been an acceleration toward the reduction of information, which amounts to bureaucratic propaganda (cf. Douglas 1971:55ff.; Altheide & Johnson 1980). The latest form this has taken is a database.

Computer formats promote as well as make databases "user friendly." Information is defined in terms of accessibility. We have already seen some examples of this with standardized educational testing, and more generally, the testing format.

As an advertisement stated, "Digital is the solution . . . We create it, store it, and most of all, share it" (Newsweek, 21 April 1986). However, since most users do not categorize, organize, and input the information, they are fundamentally unaware of basic definitions and assumptions underlying a particular database—to find out usually costs money or prestige.

A database permits manipulation and control. But this will only follow if one has access to the data. Accordingly, agencies (e.g., law enforcement, economic, academic) as well as individual citizens are buying into massive databases for information retrieval. As one microcomputer expert put it, "If knowledge is power, then the access a computer gives us to information will give the people power" (Arizona Republic, "Eye on Uncle: On-Lines Return Power to People," 14 April 1986). Moreover, the easier access is generating more interbureaucratic use of databases, which in turn serves to reify information produced for one purpose to be used for another. In one project I am working on with city officials, an effort was made to use social service records and data for providing indicators about social circumstances and community needs. The officials became very frustrated when it was pointed out by a researcher that it is common for agencies to have bits and pieces of information about clients, but a more comprehensive picture about the extent of their assistance from other agencies—a kind of horizontal view—is not available. One consequence is that workers from one agency are often unaware of aid, services, restrictions, etc., provided by other agencies!

Perhaps most importantly is the way computer formats direct information use and other activities. One example is police work. It is now more common for computer terminals (keyboards) to be in patrol cars. The intent is to use the fingertip access to criminal justice databases to facilitate police work (e.g., discover warrants, stolen autos). But these terminals also promote official information by serving as a bureaucratic account of the officer's activity: when calls were taken, answered, and their disposition. Our observations of officers in the field reveal some other uses, however. For example, an officer may decide to give a motorist a citation in order to update an address discovered on the system. The stated goal in this case was to proactively enable detectives to "keep track of that guy" should they need to question him in the future.

This kind of work also adds some more danger to police work. Since most officers we have observed are not typists, they tend to hunt and peck out messages, codes, and responses, thus taking a lot of eye contact away from the road and their surroundings. We have been told that this is dangerous, and we suspect that keyboard activity may have contributed to the death of at least one officer. Furthermore, since any individual who is stopped has prior knowledge of outstanding warrants, etc., and also knows that this information will soon be available to the officer beside his/her car, it is not unreasonable to assume that the officer would be at an immediate disadvantage, and therefore in potentially more danger. However, some of this field activity, and especially the use of lap-top computers to file reports could save time and paperwork. Notwithstanding such costs, the format of information and control is now essentially defining major facets of police work.

The construction and use of databases influences the tasks and goals. Tax rules and regulations are one example. One analyst said of our tax system, "Only the computer has spared this cumbersome system from collapse" (Samuelson 1986:68), referring to the way tax changes are tied to databases about those changes. For example, many tax lawyers, accountants, and businesses have access to a database consisting of recent tax changes. Pumping out a million words a week, the tax database service has become integrated into the way corporate taxes are figured, and apparently also informs decisions to make tax law changes; the lawmakers know that even complex changes can be made accessible through databases. After noting that the use of computers is inextricably tied to our current tax system, including the way keypunch and other errors can wreak havoc with individual taxpayers, Samuelson concludes:

> Lawyers and accountants can find obscure IRS or court rulings only by searching a database. . . . The irony is evident: an efficient new technology— computers—allows us to sustain an increasingly inefficient tax system. (1986:68)

To briefly sum, identifying communication formats in social life and assessing their effects is no trivial pursuit. How we communicate precedes and limits what we communicate. When a medium used in daily affairs operates on the basis of a distinctive logic, then communication is subject to format, which in turn informs its content and situated use. The impact is even greater when, as in the case of computers, they are legitimated as master symbols. Recognizing this format and charting its implications and effects is an act of freedom:

> According to the notion of duality of structure, the structural properties of social systems are both medium and outcome of the practices they recursively organize. Structure is not "external" to individuals . . . [and] is not to be equated with constraint but is always both constraining and enabling. . . . The reification of social relations, or the discursive "naturalization" of the histori-

cally contingent circumstances and products of human action, is one of the main dimensions of ideology in social life. (Giddens 1984:25ff.)

Computer formats operate well within bureaucratic settings because of common assumptions about rational organization and because clear distinctions exist between means and goals. From one perspective, bureaucracy looks like computerization, keyboard products and images, and efficiency. But from the interactionist interest in the definition of the situation, it is clear that process and product have not only come together, but are now Janus-like. The time, place, and manner of an expanding array of bureaucratic activity involve and reflect computer formats. Ranging from symbolic legitimacy to social control to the division of labor to development and use of databases as products, the social definition of computer technology has transcended being a tool; it is a communicative frame for transforming *topics* into *resources* massaged by a format that symbolically reifies itself through its use, while denying human agency.

Some implications of this format are suggested by first turning to the unique feature of information control implied by computer formats, including the nature and use of keyboards. Following a discussion of their social characteristics, some of the implications of keyboard formats in culture will be noted.

KEYBOARDING AS A SOCIAL FORM

The key is the contemporary communication device for use with a variety of media, governed by formats, for the recognition, selection, emphasis, presentation, and reception of symbolic information. The nature and consequences of the relationships between various combinations of these elements continue to attract scholarly attention. Especially intriguing is the relationship between a particular medium, its format, and its effect on the social order. In this sense, it may be argued that dominant forms of communication and the nature of social organization are inextricably related: how something communicates merges with what it communicates. The act of communication becomes more utilitarian as its character is influenced by other purposeful considerations. Lefebvre has noted the following about writing:

> Written matter has a further peculiarity: mental operations, coding and encoding are an intrinsic part of it, but they are not included in the message . . . [A document] can be taken for a language, for a message, and although it is given as based on a code there is nothing to stop it from cheating and delivering codes that have been tricked or truncated by "decoders" who take advantage

of the situation and mislead on the quality of the goods—namely the code. (1968:158)

It is in this sense that the social codes that underlie social order have implications for the communicative character of that order. Keyboards and their products are part of the contemporary communication order. Moreover, the form and appearance of bureaucratic rationality have further penetrated social order through keyboards, keyboard products, technique, and logic.

Keyboards, Products, Technique, and Logic

A keyboard may be defined as any device in which parts are purposefully manipulated in a social situation according to a logical scheme, in order to create, interpret, send, or receive symbolically meaningful information. What is central to the concept of a keyboard (which may not literally use keys or buttons) is that the device or tool of which it is a part cannot be manipulated directly to facilitate the communication process; rather the skillfully manipulative parts of the device fulfill the purpose (Bodenseher 1970; Hollnagel 1983). Examples include musical keyboards, such as pianos, telephone dialing equipment, typewriters, electronic tuning equipment on radios and televisions, video game controls, and computer consoles. The key to the communication process is fingertip control.

Keyboard products may be defined as symbolic information that appears as an objective track of a format. The mode of presentation and appearance conveys the message that a device has been employed to translate intention and meaning via a procedure. In this sense, the appearance and format itself constitute a kind of metacommunication.

Keyboard technique may be defined as the steps, procedures, and manner of address and operation deemed essential to effective use of a keyboard. Technique involves practical considerations, recognition, facility, and adjustment.

Keyboard logic refers to the rules of operation, grammar, and syntax by which essential operating codes are recognized, acted upon, and passed over.

When they are combined, keyboards, products, technique, and logic essentially constitute a distinctive social form most commonly associated with bureaucratic, i.e. rational-formal, organization. The nature of this association is one focus for this chapter: what is the role of the keyboard form in contemporary bureaucracy? The other aspect is: to what extent has this form penetrated the less bureaucratic realms of daily life, and what are the consequences? The significance of such queries for critical theorists has been suggested by McIntosh's analysis of Weber's views on the effect of technical rationality on human action.

> The disintegration of action in advanced industrial society has produced not an iron cage but a dilemma. On the one hand the maintenance of instrumental effectiveness requires the suppression of both the ethical and the interpretive significance of action. We are left with *mere* technical rationality. (1983:69; emphasis in original)

Contemporary life in industrial society would not be intelligible, recognizable and workable without the social form constituted by keyboards. A major reason for this bold assertion is that it is through keyboards that the form and shape of "information," "data," "issues," "decisions," "problems," etc., are recognized, focused on, selected, considered, and resolved. In short, just as contemporary life has its signatures in architecture, music and urban design, so too does the nature and shape of information "sign" for us.

To reiterate, the keyboard form communicates beyond the specific content of the printed message. The look and form are rich with meaning, significance and legitimacy; the specific content merely provides substantive information; keyboards are involved with official and recognizable action. Consider reports. Organizations involve bureaucratic forms, but a key part of this is the social form of keyboards. Only insofar as they are "keyboardable" in the bureaucratic world is there recognition for documents like memos, schedules, reports, and payrolls. In the main, only keyboard material is capable of being filed because this form indicates that something has been completed and can be recorded at a particular stage. Handwritten scribbles suggest lack of time spent, poor organization, and too much of a process still under way; rational coordination is about products, or more to the point, the appearance of products.

Keyboard Rationality in Everyday Life

Throughout everyday life, keyboards reflect, sustain, and produce technological rationality in several ways.

• Keyboards are produced and consumed on a for-profit basis. Virtually all new machines and procedures for a wide range of communication have keyboard interfaces. The best example, of course, is the flurry in personal computer sales. The major target for these products and accompanying software is the business world.

• Several modes of keyboard mastery are essential for individual survival and prosperity in an industrial order. Use of telephones, electronic tuning equipment such as television and stereos, vending machines, banking machines, "ugly" tellers (or ATMs), answering machines and a host of other devices is no longer a luxury, but is becoming routine in daily life.

• Keyboards are the major tools of bureaucratic organizations. Office equipment such as typewriters, calculators, and computer terminals are essentially synonymous with bureaucracy and organization. Not only are the organizational products unrecognizable without keyboards, but this equipment also defines the various organizational tasks, as well as the temporal, spatial, and hierarchical arrangement of an office in particular, and an organization in general. Who orders whom to operate which keyboard, for what length of time, and for what purpose provides a working model of pay, power, and prestige.

Status distinctions are increasingly marked by the substitution of keyboards for human interaction. Specifically, banking machines are in vogue because they carry out transactions without the aid of human tellers. Not only is this customer convenience more cost-effective than conventional uses of people to help people, but a customer's financial import to the bank can be symbolized by providing the personal attention that is essentially being withdrawn from less affluent customers. Inconvenience and even risks to customers accompany this shift. The inconvenience due to any errors will be up to the customer to rectify. For example, my student researchers have found a number of cases where an ID card was incorrectly "confiscated" by a machine, leaving it up to the customer to retrieve it at a branch bank during regular office hours. One of the major risks noted in recent years is an increase in the number of robberies occurring around automatic tellers. It is not too speculative to suggest that we are entering an era when person-to-person interaction, as opposed to person-machine encounters will be a badge of legitimacy; in this sense, queuing up to be served by a person will have a different symbolic meaning than queuing up for a machine.

• Keyboards are increasingly involved in the preparatory and other social skills for entering the rational-organizational-bureaucratic sphere (DiMaggio 1982). Organizational work involves keyboard manipulation, either directly or indirectly, by having the power and prestige to command others to perform these tasks (Williams 1982). While office work formerly involved training on the typewriter keyboard, another keyboard requiring mastery has been added by computer terminals with word-processing capability. Moreover, the capacity and expanded access of various computer systems have led to their more direct use by supervisors, who formerly directed typists and accountants. These skills are now routinely taught to individuals who aspire to executive status, on the one hand, while also being widely taught to entry-level data input workers, in what has been referred to as an electronic sweatshop by Dion Dennis (personal communication).

• The keyboard technology, technique, logic, and operating skills are supplanting oral and handwritten communications. Accompanying new keyboard applications are new styles of interaction. For example, as keyboards are more widely used for communication and documentation of activities not previously subjected to rational accounting procedures, the overall routine will change, and new duties may be assumed. The nursing profession is one example. With the expanded use of computer systems in hospitals, and the positioning of on-line terminals at various nursing stations, less time is available for patient care because nurses are required to participate in the accounting and billing function. Not only are medications and treatments charted for medical purposes, but these are now operationalized as charges to the patient; thus, nursing work includes keyboard work in order to expedite the billing function; the only thing that suffers is patient care.

• New keyboard procedures and equipment merge with and often replace other keyboard procedures and equipment. In terms of the modern office, typewriters—and the skills that went with them—are being replaced by word processors. Slower, dial telephones are being replaced by faster, push-button telephones, with a bank of extensions, hold buttons, transfer buttons, and similar conveniences; the telephone has become a communications center. Similarly, just as electronic musical keyboards perform like an entire orchestra, a computer can become a telephone, a typewriter, a clock, and a filing cabinet.

• Keyboards serve as transitions between the worlds of work and play; increasingly, both activities involve keyboards. As more toys and entertainment devices resemble work machinery and are essentially operated in the same way, the distinction between work and play becomes less clear. The technical rationality to have fun becomes isomorphic with at least some features of competent work. Not surprisingly, the technical rationality and skill serves in two ways to situationally blur traditional distinctions between adults and children: children and adults can both have access to a variety of keyboard tasks, such as video and computer games, and children can dominate adults in these games. In this sense, toys, tools and terminals have taken on a common form, but may be employed for a range of purposes in a variety of situations.

TOYS, TOOLS, AND TERMINALS

The ecology of communication stresses the interaction and flowing together of discrete elements to make something else, and to help the parts. As we have stressed, what may appear at a single point in time as a thing or a distinctive and separate part may also be viewed as an aspect of a process when examined over several time periods. Electronic information technology, like computers and their interfacing logic such as keyboarding, are usually associated with activities, routines, and meanings involved with work contexts. We turn now to a discussion of the way this technology can become integrated with other contexts of meaning, such as play, when keyboards and terminals are integrated, as well as help create new activities.

We have already seen that keyboards play a major role in our lives as an increasing number of appliances, communication devices, and information storage and retrieval technologies, e.g., computers, are accessible through manipulation of keys or other devices in a logical sequence. This section explores some of the ways in which familiarity with and use of such keyboards, or terminals, has potential consequences for age group identity and intergroup interaction. Terminals are now found in the adult's world of work as well as the child's world of play. The implications for traditional distinctions between adults and children, on the one hand, and the worlds of play and work, on the other hand, are discussed in terms of technical rationality and social change. Toys, as we shall see, have changed to become more like the adult perspective they were originally offered to counter.

The commonsense cliche, We are what we eat, may have a corollary in social science, We are what we experience. A host of activities, and even eating food, take on the temporal characteristics of information technology and formats. A student researcher heard an individual state, as he made a food selection from a machine, "I'll just grab something from the machine. I don't have time to eat." I would add still another wrinkle to the latter cliche: We are *how* we experience. I want to suggest that the tremendous increase in the availability and use of keyboard and other terminals in everyday life is an important change with rather far-reaching implications. But first, a brief theoretical rationale must be presented to forge a context for this assertion.

MEDIATED SOCIAL ORDER

Life through the ages has been less distinguishable by the problems in a culture than by the way in which certain perspectives and solutions to these problems have been mediated, e.g., technology, institutions, etc. and reception of information (Altheide & Snow 1991). Since virtually all tasks and activities performed by members of a culture involve some aspect of information, *medium* seems to be an appropriate concept for further explicating the nature and variety of cultural experiences, changes, and conflicts. In this sense, despite the very important differences that distinguish one culture from another, it is the way in which certain routine and mundane problems and activities have been mediated that is most distinguishable.

Common problems and concerns are mediated and resolved according to time, place, and manner. The same solution is not invoked for all problems by all persons all the time. In this sense, the techniques and procedures are more or less situation specific. Furthermore, the solutions to various problems come to be owned, or controlled or regulated, by certain individuals. And, consistent with social science lore, these individuals systematically vary according to such ascribed membership statuses as age, gender, and ethnicity/tribe. Of course, there are also relevant achieved statuses, e.g., strength, attractiveness, and skill which have some bearing on who defines, uses, and interprets a particular solution at a particular time and place and in a particular manner.

The variety of cultural activities associated with everyday life in any society is rather immense. Not surprisingly, this array of activities—implying many of the solutions noted above—is essentially distributed de facto to various members of the social order. While each of the activities will have a more or less symbolic and socializing utility for other activities, the linkage between, say, the activities of children and adults, will generally be convoluted, circuitous, or even coincidental rather than linear. I speak here of the major differences between the worlds of play and work.

The complexities of life have contributed to the similarities and differences in the worlds of children and adults. Both work and both play, but the nature of these activities has traditionally been age related. The relationship between adults' interest in the play of children has been nicely articulated by Stone:

> It is the task of society to make the lives of its members meaningful. This is accomplished by bringing little children into a meaningful communication with adults and one another, and, at the same time, by establishing their selves as objects so they can refer the other objects of their worlds to such established selves, thereby imbuing those worlds with significance. Play has a major part in the accomplishment of these tasks. (1970:548)

In our day, a lot of play happens with toys. Many historians have noted how toys as distinct items for children were further developed with the rise of a separate toy industry that accompanied industrialization and the growth of the middle class (cf. Mergen 1982). This marked a shift from children playing with ordinary material items encountered in their everyday life, to distinctive status-items produced especially for children. Other observers note how recent developments with toys promote individual play, or relative isolation (cf. Sutton-Smith 1986). Whatever holds a child's attention, then, is a practical consideration of parents and toy manufacturers alike. Danny Simpson of the Child Growth and Development Corporation explained, "[A] good toy is one that engages the child's attention for the longest time" (*Washington Post*, 25 December 1985). Computer toys using keyboards and related logic and fingertip control require—and thereby promote—focusing on a screen immediately in front, or some icon held in one's hand, rather than taking in the surround. They are task specific, with their own temporal parameter and requirements, and share this with the world of work.

Stated in the terms I have been using, adults employ different media in their activities than do children. As noted above, it is access to and use of such media that essentially defines the status distinctions between children and adults. Indeed, numerous societies mark the new membership eligibility through rites of passage that also include the right to use additional media—in order to engage in the requisite activities (solutions to other problems)—while often giving up more or less exclusive rights to the media of the prior status, e.g., a version of childhood.

The toys used by children, as we noted, are increasingly designed by adults. We should not be surprised, then, that the wishes and orientations of the latter are reflected in numerous playthings. When more of these toys involve computer applications, it seems only logical that the values of the corporation, marketing, and a host of commercial considerations in a capitalist society should complement the game format of even the most dedicated-to-games orientation of computer play. One of the most extreme examples is a game called "Barcode Battler," now being marketed in the United Kingdom. One journalist described it as follows:

> It will not even require subsequent purchases of software. But family shopping bills could rise alarmingly as a result of the game's key attraction—the ability of players to boost their scores using barcodes, the computer symbols read by shop tills to price and record sales of a vast range of consumer goods. In Japan, sales of one brand of noodle rose sharply when children discovered its code produced high scoring points when cut out, taped to cards and slid through a scanner on the toy. Each code is transformed by the scanner into a different number of points to enhance a player's "life energy", attacking power or defensive strength. No way has been discovered of predicting which barcodes possess the greatest values. The importers of the game, which goes on show at the annual toy fair in Earl's Court, west London, today and is expected in British shops by May, talk excitedly of the "thrill of the search" and forecast European sales of at least a million. Hard-pressed parents might have other thoughts as children badger them to make unnecessary extra purchases, pounce on the contents of the shopping trolley and leave behind trails of paper and cardboard as they search for the magic barcode combinations. (Randall 1993:3)

Bar codes and children's games are shaped by a context, and as we have argued, this context is itself being created by not only marketing logic, but also by the most powerful format of the twentieth century, computer logic.

Social control in a society is manifested by access to and right to use various media. One class of media I will term *tools*, and the other *toys*.

Furthermore, it could be argued that a child's world is somewhat distinct from an adult's insofar as the former does not have access to the tools and activities of the latter. And even though the adult may have proprietary rights over the child's toys, the time, place, and manner of their use will be adjusted to fit into the dominant temporal and spatial framework of the adults' use of tools. Stated still differently, toys are the major medium of children vis-à-vis adults, who excel in the use of tools, finding only leisure time for toys.

The activities of adults and children have historically been distinguished not only on the basis of certain activities, but also on the availability of appropriate media for those activities. If, for example, certain tools were available—and the jobs in which to legitimately use them—children would probably be expected to engage in some of the same work activities as adults (cf. Aries 1962). Indeed, as Randall Collins (1971) has argued, children are sent to school in order to obtain the credentials—a different kind of tool—to do the work of adults. Youth, accordingly, has been extended by the time period required to obtain additional credentials, viz., legitimacy. Nevertheless, once legitimacy was acquired, the work that followed was likely to involved different tools, i.e., media, than those previously used. This, then, is one historical sense in which the world of adults and children has been different. But a change has occurred.

THE PERVASIVE TERMINAL: PRODUCING THE "GAME BOY"

Much has been written about the way computers have changed our lives, but my focus is a bit different: I want to address how the availability of the computer-type terminal, its logic, skill, and interactional features have pervaded social life, reduced differences between adults and children, joined the world of toys and play to that of tools and work, and molded a mono-mediated culture.

Most Americans—and an increasing number of Europeans and Asians, as well—are accustomed to seeing children and adults playing with hand-held computer terminals, the most popular being Nintendo's "Game Boy." Like the miniature radio and audiotape player, the Game Boy permits one to take it along. One TV advertisement features an adult playing with a Game Boy, while waiting in line at an airport ticket counter. When he is told that his flight has been delayed for several hours, he smiles and expresses relief because, we are to conclude, he can continue playing with his Game Boy. The growth of computer terminals in the workplace hardly needs documentation. With the advent of the transistor and then the microchip, computer applications and user-friendly derivations are ubiquitous to the workplace, and now essentially define the skills and techniques needed to get a job, hold one, and advance. This transformation has gone well beyond the office and white-collar work, to include service stations, grocery stores, the postal service, and paraprofessional work of all kinds, including nursing, law, and administration.

Somewhat less apparent in the literature on social change and occupations and professions are discussions of the relevance of terminal and quasi-terminals (e.g., keyboards, buttons) in activities and media designed and marketed for children. Anyone who doubts this need only browse through any large toy department. We have seen how the vision has progressed to incorporate bar codes into games: this itself is based on a way of structuring time for fun, but highly individualistic fun.

Still another important trend is the way terminals, e.g., home microcomputers, are marketed with both adults and children in mind. An important dimension, as noted, is portability: one can always work and play, but increasingly through certain hand-machine interaction. The specific applications may differ, e.g., different software for financial planning compared to computer games, but the notion that the same thing is appropriate for adults and children is rather intriguing. Indeed, it is not uncommon for children to be more adept at some of these terminals than their parents, often leading to some situated role reversal whereby the parent requests the child's assistance!

Several things are especially important for understanding how this terminal invasion may have a bearing on social change and social control. First, adults and children are now expected to do many of the same things. Skill with terminals, especially keyboards, has come to be requisite for job security among adults and for peer respect among youth; terminal toys and tools are mediating legitimacy in different circles. Second, the change has come from the world of adults and tools rather than youth and toys. The ideology of the workplace has been infected for some time by the technological cure for inefficiency: speed and dollars are now associated with terminals and computers. But the world of children and the toys through which their lives were mediated for fun has been less influenced by the workplace ideology. Third, toys previously bore only a superficial or coincidental connections to tools. (GI Joe and Mattel M-16 automatic weapons, notwithstanding!). Now, the same skills needed to perform in jobs (e.g., computer programming, encoding commands, reading signals) are found in toys. Fourth, as I have argued elsewhere (Altheide 1985) the logic, semantics, and syntax of terminals were more commensurate with the bureaucratic and formal rationality of work than the former world of play; both are now quite similar.

CONCLUSION

This chapter examined the nature and relevance of computer formats, computer-human interfacing through keyboards, and the ultimate integration of this format into social life—the joining of the worlds of play and work, children and adults. Variation in social life is central for diversity, new directions, and creative deviance. When toys and tools using the same essential logic, modes of address, problem definition, perception, and solutions are being used by youth and adults, then toys and tools no longer exist as separate entities; they are but different versions of the same thing. Play becomes a logical derivation of work; fun becomes strange toil; life becomes more homogeneous, one-dimensional, and mediated in the same way.

The explosion in toy terminals is consistent with a movement toward cultural homogeneity. The pluralism that has always been a source of diversity, incomplete control, and a variety of cultural innovations is less healthy. Ethnic and racial groups persist, although the women's movement, complete with unisex clothing, has further eroded distinctions between men and women. Age groupings, marked by a variety of credential rules, rites of passage, and the cult of youth had persisted until now. While the lines between young and old will not all erode away, I suggest that one of those lines—that between the worlds of work and play—has been dulled by the technological infusion of terminals as tools into terminals as toys.

The Culture of Electronic Communication and the Self 3

Our approach to the ecology of communication is to combine information technology with communication formats and show their relevance for social activities and social issues. This chapter focuses on the way information technology and especially communication formats influence the culture of electronic communication, popular culture, and the self, or the internal organization of how people define and make sense of themselves in an age of new forms of information technology.

While it is widely recognized by social scientists that the *process* of meaning is implicated analytically in the *content* of meaning, the theoretical significance of this relationship for students of culture remains unclear. One purpose of this chapter is to integrate culture and communication in order to explicate how the organization and meaning of one is joined to the other through *mediation*. From this perspective, in order to understand better the stream of culture, we might ask, How is culture communicated, and is this significant for social life? We will illustrate recent changes in the way experience is mediated by delineating how popular culture reflexively joins certain mass media with formats for the definition, recognition, organization, selection, and presentation of experience.

Communication involves the interpreting, ordering, exchanging, and sharing of meaning. Certainly since the work of Boas, anthropological linguists generally subscribe to the premise that each language is a product of culture and reflects that culture. The Sapir/Whorf hypothesis (cf. Sapir 1949) delineated how language structures categorically guided, ordered, focused, and yet limited cognitive options and speakers' perceptions in the communication of meaning and therefore meaning conferral. Thus, the grammar of language and the content of ideas were related. McLuhan (1967) and others have long held that other forms of mediation, and particularly electronic media, carried with them logics and grammars that were distinctive from linguistic forms, but were nevertheless quite significant for not only adding new forms of meaning conferral, but for also challenging and often negating the relevance of the earlier forms. While McLuhan and his associates focused mainly on the technology of different media, a more culturally informed perspective locates media as a feature of organization and technology in the social context of its use.

It is in the interaction of communication forms as product and producer that everyday life takes place and social order is accomplished; *how* something is communicated is prior to *what* is communicated (cf. Peterson 1976). Identifying and locating the sources, nature, and consequences of communicative routines, styles, and patterns are therefore central to an understanding of social control as well as an explication of the politics of everyday life. A statement about what we term *mediation* is theoretically appropriate. Mediation (some people prefer *mediatization*) refers to the impact of the logic and form of any medium involved in the communication process. The following materials are offered to illustrate how media logic and formats compatible with popular culture mediate, define, and direct social interaction in contemporary urban Western society.

FROM CONTENT TO THE MESSAGE

The sociology of knowledge informs us that the communication process is problematic, and that history, context, and interaction contribute to the social construction of meaningful information (cf. Berger & Luckmann 1967). McLuhan's contributions notwithstanding, social science lacks a theory of mediation that would articulate the relationship between (1) an actor, (2) a context, (3) a phenomenon or event, (4) a medium, and (5) an audience. Each of these contributes to an actor's attention to and understanding of relevant information, as well as perception of a message (cf. Blumer 1969). This conceptualization of the communication process creates a whole from what has heretofore been regarded as discrete parts (cf. Streeter 1984). Thus, regarding political communication, sociologists have commented on the cultural, economic and political context (cf. Barrett, Corrigan, Kuhn, & Wolff 1979), the event under study (Gitlin 1980), the media organization (Epstein 1973; Altheide 1976; Gans 1979), and the audience (Gerbner, Gross, Morgan, & Signorielli 1982; Gunter & Wober 1983; Graber 1984b). And efforts have been made to theoretically join two or three of the pieces, particularly the context, the event, and the audience (cf. Lang & Lang 1981, 1984; Glasgow University Media Group 1976; Hall 1980; Bennett 1983). Missing from much of this creative work, however, is a theoretical statement about the specific medium per se, particularly how media may contribute to the process suggested by the sociology of knowledge.

Prior to modern technology in Western society, interaction occurred through rules that were constantly reestablished or mediated by the parties directly involved. Third-party mediation was largely a matter of formal institutionalized ritual, such as religious ceremony, oral history, and theater. This ecology was spatial, often occurring in public places. As we note below, things are different today; they are organized increasingly temporally. By the beginning of the twentieth century another dimension of mediation had emerged, one that developed formal properties and competency requirements independent of existing institutional norms. Consequently, an increasing array of interaction in today's urbanized world requires that people in business, education, religion, and throughout mundane everyday life must know how to operate media technology, and code and decode specialized media. It is the process, logic, and cultural impact of this competence that occupies our attention in the remainder of this chapter.

Contemporary mass communication entails active participation with rather distinctive formats, which essentially define the time, place, and manner of social interaction. It is the unique form of the mass media that draws our attention to mediation as a general feature of all communication (Maines & Couch 1988). We regard the mass media as major factors in contemporary social life, rather than merely being dependent variables affected by class, status, and power. Indeed, culture is not simply mediated through mass media; rather, culture in both form and content is constituted and embodied in mass media.

MEDIATION IN SOCIAL LIFE

Our lives are awash in media. But we are seldom aware of the role these media play because it is such a part of day-to-day experience. The major electronic media are but the latest in the human legacy and involvement with all kinds of media.

The major starting point toward a more adequate view of the audience is the assumption that social life is constituted by and through a communication process. There is a communication process at work whether one is focusing on interpersonal communication or mass communication. This view suggests two things: (1) information technology (IT), communication, social interaction, and social order are inextricably joined; and (2) scientific assumptions, concepts and theoretical frameworks that seek to lay claim to subareas of communication, e.g., mass media, will be implicitly or explicitly relevant for this more basic issue.

Media Are Visible

A medium is any process, technique, or technology that facilitates in social affairs the emergence of something visible or something tangible. Media provide the space for temporal ordering. If the major battles in preindustrial societies were for territory and natural resources, the major focus in postindustrial life is on markets. Ours is an ecological niche of time and not space, per se. As Carey notes:

> When the ecological niche of space was filled . . . as an arena of commerce and control, attention was shifted to filling time, now defined as an aspect of space, a continuation of space in another dimension. As the spatial frontier was closed, time became the new frontier. (1989:227)

Space filling is accompanied with formats that help define what is relevant, but formats do not exist apart from media. This includes not only the mass media, but also the media of everyday life; it is for this reason that we speak of life as mediated. The media we use in everyday life make thoughts, intentions and meanings come to life. Even though the media and content are joined in the communication act, these media take on a reality and importance that is independent of substantive content in the communication process. Consequently, media are more than a neutral conduit of information transmission: they are concrete action agents that come to represent or stand for the location and establishment of various kinds of meanings. Television is entertainment, news, talk, relaxation, stimulation, and so on. Through forms of appearance and action (media strategy), every medium becomes a visible agent of social affairs.

Popular Culture

Mediated experience is one of the few things we share. We now term the cultural material we all more or less share in *popular culture,* meaning the various social worlds we participate in every day, but especially the "play world" (Combs 1984:7ff.). It is suggested that media logic and formats compatible with popular culture increasingly define and direct political communication. Readers may recall recent presidential replays of popular movie dialogue: Reagan—*Dirty Harry;* Bush—*Rambo.* (Bill Clinton, during his campaign for the presidency in 1992, merely appeared as a guest performer on several prime-time shows!) It is further suggested that our understanding of political communication has been hampered by an overemphasis on the content or *what* is communicated rather than an analysis of the process and context, which involve *how* something is communicated.

Students of popular culture have serious fun with their work, especially when they inform us that people learn politics through the experience of play:

> Political culture involves the widely shared orientations of people toward themselves as a political self and the politics and government of their country. . . . We play with politics as it unfolds for us through the mass media and

popular talk about it. Our play with it helps give political culture both its continuity and changeability. (Combs 1984:16)

This view is also a cultural perspective, although it lacks a coherent theoretical statement about the role of communication in social life, and it has not been decidedly critical. A major strength is that it studies the way audience members define and use media content in their daily activities, and what this means to them. Moreover, it is not too much of an exaggeration to suggest that recent developments in cultural analysis approaches (cf. Rowland & Watkins 1984) and semiotics (Fiske & Hartley 1978) have essentially built on a popular-culture approach.

The media may differ (e.g., newspapers, magazines, periodicals, TV, radio), but we are a media-competent generation. We know how to operate media, stroke the right segment of the keyboard to increase volume, change channels, or fine-tune. And we know how things are supposed to look-read, look-view, and sound-hear. By the same token, we know how long a news report, article, story, and program should be—or at least, what is too long or too short (Zerubavel 1981; Altheide 1985). We know even more. We are experts with media grammar and syntax. For example, we know in an instant if a radio station is rock'n'roll—and whether it is heavy metal or top 40, country and western, religious, classical, or all news. With TV, we can tell even more quickly if we have tuned in a commercial, newscast, situation comedy, or movie. This competence involves media consciousness and has great implications for political communication today.

Political communication may be found throughout the media, although most social science attention appears to have focused mainly on news content and how it is constructed (cf. Lang & Lang 1968; Epstein 1973; Altheide 1976; Tuchman 1978; Gans 1979). However, there are other uses of newspapers by readers, and far more entertainment choices on the electronic and cinema media. A theory of mediation grounded in the sociology of knowledge would seek out the many faces of politics.

If the cultural analysts and critics are correct about the role of the media in legitimating certain ideological positions, then we must also consider other sources of information (cf. Edelman 1988). Specifically, the *politics of everyday life* would include those behaviors, problems, topics, strategies, and styles apparent in the selection, organization, emphasis, and presentation of situation comedies, game shows, cartoons, rock videos, as well as movies. It is the pacing, rhythm, and style of such "message packages" that makes them recognizable (cf. Snow 1983).

People carry and nurture political language and symbolic meanings through their routine involvements with mass media organized around some basic communication formats. People have such great access to this content that they incorporate the scenarios within their daily round of activities.

Moreover, experience and familiarity with these formats appear to be related to knowledge, albeit different types of knowledge, and interests about a variety of topics, including politics. For example, Gunter and Wober (1983) found that their British sample knew more specific political information if they watched TV news and read Sunday newspapers. However, in terms of opinions about issues, Gerbner, Gross, Morgan, and Signorielli (1982) claim that heavier TV viewing is related to more middle-of-the-road positions on a variety of social issues, suggesting a kind of "television mainstream." In this sense, as James Combs (1984) has suggested, popular culture becomes very consistent with political culture even though the former is not explicitly promoting the latter.

The power of the mass media goes beyond mere information transmission: it consists of shaping information along explicit temporal and spatial lines. The audience members actively participate in interpreting and giving meaning to the messages. This occurs when they recognize formats, relate a current message to previous communication, and draw on their own biographies and effective environment to provide the context for a message. This means that key organizing principles surrounding content construction, handling by the media organization, and temporal and spatial configuration of the mediated imagery must seem sensible or plausible to the individual. In this sense, the audience is also actively involved in the message process. This is where major organizing principles that join all facets of the process together come into play. The use of political language in a news conference will be used insofar as format features are satisfied:

> In the contemporary world, spectacle construction is an important part of the answer because the contriving of events and the dissemination of news about them create anxieties and aspirations, insecurities and reassurances, that fuel a search for legitimating symbols. (Edelman 1987:123)

On Mediated War and Peace

Ideas about stability and change, order and conflict, peace and war often boil down to how such things look, and what the consequences and aftermath look like. TV news tells time according to visuals, particularly videotape. Without such visuals on U. S. TV networks there is little likelihood that an event will be selected for coverage, and/or receive more than a few seconds. For example, format considerations for events featured on U. S. network TV include the following:

- accessibility—how readily newsworkers can obtain information about an event;

- visual quality—the extent and clarity of film, tape, or other visual depictions of the significant action;
- drama and action—the graphic, visual, and aural portrayal of movement, which can be used to illustrate the event;
- audience relevance—the interest an item is perceived by newsworkers to have for a mass audience;
- thematic encapsulation—the ease with which an event can be briefly stated and summarized, and joined to a similar event or a series of reports over a period of time, or within the same newscast.

When the quality and quantity of information are joined to formats, then the manner of reports is itself affected. Consider the differences in coverage of peace and war: the latter satisfies virtually all of the format criteria, while peace tends to be thought of as the absence of war, or the momentary break in war. It is conflict in general, and war in particular, that most aptly fits news formats. For example, in 1987, the major TV news networks in the United States presented nine reports about peace, although eight occurred between February 14 and 16, and focused on the International Peace Forum in Moscow. As one network correspondent, Anne Garrels, who covered the Soviet Union, put it:

> As a television correspondent, for example, I had to get pictures. Raising a camera in the Soviet Union is a bit like raising an M-16. Everybody scatters. Or else they move in and get rid of you quite quickly. . . . One other thing. There is a difference between what is reported from Washington about the Soviet Union and what is reported from Moscow about the Soviet Union. And I think that's a very important distinction. Information about the Soviet Union does often come from official sources in Washington. Such information does tend to reflect the administration's point of view. I think that's less true with information reported from the Soviet Union. . . . Therefore, I think you should look at the date line. Where is the story coming from? I think you'll notice very different kinds of reporting when you do that. (Rubin & Cunningham 1983:100–1; adapted from Altheide 1985:240–42)

But where you look for the story depends on what kinds of visuals are anticipated, and presumed to be appropriate for that kind of a story. It is for this reason that conflict and war are good angles to deal with; they are more visual because certain kinds of actions (e.g., strong statements by powerful leaders) and objects (e.g., foreign peoples) can be videotaped and offered as instances of the conflict under discussion. What we have been proposing, of course, is that the availability of such visuals informs the nature and extent of the coverage that will follow. Peace is less newsworthy because the conflictual angle (and appropriate visuals) are not so readily available:

> Political reporters demand action, or at least the appearance of action.
> Stories with two sides. Winners and losers. The notion of peace puts them off.
> Too passive. Nothing happens. (Rubin & Cunningham 1983:258ff.)

Quite simply, peace is not a good news angle or frame in light of current formats; visually speaking, peace seems to imply the lack of the kind of visual action compatible with the news code. This will involve more public relations.

> The point is that issues that get poor coverage are the issues with unskilled or no public relations. Where there is good public relations, where the event is packaged in news pegs, I think the issue gets well covered. . . . I think the media are captives of public relations, not captives of government. . . . Civil journalism depends chiefly on the public relations expertise of the peace movement. When the peace movement does a good job, journalism does a good job. (Rubin & Cunningham 1983:266)

Media formats offer another explanation of Gitlin's (1980) claim that the media coverage of the SDS activities, and New Left movement in the 1960s had the effect of influencing that movement, and therefore changing it. From the perspective we are offering, what was especially significant about some of these New Left activities for media coverage was that they were compatible with media formats, especially visual opportunities (e.g., demonstrations, signs, dress, flamboyant rhetoric). Indeed, it could be argued that such visual opportunities were central to the kind of national attention given to the peace movement in particular, and the youth countercultural shift, in general.

When viewed from the mediated-culture perspective, the problem with the peace movement, and especially most steps toward peaceful resolutions of specific conflicts, is that peace is invisible while war and conflict are visible. Unless news organizations change or adjust portions of their current format, what is less visible will not be covered and emphasized.

Because the power of media resides more in the formats that essentially constitute this communication form, we must understand the history, nature, and consequences of such formats if we are to become directors and avoid being directed. That prospects for world peace must be weighed against such considerations says a great deal about the nature and changing face of power in our time; it is mediated power and this is why nations throughout the world must come to grips with the kind of systematic bias we have been emphasizing. While later chapters will examine the significance for the ecology of communication perspective in understanding global issues like peace, war, and terrorism, it is useful to ground this perspective in the everyday-life situations that contribute to the development of a self.

FORMATS OF CONTROL AND THE SELF

Conceptualizing the interaction order as a context for communication helps us to further appreciate how social order and control is itself a feature of social process. Contrary to Carey's assertion that symbolic interactionist interest in the self was "tucked away from the questions of politics, rationality, power, and social change that Chicago sociologists had earlier engaged" (1989:146), an ecology of communication perspective argues that the nature of power, social control, and asymmetric definitions of situations are joined through communicative logics that are tied to communication formats. It is the awareness of and skill at using such formats throughout history that has provided the interactional foundation for taken for granted exchanges and shared contexts crucial for human actors to negotiate meanings and arrive at definitions of situations. In a world that increasingly is socially constructed with information technologies owned and operated by formal organizations, a plausible assumption is that the temporal and spatial order is an accomplishment that is continually mediated by a host of competing definers, who may be involved in organizational and technological processes, which bring social action together in a particular manner.

The emphasis is on the social form of communication rules that inform and make recognizable perceived options and actual behavior in types of social settings. Even using a modern library illustrates the process of information technology, organizational culture, and individual planning.

INFORMATION AND AN ECOLOGY OF COMMUNICATION

An examination of some of the elements of this culture that is part of a much broader ecology of communication can help forge a contextual linkage from the broader culture to the specific problems of information science professionals. Familiar information sources are hardly regarded as information at all, but are seen as reality. TV is the standard for today's information market. While we watch rather than read, we also tend to read what we watch. How are formats transferable to other media? What do actual and potential information seekers desire, and with what do they compare information? These are somewhat different kinds of questions for understanding information science issues, but I suggest that they are essential.

The process of inquiry and discovery shapes what we learn and what questions we ask. As information gradually is moving from a process to a product, it is important to reflect on the transformation of knowing and the information specialists who may serve as knowledge guides.

Several years ago I visited an ultramodern on-line library with my son, who was working on a project for his eighth-grade social studies class. His teacher is a dynamic instructor who treats learning as a game. A former professional baseball player, he throws Oreo cookies to students who answer questions correctly. If they miss it, he will really wind up and fire a forty-mile-per-hour Oreo at them; usually it connects with the wall and the janitor is called in for relief. It is really crazy, but the kids love it; and they work to get the answers. One of his extra-credit ploys is to challenge the students to find answers to some of the most bizarre queries you ever heard, e.g., In which direction is the Tower of Pisa leaning? (No, *down* is not the correct answer!) Or, Which country has the most subway riders? You get the idea. It is because of these questions that my son and I were venturing to a sophisticated research library (also, the local city library was closed!). I should also add that, with my children as well as my students, I have always stressed that knowing how to find answers is more important than the answers themselves, and that developing such skills of inquiry, exploration, and discovery is not only important to plan the trajectories that modern life has thrust us into, but it also saves considerable time and effort. Our trip to the library was to be another lesson in information seeking because my son is not easily convinced by talk alone.

As a senior professor who has spent more time in a library than anyone should, I was confident that a few of the queries could be answered through some reference materials, such as *Facts-on-File*. One thing I forgot to mention, however, is that it was 8:00 P.M. on Sunday evening, although the library was open until 10:00 P.M. There's another small point to consider in this tale: the library had been expanded recently and many of the materials had been moved about. (Most readers could probably have written the next few lines.)

The next thing that happened is that nothing I planned on happened. The terminals worked fine and I obtained the call numbers for the materials I sought. The only problem is that they were not where they were supposed to be. I wasn't worried; after all, I am at home in a library, it's my turf; I sweep deftly past students and other novices who are unfamiliar with the communication formats that guard information sources. Electronic language be damned, I thought; I would have some good old-fashioned oral face-to-face conversation with a fellow human being who was skilled in such matters. I knew that a reference librarian could quickly straighten things out—except they had all gone home! It was as though the library were a big machine and nobody knew how to work it! My son and I left empty-handed after investing an hour wandering through the on-line data base. This trip to the library had not worked for my son, and my modest attempt at teaching the utility and excitement of efficient information seeking had gone bust, although as you can see, it was not completely wasted on me!

There are a few salient points that may help us do an informed reading of this experience. First, our interest in finding something is *meaningful* and *emotional*. Useful information is always *my* information. The trick is to find ways to translate our specific projects into terms that permit access to appropriate information sources. Second, information procedures and issues are primarily *communication concerns*. It is within the communication context, process, and formats that information is recognizable, meaningful, and therefore applicable. Third, the context of our project guides our quest for certain kinds of information. Often we are not aware of the kind of information we need because we do not always know what is available. This suggests that there is always an *interpretive dimension* for adequate information advice and seeking. Fourth, as information increasingly is mediated by specific logics and syntax, there is a *controlling dimension* at work which tends to be exclusive and relies on experts. Fifth, information is located within the temporal and spatial parameters of bureaucratic organizations, and information workers are workers first, and informers much later. Finally, information use is *sanctioned* and evaluative. As knowledge of what is available expands, so do the expectations that it will be used. Thus, students face a different problem today than we did; we expect more because more is available.

CULTURE AND INFORMATION

The aforementioned points direct our sociological gaze away from libraries as information repositories to a more general focus on the culture of information, or its form, style, and logic; procedures of use; and meanings for social behavior. The suggestion is that a conception of self is molded from the format imposed; formats communicate control as they carry with them models of the self. Each instance of seeking out information is not the initial quest, but is rather a subsequent stage in a career with a project of some kind, like finding out some things about the Tower of Pisa.

Georg Simmel (1968; Wolff 1950) argued that cultural forms that permit certain activities also tend to direct and limit those activities. According to one student of Simmel:

> These cultural contents are produced by subjects and meant for subjects. But in their intermediate objective status they tend to estrange themselves both from their origin and from their purpose. . . . This tension in the cultural subject-object relationship may or may not lead to a rupture, but it is the fundamental tragedy of all culture that it bears within itself the element of self-destruction. (Spykman 1966:239)

This applies to information as well.

Information is a cultural form today that transcends the content or specific bits of information. While we do not teach children eternal truths, we do teach children at the primary and secondary levels to find the "correct" answers. Unfortunately, as discussed in Chapter 2, the politics of educational testing promotes this bizarre reliance on test formats for how we teach; increasingly, teachers are teaching altered versions of the tests on which the students, teachers, and school districts are being evaluated. The real challenge is to teach the students how to find out something, how to pursue their own inquiries. This approach is more relevant to a process of knowing than to specific things known, and suggests that the form of knowledge has eclipsed the content, or that which is known.

Information search is associated with uncertainty. The pursuit for new information, viz., for an information source controlled and operated in a library context, occurs when a previous source, often one taken for granted, has not worked out. Thus, information quest is a feature of a perceived failure, an inadequacy, or shortcomings of other information sources. Institutionalized information-seeking devices, techniques, and procedures constitute a dialogue with uncertainty.

With this broader context, let us return to some points noted above about the culture of information. Information is meaningful and emotional. People seek information for a purpose, but they do so within familiar guidelines and contexts. Kuhlthau's point is valid:

> Information seeking is a complex learning process which involves finding meaning. . . . Library instruction which incorporates a process approach enabling students to know what to expect can help them work through the more difficult stages of information seeking and learning from information. (1989:225)

The use of electronic databases as a tool is ideally suited for those persons who understand the logic of massive filing schemes, are at home with keyboards and electronic images, and can quickly apply computer logic to travel through menus. Electronic databases, however, are also obstacles and sources of ignorance and failure for many people, even those on campuses, including some professors (cf. Dougherty 1989:25). Thus, the process is an emotional one and has implications for identity.

The project is also salient. Why should anyone seek out certain kinds of information unless they believed that the information already at hand was incomplete? Indeed, with few exceptions, most databases are not intuitively relevant to most specific projects. It is for this reason that Durance and others have argued that librarians need to know why certain questions are being asked, rather than what the question is: "Studies of information seeking behavior have shown that what people *do* drives their need for information" (1989:127; emphasis in original).

This suggests that adequate help (and training) entails interviewing skills to assemble the general and specific purposes and meanings underlying most queries about information sources and procedures. Information seeking is primarily a communication concern. Educators have long known that people learn through association, a kind of experiential metaphor. Information science must have a foundation in communication and extensive work in social interaction in order to avoid the common fallacy of painting a communication issue with a technological brush. Durance noted, "Indeed, the lack of a good theory of information needs is considered contributory to the fact that changes in information retrieval systems are almost totally technology driven" (1989:127).

The design and eventual use of such information sources appear to be more informed by computer hardware and orientations than thoroughgoing assessments of the meaningful process of information seeking and use. Jones (1989:100ff.) argues that information systems (IS) training has been more hardware oriented and therefore quite constraining to the actual applications of information technology within a business context. How, he asks, can competitive businesses thrive when they must adjust things to a logic and format set by people who have not the slightest familiarity with the context and nuances of the particular business? Traditionally, information systems have been constructed from the computer room outward rather than from the business inward. This is not surprising, since the IS people are trained from the bottom up, first as programmers, then designers, then analysts, rather than first learning the nature of the enterprise. The key is to understand the culture within which information systems work. This is particularly true with a database system, which

> merely normalizes a snapshot of the data needed to support business objectives from a random to a more structured format. . . . [M]ore importantly, how does one decide what to store in a database? (p. 100)

Information formats like electronic databases not only provide information but can also direct inquiry. For example, one reason why statistical approaches, training, and studies have mushroomed in the social sciences is because of the widespread availability of on-line data, usually collected, coded, and organized by somebody else. Notwithstanding tremendous advances in the methodology of social behavior, social science associations seem to pay less attention to such issues in their professional journals, preferring instead to publish analyses that have been hacked out of someone else's data. Research training has been altered accordingly, as graduate students learn quick-and-dirty ways of crunching someone else's numbers, heedless to widely understand concerns about the impact of selective recoding for internal validity.

Information seeking is relevant for power, control, and legitimacy. As Simmel implicitly cautioned, electronic information systems are easily reified as certain, objective, and final. Partly because of their convenience, and partly because of the way they are used routinely, the format of databases looks official and definite. The letters are typed and not scribbled as tentative. But they can be quite misleading, as numerous people have discovered who were properly—but mistakenly—identified as matching criminal suspects, even though claims about mistakes in the computer databases were not questioned until the people had spent one or two nights in jail!

The logic of the format provides a way of recognizing, defining, and interpreting the rule. In this sense, there is no rule violation without a communication format, and this operates independently of the substance or content of the rule. Consider the following scenario, which is transforming efforts at systematic social control and regulation into electronic arenas for action. Computer-assisted telephone hookups are now being used to monitor the whereabouts and state of mind (e.g., drug use) of probationers placed on intensive probation, a kind of prison at home: It works like this in a trial period in Arizona. In addition to periodic visits by a probation officer, an individual under supervision is monitored electronically. A computer named Homer calls a number and asks for an individual. Through voice identification, the computer determines that the callee is indeed the person in question. Then Homer requests the individual to key (or dial up) a series of, say, four digits. Registering the sounds of each number played, Homer concludes, "You passed the dexterity test. Goodbye." Getting the numbers correct is interpreted as evidence that the individual is not stoned. As one spokesperson stated, "You can't fool Homer" (*Arizona Republic*, 5 April 1987).

There are several suggestive points about this disembodied interaction between a machine and an individual. (I will not dwell on the obvious point that the system can be beat by having someone else listen and key in the digits requested by the computer!) For one thing, the individual is regarded as a categorical entity subject to easy direction. Individual interpretations of the situation are unproblematic, easily predictable, and—apparently—totally derived from the definition of the social control agents' design of the communication format. Relatedly, the format itself defines what is deviant, an error, and then affords transsituational assessments of rule violation. Can mistakes in performance be made due to mishandling the telephone keyboard and/or not clearly hearing the commands? Only a very confined sense of the self is compatible with this format, which is designed and intended to operate as a bimodal switch, off or on, yes or no, compliance or not, and so forth.

As suggested in Chapter 2, there is hierarchy and privilege associated with databases and disparate access to information sources. This is where the ecology of communication joins inquiry with broader social concerns. People have differential access to sources of information because of social positions, including the fact that most electronic data sources are sold as products. While this is not the sole problem for the information specialist, it is relevant for broader social concerns since such technologies can widen further the gaps in social opportunities. In this context, opportunities include not only access, but also the transferable skills associated with the ecology of communication, including how to recognize, interpret, and use certain communication formats.

TV AND THE LIBRARY ON THE MOVE

The mass media are a source for analytical insight in the organization of communication because it is a practical problem. More is involved than merely deciding what to put on and when to air it. More fundamental is the temporal and spatial context of TV; a TV screen is two dimensional, but events in real time are three dimensional (at least!). Getting rid of that third dimension, on the one hand, and constructing messages that will also meet some organizational, technical, and commercial considerations, on the other hand, leads TV workers to develop and employ a programming logic that joins entertainment with news.

TV news essentially solves its time and space problem by defining the former in terms of the latter. That is, TV tells time with visuals that will fill the TV screen. Those visuals that are more interesting for an audience (e.g., drama, action and conflict) are the ones that will be presented. Relatedly, events that provide such action are more likely to be selected for coverage. Such considerations pervade the selection, organization, and presentation of news reports, but additional aspects are also apparent. Events that may be reported on the news are now constructed and definitely informed (albeit in problematic ways) with this media logic. For example, politicians key to ten-second one-line comments about complex issues because they know that this is the temporal extent of TV news coverage by the major networks. And they are grammatically correct, because TV grammar, like any organized form of discourse, essentially constitutes its meaning while other things are disregarded. The upshot is that the format of TV news limits what will be presented and what is appropriate, as well as controlling what newsworthiness looks like.

A press conference is another apt example of a format of control. Larry Speakes, former Reagan spokesperson, quickly acquired the skill of this arena for communication:

When Speakes joined the White House press staff in 1974, print reporters outnumbered television reporters three-to-one. He remembers how Ron Nessen, President Ford's press secretary, would prepare for questions on anywhere from 10 to 15 issues a day to accommodate the varying print appetites. Now, Speakes says, the ratio has reversed, and television reporters far outnumber print reporters. The turnaround helps explain Reagan's extraordinary ability—until Iran—to control the media agenda. With television the dominant force in the press room, Speakes says he prepared for one or two major stories a day, which is all television can handle. (Clift 1987:42)

While numerous implications of this format have been addressed elsewhere (Altheide 1985), it is nevertheless useful to consider Speakes's perspective on the relevance of the print format (and its varieties) with electronic media, and their association with audience preferences:

If you're trying to influence Middle America, you go to *USA Today*. If you want to talk to Business America, it's the *Wall Street Journal*. If you're trying to influence Washington at the breakfast table, it's the *Washington Post* and the *New York Times*, in that order. And when you're looking for impact, you go to television. (Clift 1987:42; emphasis added)

It is not coincidental that the press conference logic is informed by the media logic of TV news. Obviously, the former has become transformed by the latter, but for that matter so has the process of institutional claims-making and accounting: politics for public consumption is organized by media formats.

The format and logic have transcended organizational arenas into a general orientation. Now, the technocratic form is ubiquitous. The formats of control are different today; databases and computer techniques are the face of a bureaucratic ethos, even when applied to other activities, e.g., research. Databases are produced and sought by, through, and because of computer formats rather than other justifications, e. g., reliability, validity, as well as other scientific rationales. This "technocratic form" (Altheide & Lauderdale 1987) presents interpretive data as objective and therefore more legitimate in supporting certain claims. An extreme example of this is research purporting to show that mass media reports about suicide and homicide systematically led people to imitate these. Numerous problems with this approach were cited: (1) several reports that significant portions of unsystematically collected data were forced into categories; (2) no theoretical foundation for these claims has withstood even the most casual scrutiny in sociology or psychology; (3) it was never certain that the victims who were alleged to have committed homicide/suicide had ever been exposed to the media messages; (4) the operational definition of suicide (e.g., auto accidents or aircraft crashes occurring within a given time period) was treated as evidence that such crashes constituted suicide! In short, major questions of validity were not carefully addressed in such studies because the data were presumably reliable.

It is this lack of concern with validity that is reflected in computer formats. Validity is not merely a technical problem, an issue of access or retrievability, nor is it easily measured. Relatedly, "scientific audiences," who with their avowed competence now expect to recognize systematic data by their enumerative character, are presumed to be—and act as though they are—familiar with computer formats and the practical matters surrounding the use of databases authored by others. Accordingly, they tend to be forgiving of lack of attention to validity, and join instead with the choir of textbook writers who insist that reliability is the major test of validity.

Qualitative researchers now have available to them a variety of computer aides, even programs for processing field notes (Denzin & Lincoln 1994). However, to use many of these programs, the computer logic decrees that things be put in the proper format. This often requires extensive coding and collapsing of data before any synthesis or conceptual adventures are undertaken. This could become quite problematic because, as we have seen, the logic of formats is intended to reduce ambiguity, to define and order data so that other operations may follow. Most importantly, computer formats are communication guidelines that constitute control.

SUMMARY

The communication process is implicated in any discussion of culture. Communication and culture make each other as Simmel suggested, particularly when numerous cultural forms guide and direct social content. Nowhere is this more apparent than with the explicit mediation of an expanding array of social life by organizational-technological formats. From press conferences to database construction and use to information seeking in libraries, attributions of social competence are tied increasingly to the capacity to recognize, manipulate, and interact with electronic formats. Social selves increasingly are the identities derived in the process of mediation.

Culture is not determined by information technology or its formats. But it is experienced through these, and moreover, the very nature of plausible, intelligible experience is defined and legitimated by familiarity with formats. The culture of electronic communication increasingly is the culture of a postindustrial society. The range of topics, options, and negotiable features of routinized social action is limited by contexts of meaning. Aspects of several examples have been offered through TV news, press conferences, and computers. The aim has been to suggest how such logics have, on the one hand, been incorporated into self-conceptions and activities (e.g., public communication, research) while on the other hand, suggesting how clear communication formats have emerged that articulate the activities in the process of defining and controlling those activities.

The way we understand temporal and spatial definitions and arrangements is essential to a clearer theoretical vision of social organization. Without specifying how and what features of arenas and contexts of an interaction sequence are meaningful, interpreted, and made intelligible, we are left to infer certain avenues by which everyday actors such as gas station attendants and presidents recognize a context of action as one thing rather than another. While such recognition often takes a while and reflexively emerges throughout the course of an activity, it is nevertheless worthwhile to attempt to articulate what formal features may be taken for granted, read, seen, understood, and interpreted. Furthermore, it seems insufficient to merely posit, as learning theorists have done, that our experience teaches us and thereby gets us through future situations. Having essentially accepted the broad strokes of learning theory, it remains to delineate what it is about situations and scenarios that transforms them into recognizable arenas that in turn call forth symbolic meanings retrospectively joining the present to the future via the past.

The problem, then, is to theoretically account for how we recognize any existential moment of awareness and understand how it is actually arrived at. What does the situation look like so that we know that some things are appropriate, while others may not be, that some things would be a bit strange, but permissible, while others would have no impact or would be unintelligible in this context? This is temporal and spatial accounting at a basic level, yet the problem is routinely solved by competent actors who understand the manner of some activity; more often than not they are essentially correct about a situation and its parameters. Moreover, they understand that the operating format is not of their own making, that others have shown authorship through explicit and implicit rules of conduct. Courtrooms are like this, but so are S&M bars. Competence is assured through proper performance, or at least not violating whatever rules may be operative.

When we examine how knowing is an active accomplishment tied to biography and situations mediated through culture and history, it is imperative to attempt to clarify how the interpretive process is communicated and organized. Part of the task is to identify the source and character of how various communicative logics are regulated. It is suggested that format is a general concept for understanding the communication of control.

Information retrieval and understanding are always packaged in socially relevant contexts, like pleasing an instructor, capturing an airborne Oreo, or winning a Nobel prize. Everyone works with information but not all are equipped to be specialists, who operate within a culture of information that they help produce and direct. The main charge is to understand the full extent and impact of this culture to broader social contexts, which are joined through communication formats and the ecology of communication. We can hardly expect citizens—including students—in our pluralistic and heterogeneous society to understand and use information systems without appropriate integration and familiarity. This entails proactive accommodation by information specialists, and as I have suggested, a more general theory of the personal, emotional, and situational contexts of such information requests and interests.

As information construction and retrieval continues to become a distinctive activity in everyday life, that life process will be altered to accommodate this activity. When more activity is mediated through formally rational means, then the opportunities for control can be expected to increase as well. Information specialists are knowledge guides who can enhance citizen involvement and freedom by considering many of the points stressed above, and in particular by making such practices open to scrutiny so that original inquiries can be nurtured and developed into open-ended pursuits rather than being limited to the logic of a prepackaged electronic database. When we make explicit the underlying formats that bind us together through the ecology of communications, we are also helping to decode the very limits of human potential so that we may reflect upon them, and hopefully transcend them. This makes information seeking as important as grabbing a cookie launched by one's favorite teacher. All too often, however, we think we understand the information process well enough that we place a lot of confidence in the information we receive; when our views of the world are influenced by this information, then we have another problem. The mass media represent a compelling argument for understanding IT and formats of control.

In pursuing an understanding of formats of control, it is essential to keep in mind that these are not deterministic, but are regulative. In view of what we know about human behavior and negotiation, it would be theoretically uncouth to insert with the left hand what the right hand has taken away. No. The idea is that asymmetric social relationships abound, partly because of formats of control that influence definitions and interpretations of situations. How things look and are recognized is not inconsequential for social organization.

Human agency to challenge some of the dominant formats further suggests the relevance to understanding social order. It is not implausible that many reform and protest movements build a limited cosmology on the negation of some key formats of control in everyday life, including rhythm, style, and vocabulary.

It is neither inconsequential nor irrelevant for our discussion that a piece of youth culture includes intentionally engaging in grammatically incorrect utterances, intentionally blowing off examinations and other tests, and dramatizing as absurd a host of conventions. It is not that people can be without any formats, but only that it becomes appropriate at certain times and places to demarcate one's identity configuration from others by taking on a youthful format. Talking and walking and dressing as a kind of counter format is thereby implicated in, if not essential, for any countermovement or -organization. Recognition before action.

The language, metaphors, style, and rhythm of everyday life reflexively show their origins as well as direct the present into the future. That we are often stuck with the communication formats even as we seek to understand them, and perhaps negate them, does not dismiss their relevance for the manner of temporal and spatial order we inherit, confront, and seek to change. As with so many other features of social life, the initial act of freedom is recognition of the format and logic of control.

Dispute Transformation and the Ecology of Communication

4

INTRODUCTION

What are people to do when disputes arise? Within the collective culture stream, how do people get a level playing field, or even gain access to the ball park when the customary price of admission to the halls of justice is very steep? How is social justice to be achieved when official and legal forms of recourse such as various levels of litigation (e.g., the courts) are large, overcrowded, expensive, bureaucratic, and not terribly welcoming to outsiders who do not speak the foreign language, i.e., legalese? This chapter examines one approach that is used increasingly by a large proportion of people—a mass media troubleshooter. A key to using this alternative is the realization of the mass appeal of broadcasting the individual cases, giving rise publicly to the concerns and even fears of those agencies charged with wrongs by various citizens. It is the interaction between communication technology, formats of TV news, and the overarching sense of practical resolutions to avoid other costs, charges, or delays that contributes to the appeal and success of a TV troubleshooter. TV is more inclusive than the courts.

This chapter examines the theoretical relevance of the structure and process of communication for the transformation of the disputing process. TV as a medium (IT) has been massaged through organizational contexts to produce TV news formats, which, while distinctive from print news media formats, continue to influence the range of public information media and forums. The place of the news media and especially TV news in the effective environment for many activities is represented in Figure 4.1. This and subsequent chapters illustrate the interaction of TV news with organizational activities including dispute resolution, the creation of social issues, state policing and control, and terrorism and warfare.

The multiple purposes and meanings of television to numerous viewers in our society is apparent. More than mere entertainment, TV is now used for information (e.g., news), baby-sitting, background sound, burglary preven-

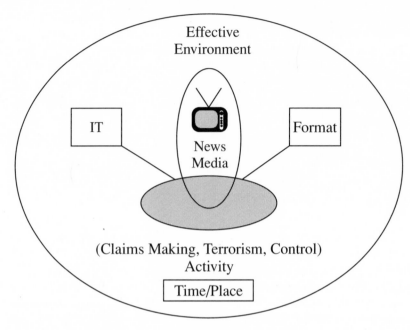

Figure 4.1. An ecology of communication and the relevance of news media for significant activities.

tion (i.e., leaving the TV on while away from home), shopping, religious worship, as well as dispute resolution. Materials from one study will be used to clarify how individual disputes are linked through a television troubleshooter (TVT) to the social and political order (cf. Mather & Yngvesson 1981) through an ecology of communication, recognized as part of the effective environment by numerous TV viewers.

The pervasiveness and impact of the mass media on various facets of everyday life (cf. Altheide & Snow 1991) have directed researchers' attention to examine whether the media can play a constructive role in resolving and sanctioning major civil and criminal disputes as well as complaints about minor injustices (cf. Surette 1992; Fisse & Braithwaite 1983). The potential relevance of the mass media for justice issues is further heightened by Nader's (1984:60) observation that complaints about goods and services have no place in the judicial system. However, Black (1984) contends that a sociological theory of compensation must identify the social conditions and the process through which compensation is administered. If the mass media play a part in this process, then they must be considered.

The ecology of communication can be useful in delineating why one forum and option for dispute processing is selected rather than another.

Communication concepts seldom have been employed theoretically to interpret differential participation in various forums for dispute processing. Despite massive perceptions of injustice (partly fueled by mass-mediated depictions of victimization), TV audiences tend to not regard formal adjudication forums and mechanisms within their effective environment. For example:

(1)   Less than one-third of American adults have been a party to civil litigation.

(2)   There is an inverse relationship between a person's geographical distance from court and the likelihood to litigate (cf. Buxbaum 1971).

(3)   Several studies suggest that 25 percent or more of disgruntled consumers elect to "lump it" rather than seek redress to problems (cf. Ladinsky & Susmilch 1985).

The structure of communication has not played a role in the deterrence or promotion of citizens' use of various dispute alternatives, including transforming and reformulating an individual dispute into public discourse, although the communication process is clearly suggested in Mather and Yngvesson's (1981:777ff.) discussion of *narrowing* (e.g., through specialized tribunals) and *expansion* (e.g., rephrasing to illustrate the relevance to third parties). Notwithstanding Galanter's observations that "[t]he central role of adjudication is mediated and symbolic rather than the direct and authoritative disposition of disputes" (1988:182), and "[d]isputants' capabilities derive from, and are relative to structures of communication and structures for organizing action" (p. 221), it remains to delineate how the organization of communication informs and reflects the social structure of adjudication and dispute transformation. This is part of our project. The relevance of work in communication for clarifying important issues about dispute resolution, including knowledge, access, public perception and use, and effectiveness, needs to be conceptualized. Informed by an ecology-of-communication perspective, the project locates the appeal and activity of a TVT within the "wider ecology of dispute processing," or various formal and informal forums for adjudication, arbitration, litigation, mediation, self-help, and avoidance (pp. 160ff.).

The organization of communication about status distinctions is central to social order, including justice guidelines and settlement behavior and procedures. As Mather and Yngvesson (1981) and others have noted, justice and legitimacy promote as well as require a communicative form and basic communicative competence. Legitimacy is coded and enlivened through patterned and institutionalized action. A key issue is how transformation occurs: "By transformation of a dispute we mean a change in its form or content as a result of the interaction and involvement of other participants in the dispute process" (p. 777).

For example, the legal process is partially constituted by rules and procedures about who talks with whom, when, and about what. However, participants' differences in experience, knowledge, and competence seldom permit balanced or symmetrical communication; asymmetry is the rule. The asymmetry of superordination and subordination inherent in legal proceedings (Black 1984:24ff.) thereby implies a communications logic and perspective.

In order for a disputant to take action to resolve a dispute that has been constituted through unfulfilled claims, cognitive options must be available to focus action and plan the next step. While Mather and Yngvesson (1981:780) are certainly correct that language, participants, and the audience help shape the transformation of disputes, it is the way in which these components are systematically organized and recognized by parties to the disputing process that must be explicated: "The forum . . . tends to develop its own distinctive views, interests and deeds. . . . Its institutional needs become one of the determinants of the process that transpires there" (Galanter 1988:158).

Each forum (or model) of dispute processing is distinguished and recognized by its format for selecting, organizing, and style of work to resolve disputes. The format and nature of discourse are particularly significant for publics to join the dispute process. Disputants recognize the differences in a general way, and thereby avoid some forums in favor of others:

> The channels of communication are especially important for explaining the dynamics of the type of expansion, since the control over those channels influences the extent to which a wider audience can be mobilized. For example, the gossip network of a small fishing village or the *mass media* in modern society play a key role in developing an audience which affects the course of a dispute. (Mather & Yngvesson 1981:810; emphasis added)

The theoretical significance of mass communication as a feature of the ecology of communication for the transformation of dispute resolution, informalism, and the radiating effects of law will be illustrated with data obtained from a sample of approximately one hundred complainant letters to a TVT during 1981–85, follow-up replies, and transcripts of cases selected for airing. These issues will be examined within the context of TV action lines, noting in particular the history of complainants' quests for compensation, why the TVT's help was sought, the complainants' views about justice, and the TVT's logic and criteria in selecting particular complaints for broadcast. Specific questions to be addressed include:

(1)   Is the communication process and the ecology of communication relevant to the transformative and radiating effects of dispute resolution?

(2)   Can the mass media (especially television) contribute to the practice and perception of resolving complaints about goods and services, which essentially have no place in the judicial system?

(3)   what kind(s) of dispute resolution are enacted by the TVT?

(4)   Does the communication process and format of television contribute to a sociological theory of compensation and dispute resolution (cf. Harrington 1985)?

THE ECOLOGY OF COMMUNICATION AND ADJUDICATION

Use of various forums for dispute resolution depends on knowledge, access, familiarity, appropriateness, and legitimacy. A key aspect of access, of course, is cost. Despite the increase in lawsuits in the United States, formal agencies of adjudication are beyond the reach and practical use of the majority of citizens. The organization and control of communication guidelines and rules are prior to any settlement process. Issues about access to and use of legal proceedings presume that various parties to such interactions have the basic communicative competence to engage an institutional order such as a highly codified legal process. Relatedly, issues about access presume that potential users of legal channels interpret formal and subtle guidelines as inclusive rather than exclusive. Exclusivity is communicated through guidelines that proclaim that specialized language and training is required, for oneself or a translator, i.e., an attorney. According to Galanter, "Adjudication is typically conducted by professional specialists who have recourse to special forms of knowledge, discontinuous with everyday understandings, and not expressed in everyday language" (1988:158). Through a process of symbolic interaction, claimants become disputants as they recognize, define, interpret, and essentially construct a meaningful course of action on the basis of familiarity and prior experience with cultural symbols comprising an *awareness context*. Prior work by Meyrowitz (1985) and others treats situations as information systems, as perceptual fields that establish differential patterns of access to information. The communication order influences the nature of the "[c]onstruction of disputes [which] entails the perception of injuries, the identification of persons or institutions responsible for remedying them, location of forums and acceptable presentation to them, investment of appropriate resources and resistance of attempts at diversions" (Galanter 1988:183).

These considerations involve awareness of criteria for inclusion and exclusion, including communicative competence (e.g., semantics and syntax), fees for service, temporal and spatial coordination, and bureaucratic-legal-rational ordering (e.g., evidence). Thus, Galanter's articulation of the adjudicative forum as reactive, rather than proactively oriented to "bring cases into itself," suggests the exclusionary character: "The forum . . . tends to develop its own distinctive views, interests and needs. . . . [I]ts institutional needs become one of the determinants of the process that transpires there" (1988:155). For example, courtroom formats have been empirically demonstrated to be exclusive (cf. Bennett & Feldman 1983; O'Barr 1982). Television formats, on the other hand, involve grammar of film—editing, voice-over, intonation, transitions—and norms for defining and emphasizing content—audience relevance, drama, tragedy, visual emphasis. The mass media in general and the TVT in particular operate more inclusively than traditional legal forums because of differing formats (cf. Altheide 1985). Inclusivity is communicated through guidelines more akin to popular culture, whereby individuals invite readers, listeners, or viewers to approach them for assistance, products, and the like.

DISPUTE RESOLUTION AND INFORMAL JUSTICE

Any mode of dispute resolution and/or the pursuit of justice reflects an ideology and constitutes a form of social control (cf. Black 1984; Harrington 1985; Palenski & Launer 1986). Legitimacy in a social order partially is fostered and often politically is manipulated through the sanctioning, control, and availability of forms of redress. The breadth, scope, and relevance of formal justice rules and procedures for ideology are manifested in their breach, when informal and other innovative modes of justice emerge or are proposed. When justice alternatives are set forth they are accompanied by a communicative logic involving rules of discourse that reflect the underlying logic and assumptions.

Unfortunately, theoretical work on communicative logic in general and the mass media in particular has not been integrated with either formal or informal dispute resolution (cf. Bennett & Feldman 1983). This absence seems compelling since communicative instrumentalities and interpretation are involved in legal discourse, interaction throughout litigation, or informal discussions, as well as the establishing and conveying of symbolic meaning between two or more parties in a dispute.

For most people in our society the business of policing and administering justice, maintaining order, enforcing public rules, and managing disputes between citizens is a state function, although there are numerous alternatives (cf. Galanter 1988). As noted above, while the state is presumed to have an interest in controlling and limiting what can be contested and potentially delegitimated, legal changes are viewed by scholars as of paramount importance for changing the social order. This is particularly important when disputing parties have unequal power and resources (Nader

1984). For this reason, access to the courts and the essential litigation to redress injustices are regarded by many as essential for promoting a just social order. Not surprisingly, many scholars caution against the use of nonlegalistic forms of settlement, arguing that settlement may actually retard justice (Odom 1986:16). From this perspective, legal precedent and legitimate condemnation of an action or policy are essential to cumulatively help *citizens qua citizens*, a more important outcome than merely helping a *citizen* redress a grievance.

Since the legal model renders courts the significant medium for proclaiming what is just and unjust, a settlement is merely that: no judgment is forthcoming, and justice is left undone. In short then, the locus of justice is societal and therefore institutional rather than personal or interactional; individual satisfaction is not isomorphic with justice. Thus, the very notion of dispute resolution is a form of social control and legitimates the status quo. Indeed, as suggested above, some critiques contend that the use of informal dispute options, including mass media action lines, essentially are supportive of state domination because they serve to misdirect attention to specific grievances rather than injustice and in particular to structural and systemic social or economic problems (cf. Harrington 1985).

Despite the prominence of the state-legal model, a variety of contrasting forms of dispute and conflict resolution exist outside the bounds of the state apparatus (cf. Gulliver 1979; Pearson 1982; Galanter 1988), although the alternatives may nevertheless support and/or affirm the basic state logic. One alternative is the self-help model of justice, a form in which "an offended party takes action on his or her own behalf . . . with or without the assistance of third parties other than those who are specialized agents of social control" (Baumgartner 1980:194). The use of self-help measures to secure justice or otherwise resolve disputes has a history predating the evolution of the state and the growth of law. While theory predicts an inverse relationship between law and self-help (Black 1984), reliance on self-help methods has persisted despite the state's effort to gain a monopoly on the "property" of human conflict (Baumgartner 1980:194).

Another type of dispute resolution is informal dispute resolution that relies on mediation by a third party(s), but is unaffiliated with a formal justice agency (Abel 1982; Henry 1983). As delineated by Abel:

> Such institutions are informal to the extent that they are nonbureaucratic in structure [and] minimize the use of professionals and eschew official law in favor of substantive and procedural norms that are vague, unwritten, commonsensical, flexible, ad hoc, and particularistic. (1982:2)

Informal dispute resolution, including various forms of mediation by third parties—arbitration and negotiation—have gained support for various reasons, including ideological consistency noted above, but also because of problems of access to courts, expenses, and lengthy delays. Advocates of these alternatives forcefully argue that most disputes dealt with through informal means would never make it to court (cf. Singer 1983:361ff.). Poor people, for example, tend to lack access to courts and attorneys, and therefore tend to not have their disputes dealt with at all (cf. Danzig & Lowy 1975). Furthermore, research suggests that many grievances do not satisfy relevant institutional and/or legal guidelines as legal issues and are therefore excluded.

There is also the issue of outcomes from various proceedings. McEwen and Maiman's (1981) study of Maine's small claims programs found that claimants were more likely to win something in mediation cases compared to adjudication cases, although the amounts were not as likely to be as large. Comparing this finding with the utility of mediation for domestic cases (cf. Mnookin & Kornhauser 1975) led Pearson to conclude:

> There is definitely sound evidence that mediation and arbitration have strengths to make distinct contributions to the satisfactory administration of justice. Based on the evidence to date, they clearly complement court adjudication in important ways. (1983:345)

Because many disputes in a technological and bureaucratic society involve consumer complaints with products and services, many dispute resolution alternatives are designed to arbitrate and/or mediate a claimant's concerns. These include ombudsmen to oversee national, state, and local governments' operations as well as complaints by individuals against the respective governments (Johnson, Kantor, & Schwartz 1977). Despite some success in foreign countries, ombudsmen are limited by varieties of political pressure as well as inadequate resources and personnel (cf. Stacey 1978; Weeks 1978).

Consumer complaint mechanisms have been established by government as well as business. With the former, legislation mandating and forbidding certain trade practices has been the most common, although consumer protection bureaus are often associated with state attorney generals' offices. These agencies have law enforcement powers, but their main thrust has been to serve as "an informal dispute resolution mechanism which focuses on solving the dispute at hand in which the individual complainant has a stake" (Johnson et al. 1977). Of course, these agencies are oriented to wrongdoing involving legally proscribed violation, and are less help to consumers in the myriad of inquiries on the borderline of illegal conduct (e.g., interpretations of warranty protection).

Perhaps the best-known consumer protection agency is the Better Business Bureau (BBB). Despite its aim to affect a large number of consumers by correcting patterns of abuse, the BBB's dependence on the business community for support has led it to serve primarily as a cooling-out agency for complaints, or to actually withdraw from a case when a business contests the customer's complaint (cf. Johnson et al. 1977:66ff.; Nader 1984:85).

ACTION LINES IN CONTEXT

Action lines often are incorporated within TV newscasts and thereby reflect that logic and those criteria (cf. Comstock 1980; Altheide 1976, 1985; Altheide & Snow 1979). While students of dispute resolution have noted that "it is critical to have an agent of transformation who can act as a broker— one who can communicate to disputants and others . . . to translate the concerns of disputants and public into the official disputing language" (Mather & Yngvesson 1981:819), action lines like the TVT have not been conceptualized as a broker, but mainly in terms of the personality, champion, or therapist who can give disputing parties insight "into their situation or themselves" (cf. Galanter 1988:161–63). Delineating the place of the TVT within the ecology of communication and dispute resolution has not been attempted. For example, what assumptions about justice and access to other forums of adjudication underlie letter writers' claims and requests? Indeed, if Galanter (p. 182) is correct that adjudication's central role is symbolic rather than direct involvement in disputes, then it would seem theoretically cogent to investigate the mediation processes and outcomes of TV troubleshooters, which is particularly relevant to clarify the radiating effects of adjudication.

TV troubleshooting is part of a general movement toward alternatives to dispute resolution that has been initiated by government as well as nongovernmental agencies. It is justice in a popular culture context of entertaining a mass audience which nevertheless is consistent with Mather and Yngvesson's argument that

> a further requirement for expansion in social contexts characterized by the kind of organizational complexity is that of a medium (such as newspapers, television, etc.) through which a broader public can be reached. (1981:819)

What is interesting about troubleshooting from a communications perspective is that the reader, listener, or viewer is already involved with the medium—the newspaper, the radio, the television. This mass medium is part of their effective environment, and they are familiar with it.

It is no wonder that TVT services attract more interest and requests than virtually all other forms combined, including state and national ombudsmen. The *Houston Chronicle* started "Watchem" in 1961. The nation's first media dispute resolution service received more than two thousand calls during its first twenty-four hours (Shapiro 1983:509). The 1960s and 1970s saw a rapid proliferation of action lines and related mass media referral and consumer assistance. One source estimates that there were some four hundred action lines operating in the United States (Mattice 1980:485ff.). Intended to increase readership, listeners, and viewers, action lines also helped fulfill Federal Communications Commission license requirements about community service and information. The most thorough review of media ombudsmen (mainly newspapers) concluded that the massive adoption of action lines in the middle 1960s was due to the "chance confluence of the interests of liberal journalists, newspaper owners and the relatively more advantaged members of the mass society" (Palen 1979:842). This particular review concluded that social justice was not fulfilled, because action lines served mainly as a referral service. Public perceptions were clearly much different, as thousands of audience members requested assistance. Indeed, in the New York area in 1976, nearly six thousand letters requesting help and information were submitted to local television stations (Palen 1979:810ff.)!

Accessible to newspaper readers, radio listeners, and television viewers, action lines shared a mediating role between an individual and usually a business or government agency. While these action lines could often help mediate a dispute or complaint (Nader 1984:83ff.) through mere expertise and competence in facilitating communication and taking some bureaucratic shortcuts, it was also clear that their voice—and letterhead—carried some legitimacy and potential clout. Moreover, it was understood that action lines could use *publicity* about a dispute as leverage in promoting quick and equitable settlements, although Mattice reports that "there may be a greater tendency among action lines to use publicity pressure against government than against private-sector complainees" (1980:506ff.).

The ability of different types of forums to facilitate general solutions to classes of problems has received little attention, despite findings that poor people will use alternative forums for assistance if access is easier, e.g., newspaper ombudsmen, who can speed the process (cf. Singer 1983:358). This is particularly important for power imbalances between individuals and the organizations from which they seek redress. This includes the way call-for-action hot lines may be incorporated into traditional legal modes of action (cf. Rothschild & Throne 1976):

> Some media action programs have succeeded both in exposing patterns of abuse and inputting information concerning recurring complaints on computers for the use of enforcement agencies concerned with consumer fraud. (Singer 1983:361)

The impact of action lines has not been well understood, partially because they have been expected to perform the same function as traditional legal forums. In contrasting two ideal type orientations of alternative complaint models, Nader suggested a "producer model" and a "consumer model" (1984:87ff.). Our preliminary investigations and review of literature suggest that action lines tend to handle complaints on an individual basis, as predicted by the production model, but they also incorporate the following features of a consumer model: the complaint system is public; product information belongs to the user public; the complaint is exercising the rights of a buyer; and actors within corporations are responsible.

The structure, operation, and overall logic of the TVT and staff in this study are similar to the profile set forth by Mattice (1980). However, as we will reiterate below, there were two important differences: First, the TVT operations studied were more oriented to publicity and broadcasting stories about specific businesses and agencies. Second, the mediating role between individuals and businesses, while helpful, was not as intense as other cases in the literature, e.g., the *Oakland Tribune* (cf. Mattice 1980:503ff.).

In brief then, self-help effort is included within the format of TV news, which in turn uses third-party mediation as a practical alternative to formal justice agencies. Individuals' complaints can be selected for airing and possibly for resolution because they are cast in TV news formats of conflict, controversy, and drama (cf. Altheide 1976; Altheide & Snow 1991; Nader 1980). Moreover, when the casting of individual complaints takes the form of individuals vs. organizations, corporations, and larger entities, as they invariably do, then a cultural thematic David and Goliath emphasis is operating to strike a responsive chord in viewers and thereby enable the TVT to help people and to maintain an audience (cf. Schwartz 1974).

THE AUDIENCE AS DISPUTANTS

In a mass society the communication order helps shape the ecology of dispute resolution (Maines & Couch 1988). The mass media are the major source of public information about the nature and variety of dispute resolution forums. It is the way media transform the temporal and spatial dimensions of one object or event to make it fit with formats that comprises media power: "There is absolutely (if not proportionately) more law stuff that invites media coverage with its built-in bias toward the dramatic, the novel, the deviant; toward innovation and conflict" (Galanter 1988:228). Furthermore, the transformation of information into the members "stock of knowledge" (Schutz 1967) that was suggested in Chapter 1 is apparent when audience members treat the media depictions as a kind of summary of "that's the way it is," translate such images back into the event itself, and then act or develop an impression of "how things are" (cf. Altheide 1985; Blumler & Katz 1974; Levy 1979). Apparently, participation and familiarity with TV technology, logic, and formats is part of the "culture stream." This suggests that individuals become viewers by adjusting to and accepting the rules and logic of the format that joins the medium with the content, and with their viewing situation.

Several implications follow from the this view about the nature and significance of communication for dispute resolution. Specifically, "mass communication should be analyzed as an interaction between communicator and audience in which both parties use perspectives and grammatical rules to perceive and interpret various phenomena" (Snow 1983:26–27). Within the ecology of communication: (1) mass media constitute a source of information on subjects of relevance; (2) mass media provide information about assumptions and perspectives underlying most attempts at learning; (3) mass media are used as legitimate and trusted agents for what is presumably credible information; (4) there are vicarious and overt interaction networks within the media industry and between audiences and the medium. It is the way such media are used and interpreted by audience members that underlies the approaches taken by action lines in general, and the troubleshooter we are focusing on in particular.

DATA AND METHOD

In 1980, a local TV station (Channel A) initiated a TVT segment of its regular evening newscast. Another (Channel B) followed suite two years later, and eventually hired the TVT away from Channel A. In terms of audience popularity, the radiating effects of this forum of dispute resolution paid dividends. Like numerous news media outlets that have attempted to expand viewer ratings with public service and the drama and excitement of investigative reporting, these stations sought to provide an alternative for those viewers whose complaints and concerns had fallen through the various cracks of businesses and government agencies and that were not likely to get much of a hearing through formal legal channels, or even the informal forums that comprise the remainder of the matrix of dispute resolution.

Our work for the past several years has involved collecting the materials, interviewing staff members, developing a protocol for data collection and analysis (Pfuhl & Altheide 1987), and testing and refining this instrument on a sample of materials. The research focus was on the nature and kinds of complaints for which people seek help, the character of resolution, which kinds of complaints are selected for broadcast, and the format for presenting the reports.

The method of study is informed by the process followed by the complainants and the stations. In addition to informal interviews with members of the TVT staff, we collected data from complainants, who were invited to write to the TVT with their collected data from a random sample of files and transcripts and to tell the TVT their concerns (cf. Mattice 1980). These letters were then read by staff members, who in turn called and/or wrote to the complainee (the business) about the problem. The following letter was sent on TVT and station stationery:

> The enclosed letter was sent to [TVT] at Channel [ ]. Because we believe the information merits your attention, we would appreciate any answer or resolution you can provide. Is there anything you can do to help our viewer? For our mutual benefit, we ask you to do the following: Communicate directly with the viewer. Send Channel [ ] a copy of that communication. Many thanks for your assistance.

The targets of the complaints often replied to the station with their view of the problem, and in many cases, what they planned to do to resolve the issue. The initial letter, follow-up replies, and miscellaneous information became the file for each complaint.

Data were collected from a stratified sample of 100 of approximately 2,600 audience letters, and transcripts of 231 TVT broadcasts of audience concerns, which were aired during the nearly five-year tenure (1981–1985) of one TVT, who worked serially at two TV stations in the Phoenix metropolitan area. When data permitted, we included the files for the cases that were broadcast in order to systematically compare them with complaints on similar topics that were not selected for broadcast. Such a comparison clarifies how TV news formats may select in favor of certain frames for complaints, rather than others.

Data analysis was carried out with the aid of a highly interactive database manager (Data Base Manager II, DBMII). Such "ethnographic content analysis" (Altheide 1987) involves both quantitative and qualitative data analysis, permitting five-level searches of key words, topics, themes, and other alphanumeric characters, and numerical values. Coding precision and narrative descriptions are important for this mode of analysis in order to enhance progressive reflection for additional insights. Accordingly, the content analysis of these documents was carried out with the aid of two protocols—one for the letters and one for the broadcasts—according to the format and logic of the DBMII for an IBM personal computer.

COMPLAINANT LETTERS

The protocols for the letters and the broadcasts contain similar categories, with a few exceptions. Key questions and concepts were operationalized as follows. In addition to case identification (and year), data were collected from approximately one hundred letters on the following variables that have been found to be relevant theoretically for TV news attention, informal justice, and dispute resolution:

1.   Date, gender, address, and census track of complainant provided data about *perceived access across a range of social categories.*

2.   Letter form and quality provided data about power imbalances, type of case, communicative competence and its relevance for inclusion within the TVT format.

3.   Appeal type—as more reasoned or emotional—clarified the *range of discourse compatible with a TVT as a settlement agent.*

4.   Information about follow-up conversations with the complainee, and whether a response was even obtained from the complainee prior to contacting the TVT, clarified *the complainant's prior efforts to resolve the issue through other informal means.*

5.   Finally, data about the bulk of the packet (i.e., documentation) and other descriptive information *provide information about the complainants' experience with other prospective settlement agents, as well as the temporal order of the complaint.*

Numeric and alphanumeric codes were developed for each of these variables. Specifically, ten types of cases emerged from our preliminary examination of the data: retail (nonauto), government, auto (sales/repair), auto (other), employer/employee, crime victim, medical/dental, public utility, tax (property/income), other. The category including the most cases was retail (nonauto), $N = 42$. The majority of the illustrative materials to follow will be drawn from these files.

AIRED STORIES

The protocol for aired stories includes data about the type of services in which the complainee is involved, a summary of what is in dispute, how the complaint/issue was cast by the TV presentation, the nature of the resolution (if there was one), whether or not the complainant or complainee appeared on camera, whether a response was forthcoming, and how much background information was provided. In addition, narrative summaries were provided about the focus of the report, what was unique about it, and whether there were any visuals. Even though these materials were transcripts, relevant visuals were noted. As data permitted, complainant letters associated with aired reports were examined in order to further compare the appeal, topic, and format features of those selected for broadcast with those which were not.

FINDINGS ABOUT COMPLAINANT LETTERS

One way to clarify why disputants select a particular forum for resolving a dispute is to examine their accounts (the letters) of their perceptions and understandings about that forum, as well as their experiences with other options. In contrast to the exclusivity of most traditional legal forums, which favor disputants with certain economic and educational backgrounds, the more inclusive format of the TVT permitted—indeed, encouraged—complainants from various social classes and ethnic neighborhoods. For example, Wieland's (1988) study of an expanded sample of 229 cases from this same database found that access to the troubleshooter as well as favorable resolution occurred in the less affluent Phoenix census tracts (26 percent), in the outer limits of Phoenix (29 percent), and in the more affluent suburbs (25 percent). Moreover, these findings hold despite the more articulate letters and complaint documentation from suburban disputants whose economic and cultural capital would give them an advantage within traditional legal forums. Clearly then, in terms of access, the TVT is inclusive.

Focusing on forty-two retail (nonauto) letters from the sample reveals the following: While most complaints in this category were about products, there were also several concerns about refunds for services not received, including complaints about the nonresponsiveness of other niches in the matrix of dispute processing (e.g., the county attorney). A stratified random sample of letters in 1981–1982 revealed that complaints were made by twenty-four women and nineteen men about motel reservations, a water bill, a water bed, a short concert, magazine subscriptions, defective tires, damage due to an automatic car wash, swimming pool companies, vacuum cleaners, faulty floor coverings and service, eviction from a trailer court, refunds on rental equipment, dead grass, and other concerns.

The data indicated a clear relationship between resolving the dispute and whether the letter was selected for a broadcast report. In the latter category, 40 percent of the complainants were favored by the resolutions, while only 17 percent of letters (retail, nonauto) that were followed up on but not selected for broadcast were resolved in favor of the complainants. However, complainees (accused) seemed to have prevailed in eight cases. The remainder, or more than half of the cases not selected for airing, were referred to other agencies and, from what we could ascertain, remained unresolved.

Equally interesting, however, was the impact of the TVT's inquiry. While only a portion of the cases were resolved in favor of the complainant, it is important to note that simply *getting a response* from a business or an organization can itself be a victory. With the exception of one case that was resolved prior to TVT action, the others appear to have been influenced by the media inquiries, albeit for the wrong reason—to avoid negative publicity rather than to provide justice.

The mediating effects of this mode of dispute resolution are suggested by the way in which some people turned to the TVT at the same time, or even prior to, making an effort to negotiate with the disputant, or seeking other resources that could help them (e.g., the Better Business Bureau, small claims court and superior court). There are a number of features common to the complainants.

1. The writers feel genuinely wronged, cheated, misled, and angered by the nature and quality of service and/or product.

2. The complaint is initiated in desperation, partly motivated by the belief that no other channel offers effective help.

3. There is a reasoned argument, usually supported by specifics and in many instances, documentation about dates of conversations, contracts, and names of individuals involved. Clearly, many of the disputants were blending and expanding a more formal and litigious logic into the more inclusive realm of the TVT. More individual consumers appear to be moving toward an awareness of what we would term the *litigate* or *formal-rational* model of dispute resolution.

4. In many of the cases we have examined, businesses were not overly responsive to initial consumer concerns.

5. The TVT's inquiries usually got a reply, although it was not always what the original writer desired.

6. As far as style is concerned, with only a few exceptions, the business replies were typewritten (compared to 73 percent of the complaints), more articulate, and more rationally presented than the complaints. The complainants' letters were written personally for the TVT, while the replies reflected a more impersonal objective style, written for the record. In only one case was a complaint letter written on the letterhead of an organization with which the writer was affiliated. (The problem involved a motel refusing to house a Pop Warner football team that was coached by the writer.) However, replies on letterhead from companies were more typical. More than half of our sample files contained responses on letterhead (cf. Palen 1979).

7. Many of the complaints concerned the quality of the service or product. For example, several writers inquired about getting refunds from con-

certs they had attended that were either too brief or where the seating was poor.

FINDINGS ON AIRED STORIES

Unlike the action lines discussed by Mattice (1980) in which the threat of publicity followed a long series of negotiations about resolving a particular case, the format of the show was oriented to publicity and transforming an individual dispute into an example of a broader class that could be recognized by the viewing audience, who in turn, it was hoped, would continue the cycle by writing to the TVT with their own complaints. Examining the reports broadcast while the TVT was affiliated with Channel A reveals that most of these reports focused on individuals' disputes and disagreements with businesses, although the latter period saw nearly an equal number of topics related to government concerns (e.g., sewage, building ordinances, flooding, traffic signals). Frequently, the writers expressed chagrin, disappointment and frustration in dealing with other agencies (e.g., the Better Business Bureau or the attorney general). Not uncommon were comments such as, "All we get is the runaround," "I am in desperate need of your help . . . immediately!!!" "I told [merchant] I was reporting him to BBB [Better Business Bureau] and [TVT Channels A and B]," "I need your help! Can you help me?" "We have exhausted all other avenues of recourse . . . we believe you are our last resort." A woman who had some problems with the government over taxes wrote, "Thank you for being so sweet to an old lady . . . may God bless you every step." One writer who was concerned about a sewer problem wrote, "My lawyer told me to get in touch with you since I do not have the money."

Examination of the data indicates that the major motive for the TVT segments studied was to improve lucrative audience ratings, while also providing a service to viewers. The aim was to broadcast interesting, worthwhile, and entertaining reports that could feature on-the-air resolution. It was assumed that such an approach promoted the station's work in the community interest, as well as promoted the station with its viewers, and indirectly, advertising revenue. Not surprisingly, elements of entertainment formats that influenced TV content can be found throughout the TVT reports (cf. Altheide & Snow 1979; Snow 1983; Altheide 1985). These include action, drama, visual juxtaposition, mythic confrontations between good and evil, right and wrong, and weak and powerful developed over a narrative story line with a beginning, middle, and end. This is relevant because at least one recent critique of media ombudsmen implied that the interests of private enterprise were incompatible with the premise of informal justice, namely, that individuals could be assisted (Abel 1982). However, this claim overlooks how TV action lines can mediate informal justice in two senses: (1) TV formats cast individual appeals for help (self-help) within an informal justice frame, and (2) the mass media aspect of TV formats broadcasts and makes a private dispute public.

It is the nature and process of publication that adds a critical and decisive feature to informal justice as a feature of the ecology of dispute resolution that heretofore has been neglected (cf. Abel 1982). Liability may be less dependent on "the efficiency of existing legal procedures to review evidence" (Koch 1984:101) than on the publication of a complaint against an organization, including a governmental agency.

The confrontation seemed to be more important than the actual resolution of a dispute, although, as noted previously, complainants' satisfaction was more likely to be forthcoming if their problems were selected for airing. For example, analysis of sixty-four files for 1984 indicates that the complainants prevailed in 25 percent (sixteen) of the cases and the complainee seemed to get the upper hand in 3 percent (two) of the cases, but by far the most common result was that the outcome of the conflict or disagreement was neither resolved nor predictable in 61 percent (thirty-nine) of the cases.

In sum, discourse was extended and dialogue did occur as disputes were transformed from private concerns to public considerations. What appears to be critical for our subjects is *communicative legitimacy*, in which the form, style, and content of the response to their complaints indicates that they are being taken seriously, and that this communication niche is accessible and responsive to their needs. The data suggest that people may intend several things when they request the TVT's assistance, and expect a range of dispute resolution options, ranging from adjudication, arbitration, mediation, therapy, to negotiation. In some cases, people requested help when other alternatives in the ecological matrix of dispute processing had failed them, but this was not always the case. On the one hand, it is clear that most cases would fall under substantive or distributive justice rather than procedural justice; most of our complainants were more concerned about satisfactory outcomes than proper procedures. On the other hand, many of the complainants expressed some satisfaction when the TVT's inquiries prompted complainees to respond.

SUMMARY

TV troubleshooters, as part of viewers' effective environment, not only help people, but also raise important theoretical questions about the relationship of information technology to the mass media, social control, law, organizations, and communications. Work to date has demonstrated that communication formats and processes are inextricably connected to issues that flow from them (e.g., communicative legitimacy, access, including the radiating effects of mass media coverage of crime, deviance, and justice). Numerous complainants reported that criminal justice agencies could not help them because no law had been violated, but that the TVT was able to provide assistance. Contrary to claims by others (Abel 1982), this aid often took the form of directing the problem to complainees or at least implying conflict vis-à-vis the TVT and complainees, including large businesses, police departments, and social welfare institutions. That this conflict was a feature of the TV format does not negate its impact and relevance for informal justice in everyday life.

The reinvention and development of action line news media formats (cf. Mattice 1980) have made it possible for individual problems to receive public attention and resolution, albeit on a case-by-case basis that may reduce public awareness of more fundamental problems (cf. Abel 1982: 267ff.). While such actions do not have the power of law, their transformative role can provide informal organizational surveillance akin to the "radiating effects of law, [of the] effects of the communication of information by/about the forum's action and of the response to that communication of information by/about the forum's action and of the response to that information" (Galanter 1988:215).

There is a major theoretical position that this study does not support. This may be called the *evil centralization thesis,* which is stated quite clearly by Carey's rendition of Innis's point of view.

> Innis principally disputed the notion that electricity would replace centralization in economics and politics with decentralization, democracy, and a cultural revival. Innis placed the "tragedy of modern culture" in America and Europe upon the intrinsic tendencies of both printing press and electronic media to reduce space and time to the service of a calculus of commercialism and expansionism. (Carey 1989:133–34)

What this study suggests, however, is that centralized electronic media can contribute to citizens qua citizens, even though the commercial and ratings interest of the TV station can also benefit from the entertaining troubleshooter segments. However, to be fair to Innis, it should also be stressed that the cases most selected by the TVT for inclusion fit the entertainment format criteria of TV news. The culture stream is channeled, albeit loosely, with TV information technology, flowing with entertainment formats. Yet more mass-mediated justice was provided for dozens of people who were excluded from the very expensive procedures needed to get them into the halls of justice. They got it on television! Thus, without discounting Innis's and others' pronouncements about the impact of information technology on social order and the activities through which it is constituted, this work suggests that it remains, as always, an empirical question; it remains theoretically critical to examine whether informal justice as mediated through TV formats can have institutional effects in resolving numerous individual complaints, as well as referring individuals to other agencies, and conversely.

This project has made a modest effort to clarify the transformative process by examining the work of one TVT in order to theoretically enhance our understandings about the practical contexts of mediation, which include circumstance, situation, and biography and history (cf. Maines & Powell 1986; Maines & Couch 1988). One implication is that practical justice can occur through the mass media court, although the formats of this framework are much different than the courtrooms from which so many people are excluded for all practical purposes. The remaining chapters examine what has happened to not only legal, but also popular conceptions of justice and the implications this can have when they are placed in the manipulative hands of media-conscious decision-makers.

Gonzo Justice

I read the news today, oh boy.

—John Lennon

With a logic similar to the underlying logic of a TV troubleshooter, the news sources responsible for the range of information about events from which journalists select news topics are very knowledgeable about the relevance of entertainment for TV formats. The experience of public life and issues is increasingly coming through electronic media formats. Court officials, especially judges, are also familiar with the criticisms made about their performances, often by people with little actual awareness of how the courts operate, except for information from popular TV programs, particularly crime dramas that focus on police officers and individual detectives or private investigators who routinely make arrests, catch "bad guys," and solve problems notwithstanding the interference and legal impediments thrown at them by the courts and judges. Moreover, since there is very little in-depth coverage about the actual operations of courts, and even less understanding about the constitutional mandates that filter most court activities, it is not surprising that most citizen-viewers (and those who use other modes of mass media engagement) are often unenthusiastic about courtroom proceedings and judges' behavior. This is especially relevant when one of the few times the standard news media carry reports about judges is when there is a problem (e.g., when a judge is bribed or a felon is released on a "technicality"). The intersection of the very different logics and formats of courtrooms and TV newscasts then contributes to misperceptions. One is not surprised when certain judges and other criminal justice officials act in a better "programming" way, which I refer to as *gonzo justice*.

Social order is experienced directly in everyday life and indirectly through mass media images and messages. If we take seriously the proposition that experience is communicated and interpreted, then the varieties of such experiences, including mass-mediated content and discourse, must be taken into account. A compelling feature of one's experience is the nature of order and disorder, repair and disrepair, problems and solutions. This chapter seeks to clarify further the implications of public discourse about disorder, repair, justice, and social control.

Formal agents of control (e.g., criminal justice agencies) derive their legitimacy from the promise that their expansive—and expensive—efforts to patrol and repair breaches of social order are successful. However, when counterclaims are made, that is, when doubts arise and are widely publicized that formal agents of control are not adequately protecting the public (order), then extraordinary steps may be taken by those agents to demonstrate their resolve, if not their effectiveness. This may involve routine undercover and even sting operations, whereby state agents intentionally violate laws in order to demonstrate that other suspects are felons (cf. Marx 1988). Such steps often involve the news media, not as *chroniclers* of disorder, but as *instruments* of repair. We do not refer to the widely documented use of social control agents as news sources, but rather to the direct participation of journalists and news organizations in the process of control and punishment. The use of the mass media to stigmatize and presumably curtail future deviant behavior like white collar and corporate crime (cf. Fisse & Braithwaite 1983) is now institutionally accepted.

Consider a few examples. This one is from Pennsylvania:

A 311-$\frac{1}{2}$ pound man who hasn't made child-support payments for more than a year because he's too overweight to work is under court order to lose 50 pounds or go to jail. . . . "I call it my 'Oprah Winfrey sentence,'" [Judge] Lavelle said. . . . It's designed to make him lose weight for the benefit of his children, while Oprah lost weight for the benefit of her job and future security. (Arizona Republic, 18 June 1989)

And another, from Tennessee:

A judge ordered Henry Lee McDonald to put a sign in his front-yard for 30 days declaring in 4-inch letters that he "is a thief." U. S. District Court Judge L. Clure Morton instructed McDonald to erect the sign Tuesday as part of his three-year probation for receiving and concealing a stolen car. . . . The sign must be painted black and have 4-inch white capital letters that read: "Henry Lee McDonald bought a stolen car. He is a thief." (*Tempe Daily News*, 5 January 1984)

Readers of the *Arizona Republic* were dealt this sentence from Rhode Island on p. 1:

Saying there isn't enough public awareness of sexual abuse of children, a judge has ordered a child molester to buy an ad and have his picture in a newspaper with a caption urging others to seek help. . . . The judge told [accused] that as a condition of his [35 year] probation, he will have to place a 4- by 6-inch ad in the newspaper with his picture and a caption that reads: "I am Stephen Germershausen. I am 29 years old. On Oct. 26, 1989, I was convicted of child molestation. I received a 35-year suspended sentence with 35 years probation for my crime. If you are a child molester, get professional help immediately, or you may find your picture and name in the paper, and your life under control of the state." (9 November 1989)

News reports like this can simultaneously contribute to our understanding of social control, the role of the mass media in the drama of everyday life, and how to evaluate documents and sources of information. The latter consideration entails, first, developing a general approach to *relevant information as documents*, and second, placing these documents in a context of meaning in order to interpret them. These points have emerged from some recent efforts to develop a conceptual framework for the qualitative study of documents. One concept that joins these concerns is gonzo justice, or the use of extraordinary means to demonstrate social control and moral compliance, often through rule enforcement and punishment designed to stigmatize publicly (e.g., the mass media) and to demonstrate the moral resolve of those mandating the punishment.

With apologies to gonzo pioneers like Hunter Thompson (1971), who locate themselves in an activity in order to tell an ironic—and usually outrageous—story about it, I choose to look for the institutional arrangements that promote social definitions and conclusions through outrageous stories. It is the character of such public accounts that concerns me, and in particular the way in which authorized and legitimate agents are celebrated for their gonzo acts. I draw a distinction between an act and its publication career through an interpretive and communicative process that defines it for a purpose. My interest, then, is not to explain why these kinds of sentences were issued by state agencies, but that they were widely publicized through the mass media. I will focus especially on the reference to justice in these reconstructive efforts.

The method used in this study is best described as qualitative content analysis of documents—primarily news reports—which are collected and analyzed for recurring themes and patterns. As noted in previous work (Altheide 1987), this is a reflexive process of theoretical sampling, filing, constantly comparing, and conceptually coding. The original sensitizing concept was termed *extraordinary measures,* as, for example, in a case discussed below, where a judge ordered a woman to remain on birth control "for life." While there were numerous accounts by colleagues and others, as well as much smaller circulation publications (e.g., criminal justice newsletters), the sample was restricted to mass media publications, largely because previous work indicated that messages contained in such media have implications for public perception about order and disorder. This report focuses on some three dozen news reports collected over a seven-year period in which legitimate agencies of social control ordered individuals to place public advertisements/statements about their untoward activity and, in effect, self-stigmatizing conduct.

POWER AND COMMUNICATION

Power, control, justice, and communication are reflexive.

One aim of social control is to define the time, place, and manner of appropriate behavior. Social control is manifested through images and claims about order and disorder, stigma and identity, enforcement, and moral denunciation. Underlying all social control is an ontology of normalcy, perfection, and disrepair, although the content of each may be contested. Such contests constitute the meanings of justice and injustice. For example, the attempt to repair something with the symbolic glue of evil characterizations provides a glimpse of the social meanings of disrepair.

In every social order, persons and agents with access to the major communication outlets have more opportunity to do social control work by interpreting problems within their domain as problems for all of social order. However, ideas and programs carry with them the discursive elements of cultural meanings and logics underlying all communication.

Statements about public order are shaped and transformed by the way in which they are mediated by, or cast within the major news media. In terms of issues about justice and injustice, this means that efforts to promote claims about public order entail joining at least two components: notions of justice, including the recipe for overcoming its breach, and a means of communication. The upshot is that the ability to employ the mass media to assist in defining situations, events, and issues as one thing rather than another—as a threat to social order or as a measure to repair social order—is a major act of power that has tremendous implications.

THE NEWS MEDIA IN RELIEF

A great deal of public life takes on the frames or interpretive perspectives offered by the mass media, and especially TV news. News is the most powerful resource for public definitions in our age. The legitimacy of media logic now underlies claims about the nature of public disorder, which in turn points to the constructive process for social worlds (cf. Altheide & Snow 1979, 1991; Hall 1980; Couch 1984; Snow 1983). The renewed interest in culture and the symbolic systems and processes through which social order is constructed, constituted, defined, interpreted, and enacted calls for an expansive perspective incorporating the processes of communication, interpretation, and meaning. This awareness has taken us beyond the point where the mass media merely set the public agenda (cf. Altheide 1976, 1985; Carey 1987; Ericson, Baranek, & Chan 1987, 1989; Maines & Couch 1988; Meyrowitz 1985). We have also moved well beyond the old arguments that the media are subservient to more powerful economic and ideological interests, and simply do their bidding (cf. Morrison & Tumber 1988; Schlesinger, Murdock, & Elliott 1983).

The most creative students of the mass media now take it for granted that power and ideology are implicated in all media content, and conversely that power is exercised through communication channels and formats. Ideas, interests, and ideologies are clothed in communication logics and formats; it is the negotiability of the latter that enlivens the former. The research agenda for innovative work in mass communication will involve its cultural reflexivity, including how news codes, entertainment codes, and mediated logics, styles and rhythms have transformed our postmodern experiences through a complex ecology of communication. For example, recent work shows that significant news sources (e.g., the police and politicians) now use the reflexive media logic and formats through which they have learned to successfully communicate via news media agencies to their various publics. Indeed, the media increasingly control the negotiation process for setting the themes and discourse through which those agenda items are to be addressed (cf. Ericson et al. 1989).

Public order increasingly is presented as a conversation within media formats, which may be envisioned as a give and take, point-counterpoint, problem-solution (cf. Ferrarotti 1988). For example, when mass media depictions stress the breakdown of social order and suggest a failing by agents of social control, we can expect those agents to present dramaturgical accounts of their resolve and success in order to increase citizens' confidence in them.

The combination of various media constitutes an *interactive communication context*. For example, in a study of the "missing children problem" (discussed in Chapter 7) we found that similar messages about "thousands" if not "millions" of missing children who were abducted, molested, and mutilated by strangers were carried on TV news, docudramas, newspapers, billboards, posters, T-shirts, mailings, and milk cartons (Fritz & Altheide 1987). Such claims were exaggerated and traded on widespread beliefs about crime and danger. This can also be illustrated with crime news that seemingly celebrates the inability of the state agencies to protect its citizens. In some cases, this will involve vigilante scenarios by individuals, while in others it will involve vigilante actions by entire audiences. An example is the TV program "America's Most Wanted," hosted by John Walsh, the man behind much of the missing children furor. This show draws some five thousand calls per week from viewers who report that their neighbors, work associates, and fellow-consumers fit the description of a wanted suspect flashed on TV.

While news is replete with propaganda and ideological content, it is produced through organizational work governed by format considerations, including attracting an audience, relying on routine news sources that are largely state bureaucracies, and being consistent with other information sources about social problems and injustices, including a range of popular culture and entertainment programming. Extraordinary claims about individual and organizational resolve to promote justice by punishing injustice accompany prolonged periods of published reports suggesting that crime is rampant, no one is safe, and the evil dramatized through popular culture is on the rise.

TIME FOR GONZO

Gonzo justice has emerged as a new cultural form to address the mass-mediated public perception of unsuccessful social control. Popular culture provides a way to participate in or play with horror, banditry, crime, and justice, as we are presented a range of scenarios and enactments through which we can interactively arrive at meaningful interpretations. For example, it is common for youth to view horror or slasher films in groups that educate, direct, and limit interpretation and action (cf. Roe 1983). This is also true of competent news watchers, who soon take for granted TV sequencing, use of examples, and distinguishing segments of a report from the whole. However, plausible interpretations are limited by the news code itself (Altheide 1985:97ff.) as certain metaphors, scenarios, and relationships are repeated within and across various media.

The scenario of out-of-control evil calls forth a heroic retort as a kind of narrative response in the mediated drama. I refer to this as gonzo justice. The examples noted above illustrate how media logic and formats permit the legal system to show outrage and affirm to various publics that specific agents are doing their job.

A combination of "public spectacle" (Edelman 1971, 1988), moral authority, and news legitimacy, gonzo justice is specifically oriented to mass communication formats, and is often celebrated and applauded by mass media writers and commentators. For example, in 1987, a young mother who had left her two infants sweltering in the Arizona heat alone in an apartment for three days was put on probation, with the judge's proviso to remain on some method of birth control, "for life." About a year later,

George Will's syndicated column addressed the "philosophical issues" underlying such a sentence, noting that while one could sympathize with the judge—a woman, the sentence is a step down a dangerous path since "pregnancy is not an illness," but "bad behavior—irresponsible procreation." Will argued that a more just option would have been to send her to jail! Will propped up his verdict by saying, "The law should appeal to conscience by stigmatizing certain behavior, and should pose a threat to be feared" (*Arizona Republic*, 29 June 1988). Several months later, another report appeared in the *Arizona Republic* with the headline: "Child Abuser Pregnant; Birth-Control Edict Fails." The sentencing judge, a prosecuting attorney, and defense counsel were featured in several statements, including the woman's attorney's request for a clarification as to whether "abortion is a form of birth control and whether [the woman] should obtain one to abide by the terms of her probation." No, replied the judge,

> I'm not going to send her to prison because she is pregnant. . . . However, . . . she intends to modify the terms of Forster's probation to provide health safeguards for the unborn child [including] prenatal checkups . . . and urinalysis to make sure that the defendant isn't using illegal drugs.

When an attorney representing the American Civil Liberties Union (ACLU) argued that "the order is unconstitutional because it is an invasion of privacy, is tantamount to 'cruel and unusual punishment,' and violates freedom of religion" because Forster is a Roman Catholic, and besides, the national attention has been cruel and stigmatizing, the deputy county attorney replied, "She's got to use birth control," for purposes of "rehabilitating the defendant and protecting others." The original sentence was subsequently appealed!

Analysis of these materials suggest some identifiable features of gonzo justice that join the news media to legal authority:

1. There must be an act that can be defined and presented as extraordinary, if not excessive and arbitrary.
2. It must be protective or "reclaiming" of a moral often mythical. dimension.
3. Individual (rather than "organizational") initiative is responsible for the reaction.
4. The act is expressive and evocative.
5. The act is intended to be interpreted and presented as an exemplar for others to follow.
6. Audience familiarity with other reports about the problem provides a context of experience and meaning.
7. Reports seldom include contrary or challenging statements.

Individual acts of heroism or taking the law into one's own hands—including homicide—may qualify as dispute resolution, but they are different from gonzo justice. What makes gonzo justice peculiar and unique is that we can expect it to be associated with those agencies and roles less likely to be seen as affirming and supportive of the cultural myths. For example, in the general realm of criminal justice, we would anticipate that more of the emphases would involve the courts and judiciary partly because this is where formal sentencing occurs. More importantly for our argument, the judiciary has also been the most maligned for not enforcing laws and not protecting the public good, including "tying the hands of the police." In many instances, it has been contrasted with the bravado of "street cops."

It is an understatement that a large number of Americans do not understand or simply do not accept the philosophy and function of our courts, and in all likelihood, the Bill of Rights. One consequence is that many people do not intuitively grasp how "those who probably committed acts" can be released due to "insufficient evidence," on the one hand, nor do they understand how overcrowded prisons can lead to the court-ordered releases of convicted felons. Certainly one reason for this lack of understanding is the inordinate attention of our public and popular culture to the police function, individual discretion, and heroics, which are often foiled by lawyers and courtroom procedures. (Recall that far more people can identify Judge Wopner of the TV show, "The People's Court," than can name the chief justice of the Supreme Court!)

The news media are just as culpable. Press reports are widespread about plea bargaining, lack of concern with victims, and in general, the justice system not doing enough to "put criminals away." Moreover, the complex legal tradition, statutes, and organizational considerations (e.g., crowded prisons) within which adjudication takes place make it very difficult for uninformed journalists to report routinely on the legal process (cf. Ericson 1989). Indeed, it has been widely documented that the administration of justice in courtrooms involves applying averages of previous sentences (i.e., plea bargaining) rather than case-specific negotiations (cf. Eisenstein, Flemming, & Nardulli 1988; Nardulli, Fleming, & Eisenstein (1988). With judges less receptive to cameras and thereby to public understanding, publics are left to their own devices—and accounts mainly made by the police—to explain why crime and evil are rampant throughout society. For example, a Washington state senator explained why she supported a bill to reduce prison sentences of persons convicted of sex crimes if they underwent voluntary castration:

> Craswell . . . said the Senate's 25-23 vote for castration was the ultimate sign of frustration with a criminal-justice system that is incapable of keeping the most dangerous criminals behind bars. . . . While acknowledging that the

bill's chances in the House are slim, Craswell said the Senate action has given new credibility to the possible use of castration. (*Arizona Republic*, 14 February 1990).

When such a view is not uncommon among state and federal representatives who, presumably, are better informed than most of those they represent, it is not surprising that workers in the criminal justice system, especially the often maligned court officials, may seek to use popular culture to demonstrate their own compliance and values. Thus, from the perspective of a court official, it is hardly newsworthy to carry out one's judicial tasks of hearing, evaluating, and passing sentences; something more is needed to communicate moral resolve.

Consider a few examples of efforts to achieve what may be termed effective public communication. A judge in Texas granted probation to a man who had been convicted of cocaine possession four times, but he warned him that any violation of the terms of his probation would result in a life sentence. When the man was picked up for driving with a suspended driver's license, the judge sentenced him to sixty years in prison (*Arizona Republic*, 2 June 1989).

I am suggesting then that gonzo justice permits judges to act like moral enforcers who are committed to preventing crime and social disorder, i.e., to act just like police officers are perceived! For example, in 1976, juvenile officials in New Jersey "sentenced" a group of juvenile offenders to spend time in Rahway State Prison where they would be "scared straight" by associating with lifers who enacted their roles so well that a documentary film *Scared Straight* was soon made and shown throughout the United States. The film showings were often followed by a panel of police officers, business people, and court officials, who together with telephone callers bleated that "something has to be done," and "we should try it." Editorials in newspapers and on TV stations gushed with approval as some thirty-eight states developed programs. When studies indicated that the program was ineffective and often made matters worse, the media attention subsided. The evocative nature of this program is suggested by Cavender's conclusion:

> "Scared Straight" is a media-generated phenomenon. The public was enticed to watch it by publicity efforts, akin to "previews of coming attractions" that promised a shocking and vulgar film—one that might contain a solution to the crime problem . . . Based on the distorted reality, the film offered a solution to crime, one that was kept before the public with supportive media coverage, both before and after the documentary was aired. (1984:257–58)

What is important here is that even though court officials and police officers have explicitly different roles in the criminal justice system, occasions like the one noted above put them on the same moral and rhetorical footing (e.g., something must be done, we are not doing enough, we are failing, and tougher enforcement and punishment is the answer).

What must be remembered, of course, is that this collapsing of occupational roles and distinctive mandates occurs at the pleasure of the journalists, who are often uninformed about the intricacies of the criminal justice system.

Not surprisingly, when extraordinary—and usually sanctionable—activities of the police do occur, they may be applauded by journalists and columnists. My materials provide some interesting examples of journalists' approval of the vigilante theme, or the notion that taking the law into one's own hands in order to exact justice is admirable if not formally permissible. The key is their expressive and evocative nature, which joins the author to the reader as members who share a situated solidarity relationship. As Seckman and Couch stated about employers and employees, "Our observations suggest that much relationship work within mature relationships is completed by evocative transactions, not by negotiating" (1989:340). While the print media rely more on discursive than expressive symbols than visual media like TV, the interpretive process permits the audience members to draw on a range of other experiences, including previous media accounts, to inform their emotional response. Moreover, even discursive accounts of gonzo justice provide an evocative occasion between friends, co-workers, and rapid transit passengers.

Two examples by Mike Royko, syndicated columnist for the *Chicago Tribune*, come to mind. The first, regarded as one of his favorite columns, appeared on June 19, 1979. A thirteen-year-old boy, described as a compulsive thief, was sat upon by two adults, one a police officer, the other the owner of a car the boy was attempting to steal. When he tried to get away, they severely beat him. Royko adds,

> And if you strip it down to the basic facts, it does sound unfair: two grown men, one of them a cop, beating up a 13-year old boy. And, as a rule, I'm against police brutality. . . . But on the other hand, I'm in favor of appropriate punishment which is something that is rarely applied. The fact is, the amount of crime in this country greatly exceeds the supply of punishment. And the imbalance is growing all the time. . . . So the question is, what can be done? And the answer is, not much. . . . [But] it might also involve a hard smash in the mouth. That, I think, is educational. And I just wish more of us had the chance to be the teachers.

Reflectively, one could ask, what does he mean by "appropriate punishment" and how does he know it is in short supply? But this is hardly his point, and it is surely not likely to be asked by many of his readers because the column is intended to be evocative, with a nod of one's head and agreement with fellows indicating shared group membership and common-sense awareness of how the world "really is."

Another Royko column celebrating vigilante justice described how a police officer, Whitey, unofficially brought to justice a man who would routinely get drunk, go home, break apart the furniture, and beat his elderly mother with whom he lived. (Note that the significant feature of this account for gonzo justice is not the actions taken by the officer, but rather that it was reported, with approval, in a Royko column in a respected newspaper.) After Whitey's trouncing interrupted the man's levity, "A squad found [the man] out in the backyard, unconscious in the flowers. He had cuts, bruises, loose teeth and a nose that had been completely rearranged" (*Tempe Daily News*, 2 May 1989). When Whitey reappeared at the station and was told of the mother's complaint that someone who was "11 feet tall, weighing about 1,000 pounds and had nice rosy cheeks" had beat her son, he was asked if he could solve this crime. Royko ended the column with a quote from Whitey, "Of course . . . the son might not ever act like this again—and then we won't be able to solve it, will we?" This is evocative. How many of the thousands of *Chicago Tribune* readers would openly disagree with Royko when riding the el with fellow commuters?

While Royko's celebration of such individual acts against injustice and brutality tell us a lot about how he perceives the point of view of his audience, it also provides a teaching tool for others in the criminal justice system to present their moral authority by teaching a lesson to the accused, which often becomes a mass-mediated lesson to the entire class. If police officers can be lauded for such extraordinary activities, why not the judiciary? The first problem, of course, is establishing with various publics that such activities can occur in court. When John Zucker was arrested in Gainesville for burglarizing vehicles, he may not have known how a local prosecutor was operating. A prosecutor in Tampa is

> having criminals apologize for their crimes in newspaper advertisements as punishment, in return for probation and dropping of some minor charges. "I've admitted my guilt . . . I've been punished. It was not worth it. I'm sorry," an ad purchased by John Zucker said. (*Arizona Republic*, 18 October 1988)

Consider another case involving a child molester in Florida:

> A man who pleaded guilty to molesting a 7-year old boy has been ordered to write the phrase, "I will keep my hands off other people" 25 times a week for 11 years. (*Arizona Republic*, 3/3/85)

The molestation theme can be expanded by creative headline writers. Consider another case from Florida: "Crab "molesters" Must Wear Signs Advertising Guilt." Four young men who were "a little bit drunk" were caught pilfering about twenty-five crabs. One part of their plea agreement was to pay the crab fishermen five times the cost of the damage and lost crabs. The other part was to wear placards:

The signs, which were to be on poster-board-size placards and readable from one hundred feet, had to carry the following message: "It Is a Felony Punishable by Five Years in Prison and/or a $5,000 Fine to Molest Crab Pots. I Know Because I Molested One" (*Arizona Republic*, 9/9/89).

Gonzo justice is a completed narrative about morality and norms, values, and sanctions, but it also suggests counterfactually why the breach occurred. This is illustrated by several of the previous examples, and includes lack of thought and inadequate self-control. Thus, an explanation and view of social order is implied by the sentence.

The symbolic use of gonzo justice to construct an image of propriety by celebrating its breach is illustrated in a report from Atlanta about seven ex-Klansmen who were sentenced to "get lessons in brotherhood as punishment." The KKK members, who were involved in an attack by robed Klansmen on marchers led by the Southern Christian Leadership Conference (SCLC), agreed to take a course in race relations taught by civil rights figures. According to Dr. Joseph E. Lowery, president of SCLC, the intent was "not to denigrate or humiliate but to redeem" the Klansmen. While one Klan member was reported to have said that he hoped the "classes could improve understanding on both sides," James W. Farrands, Imperial Wizard of the Invisible Empire, Knights of the Ku Klux Klan, described the agreement as "cruel and unusual punishment," and added, "I think it's a form of forced brainwashing. They'd have to lock me up forever before I'd do it" (*San Diego Union*, 25 September 1989).

Gonzo justice is not synonymous with the news media, but the extraordinary measures, particularly in terms of formal sentencing, fit comfortably with news media formats, while the moral-myth statements virtually ensure an interested audience. An agents' view of social order is enhanced through the mass-mediated formats designed to promote circulation and TV ratings. It is difficult for judges and others involved in adjudication to gain stature among the media-dependent publics, which are more oriented to the police perspective celebrated through entertainment and news presentations. One way to bypass this bias is to promote yourself as tough and decisive.

The extraordinary sentences under review are seldom criticized in the press by anyone other than the American Civil Liberties Union (ACLU). For example, when a judge ordered a woman who had falsely accused a man of raping her to take out radio and newspaper advertisements apologizing to him, the Nebraska Civil Liberties Union argued that the sentence may constitute cruel and unusual punishment:

A judge ordered . . . in a half-page advertisement in every newspaper and a spot on each radio station in Dawson County, a county of about 22,000 in central Nebraska. The media campaign was expected to cost about $1,000. . . . She also was sentenced to 180 days in jail and was placed on probation for two years. A panel of attorneys from the state Civil Liberties Union who reviewed the case said the sentence may violate Richardson's constitutional rights against cruel and unusual punishment. . . . "Suppose someone is arrested for shoplifting. Are we going to make him wear a sign saying he's a convicted shoplifter?" (*Arizona Republic*, July 3, 1990).

Of course, we have already reviewed examples where some judges answered affirmatively.

When the sentences are harsh, but later revealed through judicial review to be unwarranted, we have a "mistake." Such a mistake occurred in the case of Louis Woodrow Freader of Phoenix, who should have received a maximum sentence of seventeen days on September 28, 1983, for failing to pay a fine for resisting arrest. When the full fine was paid, Justice Marilyn Riddell, of the Maricopa County Superior Court, denied a motion to have him released (*Arizona Republic*, 16 January 1985). Two years later the Arizona Court of Appeals reversed the ruling, stating in the words of one justice, "justice was not done. Rather, it clearly appears that an injustice has taken place" (*Arizona Business Gazette*, 16 January 1985). Nothing was stated about the judge's arbitrary ruling.

The issues raised by the ACLU and the theoretical points underlying this essay appear not to have been lost on all newspaper editors. Indeed, there is a glimmer that some editors may be more attentive to the constitutional issues undergirding the ACLU's point of departure than certain judges. Consider a case in Florida in which the chairman of the *Pensacola News Journal* rejected a court-ordered advertisement placed by a man convicted of drunken driving and other misdemeanors on the ground that the press should not be "a vehicle for court-ordered public humiliation" (*New York Times*, 26 January 1991). Another newspaper accepted the ad:

The weekly, *The Gulf Breeze Sentinel*, ran the first advertisement on Jan. 17, complete with a photograph of the defendant. . . . The advertisement ran three days after Judge William White of Escambia County gave Mr. Whitfield a choice of buying a 2-inch square advertisement in *The Sentinel* or going to jail for two days after he pleaded no contest to a charge of driving under the influence of alcohol. "I think it is worth it if it will help as a deterrent," Duane Cook, editor and publisher of *The Sentinel* [said], adding that there was no difference between publishing such advertisements and publishing news articles about crime. (*New York Times*, 26 January 1991)

Clearly, in our age the distinction is blurred between the courts and the press, as both operate as agents of control.

CONCLUSION

Horror is usually visited upon humankind through the rhetoric of justice. Human beings are slaughtered, cities destroyed, genocide perpetrated, and worlds made orderly through public discourse of justice.

Getting tough is good news, and gonzo justice is how toughness is publicly celebrated and legitimated. Public discourse is important in making the extraordinary ordinary. More seems to be involved than the long-standing approach of shaming through stigmatizing; public notice of untoward behavior becomes celebrated through the blurring of distinctions between agents of control and enforcement on the one hand, and those media that have edged closer to moral enforcement, even as they increasingly retreat from the appearance of mere chroniclers of order maintenance, on the other hand. I have suggested that when viewed from an interactionist perspective, gonzo justice integrates mass communication formats with efforts to control the symbolic order through the definition of the situation of moral violations, reconstruction, explanation, and prevention. While the justice motive underlies most commonsense interpretations of social problems and issues, the challenge is to understand the process, meaning, and consequences of different ways in which this motive may be manifested and, in particular, how it is published and celebrated.

It may be argued that gonzo justice underlies numerous changes and adjustments in social relationships and even institutions. And there is evidence that the effect is cumulative, rather than case by case. Practitioners and audience members become accustomed to the increased span of control. Circumstances often assume the identities attributed to them by mass media characterizations. Gonzo justice becomes a feature of propaganda. For example, police undercover and sting operations are now accepted by our courts and citizens. What should not be forgotten, however, is that the use of video cameras not only provides visual evidence for the court but also terrific material for the evening news.

When police agencies and prosecutors release videotapes and newspaper transcripts of sting operations before court proceedings, the mass media become active players as prosecution gives way to public humiliation and persecution; a version of justice can be obtained without the complexities of court trials, including concern with due process and other civil liberties. Chapter 6 examines an eighteen-month-sting in 1990–1991, by the Phoenix Police Department and the county attorney, led to the successful videotaped bribing of several state legislators and lobbyists. When the police and other authorities were notified by alert legislators that a suspicious person hanging around the statehouse had attempted bribery, the police dissembled and assured them that it was being investigated. In this way the informal checks to prevent someone from violating the law by offering a bribe to a public official were circumvented, and the illegal behavior was soon embraced by an ever-widening circle of police and prosecutorial agencies. The million dollar expenses were provided by discretionary funds the police department had obtained through previous seizures in drug cases. Several "suspects" used the funds during their election campaigns, thus compromising the democratic process. Video scenarios were released to the news media, one at a time, in order to ensure that there would be successive reporting of the legislators accepting money. It was hardly surprising that opinion polls indicated that the Arizona citizens trusted their police more than their elected representatives.

From a sociologically informed communications perspective, foreign policy has an individual look, self-described and self-attributed with clear moral characteristics. International conflicts between the United States and Libya, Panama, and Iraq involved dramatizing the evil of, respectively, Muammar Khadafy, Manuel Noriega, and Saddam Hussein (Chapter 9). These men became symbols of entire societies and their identification as criminals in need of extraordinary measures helped set the stage for the extraordinary sentencing that was carried out: Operation Just Cause (Panama) and Operation Desert Storm (Iraq). The subsequent invasion and slaughter in Panama might not have occurred without the previous invasion of Grenada; the heads of state delivered public opinion by engaging in the dramatization of evil and the characterological attack on Manuel "Pineapple Face" Noriega as a philanderer, drug merchant, and practitioner of "voodoo." On January 16, 1991, one year later, the majority of people in the United States supported bombing Baghdad, which resulted in thousands of deaths and untold destruction at a cost in excess of one billion dollars per day. The most visible enemy in this case was Saddam Hussein, who was mass mediated as evil, "another Hitler," "a madman."

Individual culpability can be assailed against a backdrop of anticipated outcomes if the audience is properly prepared. If the long historical look backward is correct that virtually all routine social arrangements emerged through acts of power to offer and sustain a definition of a situation, then we should not be surprised if extraordinary and draconian measures today become commonplace in the future. Consider how testing originated, how it has been applied in recent years to illness and drugs for employment, and how it may be accepted in the future (e.g., for all employees of federal and state agencies). Recall some of the points we made about IT and testing, and consider the case noted above about the pregnant woman who would not be sentenced to prison, but would be "tested."

The myth of social control is that *illegitimate* agents pose the greatest challenge. In fact, social control expands through the pursuit of exceptional and extraordinary methods by *legitimate* agents. One way to check its expansion is to reinvigorate our efforts to identify the communicative modes that constitute public concerns, crises, and the formats for noteworthy action. The significance of gonzo justice, with help from IT and formats of control, for public life, is illustrated in the next chapter by a city police department's sting operation—of elected officials!

Gonzo Democracy:
The Case of Azscam   **6**

Something happening here, what it is ain't exactly clear.

—Buffalo Springfield

Originally cast as an antiwar song in the 1960s to celebrate a growing awareness of expanded social control, Buffalo Springfield's "For What It's Worth" is now incorporated into a news-music-video urging viewers to watch for criminals! The following comments address how news media formats and communication logic are embraced by social control agents in a dance of domination.

INTRODUCTION

Social control, power, and communication have been joined throughout history (cf. Innis 1951; McLuhan 1962). If the essence of power is the ability of one person to define the situation for others, then the capacity to communicate that definition becomes paramount. (For a different perspective on social control, see Gibbs 1982.)

The intersection between state control work and public order, as discussed in the previous two chapters, increasingly occurs through the mass media. Just as judges use gonzo justice to demonstrate (and promote) their moral character and resolve to audiences who know little about their work routines, other bureaucratic workers, like politically ambitious county prosecutors, rely on the news media to not only publicize their achievements, but to actually work with and through the news formats to "do good work." The case we call Azscam illustrates how the ecology of communication proves to be a useful concept in clarifying a strange development in the way law enforcement officials increasingly are using information technology and communication formats to do their work even as they provide good news material. Great entertainment!

Our purpose is twofold: first, to clarify how the communication order is implicated in the way formal agents of social control (FASC) representing state structures may shape, use, and be influenced by communication media and their attendant logics, particularly in regard to journalism; second, to delineate some new ways in which formal social control work and news work are folded together. This inquiry is grounded in a case study of a sting operation (Azscam) of the Arizona legislature, by the Phoenix Police Department, in which bribery transactions between a government stooge and a number of Arizona's legislators, including seven (8 percent) who were subsequently indicted, were recorded on videotape that was strategically released to the news media prior to any trials. While the majority of those charged resigned their positions and/or accepted plea agreements, the defense efforts of the one who opted for a hearing to put the evocative pretrial images in a different context were stymied by the replaying of a barrage of guilty-looking visuals for more than a year. Jury selection became a major problem. As one prospective juror stated, "I think you would have to be Ken or Barbie not to have some thoughts on it" (*Arizona Republic*, 10 April 1992).

Our topic of investigation concerns the social context, rationale, and the way these video images informed the entire sting operation, including how they were obtained, released by officials, and used by news media, and their ultimate impact on the case. Materials for analysis include TV reports, articles from two newspapers, legal briefs, and interviews with several journalists who worked on the story. Following an overview of some connections between power, communication, and information resources that had previously been controlled by police departments, we will examine the changing face of journalism and information technology. This will be followed by an analytical summary of one of the first video stings, Abscam (1979–1980), in order to illustrate how FASC altered their use of the mass media for Azscam (1990–1991). Some of the consequences and implications for formal social control, journalism, and TV newswork will be noted.

COMMUNICATION TECHNOLOGY AND LOGIC

Power and communication are not symmetrical (cf. Hall 1988). A central part of the communication process is the information technology, and how it is organized and used, including the guiding logic or rationale for its operation. Innis (1951) suggested some general relationships in early attempts to chart the nature and implications of state control versus market control. While state authorities are dominant news sources in any social/political context, there is a difference when the mass media are operating under state or market auspices. For example, when the technology and news organizations are controlled solely by the autocratic state, then messages (content) are likely to fully reflect the ruling elite's interests, i.e., propaganda, regardless of audience preferences. When, on the other hand, marketing logic, or what the audience approves of or buys, informs message selection and production, then the whims and interests of the elites will be less definitive of content. In the context of journalism and news, messages will reflect those values and issues most likely to attract the largest and/or most lucrative audience. In the second instance, Innis (1951) and others have argued that the underlying market principle of these media actually promotes more democratic state structures, because the audience members are an important factor in the success or failure of a newspaper or television news station. [We will not engage the argument here that the market and the state are two sides of the coin of domination (cf. Schiller 1971, 1989).]

The way in which interests can be served through the use of information technology by journalists and FASC remains a significant issue. As work by Couch (1984) and others has shown, regimes throughout history and across cultures have grappled with the nature and consequences of controlling the technology (oral, print, or electronic), process, and substance of communication. There remains the important question of how the dominant media are contextualized within a social order:

> I advance the proposition that the relationships between the media and social structures are multilateral; that the consequences of a medium are different when it is contextualized by economic structures than when contextualized by state structures . . . [when the latter] it will reflect the interests of state officials. (Couch 1990:112)

It is this relationship between market or economic logic and state or autocratic logic that informs our inquiry into the changing role of the news media, and especially the electronic media, in social order. Within the context of an ecology of communication, it is not enough to do a job (e.g., stop political corruption), but rather, one must show the political corruption in a way that is recognizable by relevant audiences. Today, this means entertaining material that will be compatible with TV formats. We are particularly intrigued by the role of video imagery and its multifaceted uses by laypeople, news people, and state workers, particularly FASC explicitly charged with order maintenance, including the interpretation, surveillance, regulation, apprehension, and sanctioning of proscribed behavior (and intentions). The reader is invited to adapt the activity scheme to control—order maintenance and exposing political corruption (see Figure 4.1).

The following case study of a major political sting operation in Arizona provides a vantage point for investigating the changing face of communicated power, both as public discourse and social epistemology—"I saw it on TV." With an escalating number of interest group concerns, the domain of state control has expanded considerably, and the orientation and tactics of state power have also increased beyond the traditional domains of public life to more proactive investigation and surveillance. As Marx notes:

> Social control has become more specialized and technical, and, in many ways, more penetrating and intrusive. In some ways, we are moving toward a Napoleonic view of the relationship between the individual and the state, where the individual is assumed to be guilty and must prove his of her innocence. That state's power to seek out violations, even without specific grounds for suspicion, has been enhanced. With this comes a cult and a culture of surveillance that goes beyond government to the private sector and the interaction of individuals. (1988:2ff.)

The exponential growth of the surveillance and undercover options across international, nation, state, county, and city jurisdictions has been widely documented (cf. Marx 1988). While much of this work has focused on the increased use of *agents provocateurs*, our interest is in the way certain state tactics and orientations can be blended with prevailing mass communication routines and patterns. We now turn to some important changes in the nature of journalism.

FROM JOURNALISM TO POSTJOURNALISM

We choose to examine the nature, use, and contextualization of information technologies as they apply to organized journalism in nonautocratic societies. We regard journalists as the important regulators (if not owners) of an information process about public concerns and issues. We are particularly interested in the expanded use of video in everyday life as a context for the transformation of public discourse, including courts of law. The argument we are addressing can be simply stated: The Azscam case illustrates a major refolding of social control and mass communication through a shared media logic, which has joined the market orientation of news agencies to the autocratic control of state agents. Stated differently, journalists and their sources now use common logics and procedures that are associated with visual formats. In order to complete the context for an event like Azscam, it is helpful to set forth a conceptual summary of the relationships between journalism—especially the television format; market orientation (or commercialism); sources—especially FASC; and electronic technology—including TV visuals and formats.

The power of visuals, derived from our ecology of communication, is another key element in the changing relationship of state structures to communication and social control. News media workers, and especially TV news workers, entered the TV age with a radio and newspaper orientation. It took nearly thirty years for a widespread and distinctive television journalism perspective to emerge (cf. Epstein 1974; Altheide 1976; Schlesinger 1978). One emergent approach for TV journalism was to use *visuals to tell time.* That is, since journalists wanted to maintain their audience, they assumed that brief reports with plenty of entertainment value—visual drama, action, conflict, and emotion—would be the best formula: *movement on the screen was the key.*

As stressed throughout this book, the realization that visuals matter more than dialogue and abstract meanings became the guiding format for TV journalists: If the visuals could be about crime, death, mayhem, and combat, so much the better, because this content had already long been the staple of newspaper news; the covenant of social control agencies and news organizations to protect order could be enhanced, and audiences would grow, if the action of crime, drama, emotion, and conflict could be shown on the evening news. A new working formula developed: the more visual the action, the more time and attention the report would receive. Research has demonstrated that TV journalists preferred news sources that could provide enough advance warning and access to such events (Epstein 1973; Altheide 1976, 1985). To paraphrase a compelling line from the movie *Field of Dreams,* we can state that as far as TV news goes, "if they can film it, people will come."

The format of commercial TV news is thus a kind of template or predictor for what an interesting news report will look like. Furthermore, those sources that provide the best stories compatible with TV news formats are more likely to be selected for coverage. This realization by the dominant institutional news sources, which include a number of FASC, led to the development of stories that were selected/produced with TV formats in mind: The sources essentially adopted TV media logic in preparing events for the news media to cover (cf. Ericson et al. 1989). We have referred to this situation elsewhere as

> "postjournalism," in which journalists essentially are reporting on events that have been arranged for them and their criteria; while the journalists and their procedures were always implicated in what they covered, we are in a new era when the sources and events of coverage are no longer distinguished from the journalists' own perspective; the sources now essentially construct their activities with media logic that was once the province of news workers; it is now part of public discourse, with the consequence that the object of journalism has disappeared (Altheide & Snow 1991).

A pervasive marketing orientation further shaped the present context.

INFORMATION TECHNOLOGY AND THE MARKET CONTEXT

The ecology of communication operates within a cultural context that simultaneously reflects, yet also guides additional applications. American journalists' work is primarily market oriented, while that of FASC is not. However, journalists and FASC have more in common today than they used to. As specialists who focus on and are guided by information technology of the mass media, the work of contemporary journalists—and many of the sources they rely on for information—reflects this logic. As we note below, even though both have had an interest and orientation in "preventing disorder," (cf. Ericson et al. 1989), FASC were primarily a *source* for the journalists to use in presenting news reports about problems and issues.

Historically, journalists controlled the information technology, the access, and the audience. FASC controlled the character and access to many events that were of interest to a market-oriented journalism; readers (and, later, listeners and viewers) were interested in crime news coverage. Thus, the perspective and interests overlapped—they were not isomorphic. However, over time, journalists *taught* FASC the logic and perspective of information technology and news formats. This awareness enabled FASC to move beyond the separating hyphen of the journalist-source relationship *to become the news*. A key mediating influence for their coming together was the gradual realization among FASC that their services and demands were also subject to marketing considerations; they realized that they had to compete for the support of publics whose perceptions of social order, problems, and issues were increasingly mediated by entertaining programs, including TV news.

ENTERTAINMENT AND SOCIAL CONTROL

The thrust of the journalists' efforts to maintain their respective audiences in our era may be characterized as an entertainment orientation. From the audience member's perspective, entertainment implies a contrast with the mundane, providing spontaneous enjoyment and with potential for vicarious involvement (Altheide & Snow 1991, 16). Extraordinary crime, violence, conflict, and destruction seem to qualify. It is partly for this reason that Park (1940), Hughes (1940), Chibnall (1977), Schudson (1978), Ericson et al. (1987, 1989), and many others have noted that crime news, scandal, tragedy, and other human interest events and issues are the stuff of news. Numerous students of the history of news agree that crime news and issues about social order, especially disorder, have not only been part of the history of journalism, but also that journalism is essentially part of the repairing mechanism for breaches in the social order. As Ericson et al. note:

> The defining characteristic of journalism is that it visualizes deviance and control as these relate to visions of social order and change. The journalistic search for procedural strays and signs of disorder is a means of charting the consensual boundaries of society and acknowledging order. . . . News of deviance is a discourse of failure and, as such, is essential to imagining what might be better—the discourse of progress. (1987:8)

Equally important is that entertaining news came to be viewed as very similar to crime news. As noted, this history and mutual interest in order/disorder is partly responsible for the very close relationship between news organizations and news sources, especially FASC (e.g., the police). The relevance and impact of this relationship on social order have informed mass communication research for several decades (cf. Surette 1992).

To briefly recap, a plethora of work on news organizations and news sources has documented the complex ties between contexts, commercialism, news routines, sources, and perspectives (cf. Epstein 1973; Altheide 1976, 1985; Tuchman 1978; Fishman 1980; Gitlin 1980; Snow 1983; Ericson et al. 1987, 1989). While there are a number of disagreements among news researchers on a host of complex issues, students of the media agree that the relationship between journalists and sources is a strategic locale for clarifying large questions about news bias, ideology, and hegemonic control. Much of this work documented the differences and sometimes the similarities of the perspectives of journalists and news sources.

Even though journalists were interested in order maintenance, they were distinctive from their sources: they had a perspective, a market orientation, and clear organizational work routines and procedures for covering the news. Stated differently, the journalist had a craft orientation and a discourse consisting of news frames for emphasizing newsworthiness, relevance, and connectedness, which could be applied to any *item provided by a source*; journalists had an occupational perspective that included viewing the world of experience in terms of potential newsworthy items.

Things were different for sources largely because their primary orientation was to the more specific view of their work and its points of interest to journalists. We already noted that the police, for example, had their discourse and frames for doing their work, and that their problems were of interest to journalists because they dealt with examples—if not issues!—of social order. However, until relatively recently, formal control agencies were not primarily market oriented; they were state mandated.

Changing economic conditions, assumptions, and some key political events contributed to an expanded media perspective by state agencies (cf.

Altheide & Johnson 1980; Schlesinger 1991). The demands for more efficiency and accountability combined with historical events to increase public interest and questioning of the legitimacy of state authorities and services.
The state agencies, especially the police and the military, became more
market oriented and embraced the media logic perspective of the journalists
who reported on their activities. The stature of the more authoritarian apparatus was called into question, and its legitimacy challenged regarding the
nature and necessity of its services (e.g., the civil rights movement of the
1960s, and the Vietnam War). Part of the delegitimation effort involved
the news media, especially TV journalism and investigative reporting. Many
state control authorities perceived that news revelations on topics ranging
from the Gulf of Tonkin Resolution to the Pentagon Papers to several presidential commission reports on civil rights violations (cf. Marx 1988), including the events of Watergate, and a host of others, contributed to increasing
public doubts about the efficacy, necessity, legitimacy, and standard operating procedures of state control agencies.

Such perceptions led numerous authorities to become more market oriented in the selling and promotion, if not the actual operations of their
organizations. The slide toward a market orientation among FASC was proceeding at about the same time as TV news was becoming more sophisticated in its use of visuals and electronic signaling and editing.

From the 1970s on, it was clear that a media consciousness would inform
national, state and local enforcement strategies (cf. Heinz, Jacob, & Lineberry 1983). Widespread public relations changes were instituted at the federal,
state, and local levels. For example, police departments became more proactive as they discovered public relations, positive mass media coverage,
and above all a clearer sense that they had enemies—including the press.
There was also more competition for funds from social service agencies such
as local fire departments and probation offices, which sought additional
resources that had previously been controlled by police departments. As
relationships between agencies and political interests became more competitive, the state agencies began to adopt more of a market orientation to
promote their organizations and activities as necessary public services. They
started to pay more attention to the news media and to expand their efforts to
influence news content in order to send the most advantageous messages to
significant audiences.

The national change can clearly be seen with regard to war information.
Disappointed with the news coverage of the Vietnam War, the military
changed its strategy (cf. Braestrup 1978). The military's control of the press
during the invasions of Grenada and Panama, in 1983 and 1989 respectively, illustrates the national response, which culminated in the high-tech
video war with Iraq in 1991. This TV war was heralded as a resounding
success, largely because of new technology that was available, including

gunsight visuals of "smart bombs" decimating targets, as well as Patriot interceptor missiles knocking down Scuds. The accolades of a high-tech success notwithstanding, it took more than a year, in March 1992, when a congressional investigation brought to light a report by the Department of Defense showing that only a fraction of the Patriot missiles actually hit their mark, and that when a worldwide audience thought they were viewing Patriot hits on Cable News Network (CNN), they were being deceived: *They only looked like hits.* (See Chapter 9.)

The evocative impact of crime and war visuals coming from familiar television receivers in the personal and private space of viewers' homes is also part of the context for the changing market orientation of FASC and what eventually happened with Azscam. (Indeed, the first news of Azscam shared the front page of the *Arizona Republic* with speculations about the start of the ground war in Operation Desert Storm!)

FROM ABSCAM TO AZSCAM

Mass media formats have been explicitly incorporated into the planning, execution, and outcomes of formal social control (cf. Surette 1992). We are referring not only to the plethora of undercover, *agent provocateur* operations that have been delineated by Marx (1988), but our interest is also on a new genre of such activities in which agents of control adjust their activities and discourse to fit news media formats in order to ensure public interest. *On television, interest is predicted by entertainment values.* As we have stressed, getting public attention means gaining access to the news media, and especially television. This requires the sense of something extraordinary and entertaining. One example is gonzo justice, as discussed in Chapter 5 (Altheide 1992). Another example is the changing character of government sting operations in which an *agent provocateur* provides the opportunity and usually encouragement for someone to commit a crime before hidden video cameras, capturing evocative visuals for broadcasting to millions of citizens. Azscam and its predecessor by a decade, Abscam, illustrate this convergence.

Our present focus is on the way video materials are obtained not only for use as evidence in criminal trials, but more importantly how an entire operation is organized around the collection of such materials, in order to display them publicly in entertainment formats, so that the accused (implicated) will either withdraw or, in the case of criminal charges, plead guilty in order to avoid a trial. While we cannot discuss the legal problems associated with stings here, it is important to simply note that the entrapment feature of such operations continues to plague prosecutors. However, entrapment as a defense usually comes up during a trial, and so the entrapment defense can be avoided by avoiding a trial.

Azscam represents a new genre of mass-mediated justice, but it emerged through a decade of experience with stings for crime stoppers and for audience members, as well. It began with Abscam (from "Arab scam," but initially "Abdul scam"), the two-year FBI sting that netted a dozen elected officials, including six congressmen, a United States senator, the mayor of Philadelphia, and several city council members.

The scenario was to entice these elected officials to accept money from a representative of an Arab sheik who desired, among other things, a new immigration bill. All were captured with the aid of hidden video cameras as they discussed elements of bribery and conspiracy involving immigration legislation, gambling, and real estate deals. The undercover and taping work ended in February 1980. With hidden video cameras catching the action, Congressman John W. Jenrette, Jr., agreed to introduce such an immigration bill for an initial payment of fifty thousand dollars with the understanding that more would follow.

The videotaped materials in Abscam were collected and used primarily as legal evidence in a court of law. News agencies first reported this operation and pending indictments on February 2, even though the initial indictments were not issued until May 22, with Congressman Jenrette's on June 14, 1980. However, no actual evidence, i.e., video or audio materials, was presented by the TV networks until October 14, when the Supreme Court gave approval to show videotapes that had been used as evidence in the first Abscam trial. Within hours of this decision, all three networks led off their evening news programs with excerpts from the tapes. From the court's perspective, the key point was that one trial had already occurred. Referring to the "common law right to inspect and copy judicial records," the court found "a presumption in favor of public inspection and copying of any item entered into evidence at a public session of a trial" (New York Times, 18 October 1980). Notwithstanding the impact such coverage could have on other defendants who had not yet had their day in court, the fact that at least one trial had occurred was critical in the timing. Our point here is simply that the video material was first used as evidence, and only later, following some four months and rather complex legal proceedings, were the tapes to be broadcast through TV news formats and other outlets.

Continuing with Abscam's success at visually capturing members of Congress using foul language, various states have used hundreds of such operations to trap burglars and other street criminals. Indeed, most legislators across the country have supported such methods as essential to fight crime. But the nature of such operations, especially when they involve public officials, was a concern to a congressional oversight committee, whose review of Abscam pointed out major problems regarding public trust, civil liberties, and especially entrapment, stressing that the "tyranny of unchecked crime and the tyranny of unchecked governmental intrusion" be avoided (*New York Times*, 17 December 1982). More recently, South Carolina and California have used bribery stings to fight corrupt legislators. Even though it is against the law to attempt to bribe public officials, these operations have been carried out by state police agencies, which have expanded their usual reactive agendas to more proactive efforts with elected public officials. All of this is the context for Azscam.

Azscam or Arizona scam, joined the work of journalists and FASC through the TV news format as the criteria and perspective of the former essentially dominated the legal perspective and format of the latter. This was accomplished by combining several features of Abscam, and rolling them into the context of a decade of reports about numerous police sting operations, usually of street criminals, drug dealers, and the like. Such reports served to accustom Arizona citizens (TV viewers and newspaper readers) to such practices. However, there were some rather important differences from Abscam. (See Table 6.1): (1) For one thing, the operation, which ultimately changed 8 percent of the state legislature, and also influenced an ongoing election, was orchestrated by the Phoenix Police Department and the Maricopa County Attorney's office! (2) While Abscam agents went after specific individuals who had a history of "suspicious" activities, Azscam agents offered bags of money to numerous legislators in order to find out who could be tempted to support organized gambling legislation. (3) The liberal use of racketeering statutes, or RICO legislation, which permitted property forfeitures and seizures, gave the local authorities in excess of one million dollars to use at the discretion of the county attorney! These funds bankrolled Azscam. (4) A point to which we will return below, the videotaped materials and transcripts were warmly permitted to be published prior to any legal hearing. This was all part of Azscam.

Azscam was a sting operation designed to ferret out any legislators who might be susceptible to a bribe or influence money to get them to support legislation for organized gambling in Arizona. Unlike Abscam, in which the prime targets had been previously suspected—and in a few cases, actually charged—with inappropriate conduct, those persons involved in Azscam did not have a background of unethical or near-criminal activities. Indeed, several of the indicted legislators had been vocal supporters and sponsors of social gambling bills for several years. Nevertheless, all indications are that numerous legislators were directly or indirectly approached, in a grab bag fashion to see who would bite.

The plan was to have the bag man, Joseph Stedino (a.k.a. Anthony Vincent), go from one legislator to another and offer money to anyone interested in working to support the legalization of organized gambling in Arizona. A 1987 Arizona law forbade gambling, but an amendment in 1988 and 1990 (*Arizona Republic*, 13 April 1991) did allow amusement and social gambling. The Phoenix police chief, the county attorney, and the other FASC

Table 6.1. A Comparison of ABSCAM and AZSCAM Stings

	ABSCAM	AZSCAM
Date of indictment(s)	May 22. 1980	February 5. 1991
Place	Washington, DC	Phoenix, AZ
Agency	FBI	Maricopa County Attorney General's Office Phoenix Police Department
Targets	Specific U.S. congressmen and senators referred by "middlemen"	Numerous members of Arizona legislature
Evidence	Video/audio recordings	Video/audio recordings
Charges	Bribery, regarding immigrants, gambling, and real estate	Bribery regarding gambling legislation
Number of people charged	12	20
Legal action	Trials	5 trials (7 people) (pending)
Outcomes	12 convicted 2 overturned (entrapment)	12 guilty pleas
Tapes released to media after	4 months. 1 trial	1 day

opposed even this form of gambling. Other lawmen soon came on board the operation.

On February 5, 1991, seven members of the Arizona legislature, four lobbyists, and several others were indicted on a range of charges pertaining to the legalization of casino gambling in Arizona. The eighteen-month investigation was funded by drug forfeitures and seizures, and coordinated by the county attorney's office and the Phoenix police department. Others were later named in conjunction with a civil racketeering suit filed to recover the one-million-dollar cost of operation Azscam. In one case, a justice of the peace of a Phoenix suburb was named in the suit because he agreed to fix a speeding ticket given to Joseph Stedino, the *agent provocateur*, a former Las Vegas TV personality with a long police record. (He was very good at his work.)

Twenty people were indicted altogether. Of the seven who were legislators, (there was also one former legislator) six pleaded guilty to various charges ranging from bribery to accepting illegal campaign contributions. The amounts of money accepted from the bag man ranged from $660 to more than $60,000. All but one of the six received prison terms ranging from six months to five years, supplemented by fines ranging from $2,760 to $200,000, and the attendant probation sentences (eighteen months to seven years), with ample community service.[1]

Some members of the Arizona legislature had become concerned during the sting that a "shady character" was attempting to spread influence in an untoward manner, and they notified the proper authorities. It is at least a Class 4 felony in Arizona to offer a bribe to an elected official, with a presumptive sentence of two to five years in prison. Like most sting operations, the FASC elected to break some laws in order to capture any legislators who would accept money to work for the passage of organized gambling. Nevertheless, indications are that the process was working to prevent the corruptible from being corrupted. During the operation, several members of the legislature mentioned Stedino's behavior either to their colleagues or law enforcement authorities.

While we remain uncertain exactly when some officials learned about the operation, there are indications that upon consulting with the county attorney, they were let in on the operation. However, they did not tell the legislators. This is important because had the police and other enforcement bodies taken their usual course of action when such suspicions were brought to their attention, Stedino would have been questioned, chased away, and the threat would have disappeared. The "corrupt" legislator would not, in fact, have been corrupted. But that was not the plan; the intent was to tempt Arizona lawmakers into accepting bribes, document it, and then indict them. Published news reports indicate that the state attorney general, Robert Corbin, first learned about the sting as a result of a telephone call from legislator Jack Jewett, whose call preceded other legislators' inquiries noted above.

Jack Jewett was approached by Stedino flashing a large amount of money. Jewett described him as coming "off in my judgment as a real sleaze". Jewett told a reporter, "It was obvious he wanted me to see it [money]. . . . [This] confirmed my worst suspicion that something was wrong with the whole setup" (*Tempe Daily News*, 7 February 1991). The next afternoon he returned to his home in Tucson and telephoned the attorney general, who told him he would look into it and that an investigator would contact him. What occurred next was quite remarkable. The investigator called later in the afternoon and said "that I was not to talk to anyone about this incident, that they were going to investigate it. I complied with that request" (ibid.). According to Attorney General Corbin, this was when he, the highest ranking law enforcement officer in Arizona, made some inquiries and learned about the operation. Yet, he stated that he could not inform Jane Hull, Speaker of the House, about the operation:

> "By then I knew what was going on, but I couldn't talk about it. I just told her that we were aware of it and to sit tight. We were investigating it" (ibid.).

Thus, one of Arizona's most important elected representatives was misled by the attorney general, who was receiving direction, apparently, from the county attorney and the chief of the Phoenix Police Department!

It is not irrelevant to our concerns that Jewett's account was published on the opposite page, where a spokesperson for the American Civil Liberties Union, Louis Rhodes, protested the activity, opening his discussion with the assertion, "The job of the police should be to discourage crime, not create it." He concluded, "The bottom line is only those who it appears were already engaged in criminal activity should have been targeted" (*Tempe Daily News*, 7 February 1991).

PUBLIC DISCLOSURE AND MEDIA LOGIC

Arizona, like many states, has a public disclosure law that permits public access to a range of information collected by public officials, including FASC. Journalists routinely make requests for such material. The videotapes and transcripts of legislators and the government stooge would fall within the scope of this statute. Ultimately, of course, it is up to the FASC to grant the request. And, given the market orientation of most FASC, they were usually eager to cooperate in the release of information. One reason for not honoring a request would be if an investigation was continuing. Journalists understand that this is somewhat self-serving, since virtually any investigation can be said to be continuing. As one TV journalist explained in an interview, "access delayed is access denied." Journalists understand, in short, that ultimately it is up to the FASC to release the information or not.

The newspaper and TV journalists interviewed agreed that the county attorney's office was very helpful in getting very quick access to selected videotapes and transcripts. Several of the reporters interviewed could not recall such cooperation from FASC, especially when compared to a case several years prior involving drug charges against popular members of the Phoenix Suns basketball team, in which very little information was forthcoming. He explained that in the Suns' case:

> What the prosecution did was to subpoena all reports under the cloak of the Grand Jury. They subpoenaed their own records "as part of an ongoing investigation!" . . . When the agencies want to cover themselves or not be cooperative, they may invoke an "ongoing investigation." (author's field notes).

Azscam was treated much differently by Arizona FASC. Even though the prosecution claimed that more indictments would be forthcoming—and more were—the ongoing investigation criterion apparently did not apply to the video and audio materials that were released to the press. A motion to dismiss the charges against one defendant on the basis of pretrial publicity stated,

> Not only did the prosecution team do nothing to deter the dissemination of pretrial publicity, a helping hand was offered the media in obtaining any and all material in the prosecutor's possession, including, but not limited to, video and audio tape recordings which the prosecution knew would be used as evidence at the trial. The reporters were given *carte blanche* access to three long shelves of videotape and 39 notebooks of 400 pages each of transcripts. In the words of one reporter, evidence in the case was literally "pushed on us." While the Phoenix police chief was making almost daily comments, the evidence in the case was being made available to the media in whole-sale lots, with the video provided by direct "uplink" from police headquarters. The "uplink" was necessary so the various television stations could review and edit those portions which they intended to show on that particular night's news. Copies of transcripts and other materials were prepared in advance for media distribution. (State of Arizona v. Ronald G. Tapp, Motion to Dismiss—Pretrial Publicity, Superior Court of Arizona, July 30, 1991).

The indictments were made public on February 6, 1991, and the tapes and transcripts began to be published the next day. But they were not all turned over at once, so that widespread editorial discretion had to be used. The "juiciest" transactions, taken out of context, were released serially to the news media, one segment at a time, one day at a time. Interviews with some reporters suggest that this was intentionally done in order to promote the mass media presentations on local TV news in particular, and printing the transcripts in newspapers, in general. Several selections were replayed dozens of times on local TV newscasts during the next fifteen months. Typically, brief transcriptions in the newspapers were accompanied by photos lifted from TV broadcasts and reproduced on the front page of the newspapers. For example, the *Arizona Republic* included the following transcript of a conversation between one of the people indicted, Raymond, and "Vincent," the bagman:

> Raymond told Vincent: "I do deals." Raymond said: "I like the deals of the Legislature." . . . Vincent told Raymond: "If you can deliver 14 votes, and if you're gonna vote yes on my issue and help, there's nothing in the world I won't do to help you." . . . Raymond told Vincent that he controlled the majority of the votes in the caucuses. . . . Vincent asked Raymond what he could do for him and Raymond said: "I have to raise about another $10,000. From a dollar to whatever you can help with, that's just fine." . . . Vincent handed Raymond $10,000 in cash. Vincent said: "When Tony does business, he does business." Raymond told Vincent that his favorite line was: "What's in it for me?" (Feb. 7, 1991)

The publication of the transcripts and video vignettes of shadowy figures exchanging greetings and packages continued for several days. The pretrial propriety of this activity did receive some attention. On February 10, a law professor at Arizona State University wrote in a "Perspective" piece that while it is certainly understandable and inevitable that the issue should be covered by the press,

> What is not inevitable, and what seems to me to be extremely questionable, is the pretrial release by the prosecutor or police of masses of evidence in the form of hundreds of hours of video and audio tapes and transcripts. The evidence of guilt, I had thought, was supposed to be introduced at trial. (*Arizona Republic*, 10 February 1991)

On February 12, 1991, Judge Ronald Reinstein refused to impose a gag order on lawyers, police, or witnesses, stating that the documents were public records available for media review under state law. He also stated that "sealing the documents was no longer an issue because media has had liberal access to them since last week" (*Tempe Daily News*, 13 February 1991). [Paradoxically, Deputy County Attorney James Keppel told reporters on February 11 that "Judge Reinstein has urged us not to talk about the case, so I'm going to abide by his ruling" (*Tempe Daily News*, 12 February 1991)]. The news sources had cleverly transformed the prosecutorial function into one of shaming, persecution, and overwhelming presumption of guilt.

By April 17—about nine weeks after the indictments—all legislators except one (and one former legislator) had pled guilty, arranged plea bargains, and resigned their posts. This was 8 percent of the legislature. Moreover, the democratic process had been tainted by this operation since a number of the people who were indicted had used these funds to aid their own campaigns, and thus received an extra advantage over their opponents. Following the resignations, alternative representatives were appointed—not elected.

Arizona citizens had experienced yet another soap opera, following the impeachment of a governor, the implication of both U.S. senators in the Savings and Loan debacle of antipornographer Charles Keating, and the failure of Arizona voters to approve a Martin Luther King Holiday, which cost them the 1993 Super Bowl and substantial convention business. But this was different: the coverage and the lack of broader perspective on Azscam painted a picture of inept and corrupt officials who could only be kept in line by undercover sting operations. Some of the opinion polls were not comforting. They showed that immediately following the sting, opinion was very negative about the legislators and elected officials, and quite supportive of police and law enforcement agencies.

There were other effects as well. The chief of police, Ruben Ortega, received some criticism for not checking with any of his superiors, such as the mayor or the city manager. Following some sparring over whether or not future operations should remain so secretive, the city manager relented, but Ortega resigned anyway.

Perhaps one of the most bizarre instances of the abuse of power involved Fondia Al Hill and Lillias Apland (*Arizona Republic*, 16 February 1994). Hill, a former professional football player, was an aspiring entrepreneur. He had an office next to Azscam stooge Stedino. An undercover officer posing as Stedino's secretary learned that Hill had a video on his desk, *The Crayon Lady*, and assumed that Hill was involved with child pornography. This tape, which was never viewed by the investigators, was actually an art instruction video produced by seventy-two-year-old Lillias Apland, who had given it and twenty-five thousand dollars to Hill to produce and market it. Through a series of complex twists and turns, Hill was lured into attempting to earn several thousand dollars provided by Stedino by tracking down child pornographers. Even though Hill had no such contacts, the opportunity was appealing and so he attempted to scam Vincent. Hill traveled to Amsterdam to purchase over-the-counter pornography tapes which he sold to Stedino for a handsome profit. He was later arrested and served several months in jail because he could not raise the one-hundred-thousand-dollar bail. As for Apland, her name and tape got associated with Stedino, who, in a book he later wrote, linked her to kiddie porn.

The *agent provocateur*, Stedino, like so many agents, was recruited because of his expertise in criminal affairs. He was a star, and was found

deserving of a four-part series in local newspapers. True to our media condition and his background in television, he approached several people to write
a book, to be made into a movie, but was temporarily derailed in this effort
when other questions were raised about his conduct and the role he would
play as a witness if there were to be legal proceedings. As the date for the
first trial approached, Stedino was found guilty of perjury when he falsely
testified that he had not had a social relationship with a key official from the
county attorney's office. Stedino's attorneys requested that if he had to testify
in court, TV cameras be banned, since they were concerned that his life and
reputation might be damaged via the coverage! This is no small irony considering how central TV was in his entire operation! Proofs of his book
appeared during the trial of one of the defendants, Carolyn Walker. Stedino
noted that he was savaged in the media, and that although news coverage of
the politicians in the sting was cruel, he felt no remorse since it was "Tony
Vincent that did it, not Joe Stedino" (*Arizona Republic*, 15 May 1992).

Finally, the RICO statutes, which not only funded Azscam but enabled
Phoenix and numerous cities in Arizona to brazenly confiscate money and
property, came under scrutiny. Through a series of award-winning investigative newspaper reports published in November 1993, details of how more
than thirteen million dollars worth of property and money confiscated from
individuals, few of whom were convicted of a crime, became a staple of law
enforcement budgets. In 1994, the Arizona legislature revised the RICO
statutes, but not in time to help the Azscam defendants. Jim Hartdegen,
charged with accepting improper campaign contributions totaling $660—
reported to have come illegally, from a single source—was ready to fight, to
go to trial, and to defend his reputation. However, he relented when the
Maricopa County Attorney's Office put a racketeering lien on his house, five
acres of land, and his truck. "They explained that just because you win the
criminal charges doesn't necessarily mean they will drop the RICO
charges," Hartdegen said (*Tribune Newspapers*, 21–26 November 1993). In
addition to resigning from the legislature, he pleaded guilty to three misde-
meanor counts of falsely reporting campaign contributions, was sentenced
to eighteen months of probation, and was assessed a $2,100 fine. Then the
prosecutors dropped the RICO suit.

CONCLUSION

Sting operations have apparently been accepted by elected officials, official control agencies, and a growing number of citizens. This work has
accompanied the expanding effort by FASC to demonstrate their need to
control threats to social order. When this can be demonstrated through

electronic communication formats that are evocative and resonant rather than discursive and more object oriented, journalism and FASC share a common language and perspective: what makes for good news also makes for good control, i.e., the image of evil is checked through electronic symbolism. As Couch instructs,

> The biases of electronic broadcasting that favor evocative symbols infuse the head of state and citizen relationships with more emotionality than does print. . . . Forceful acts and appearances have greater appeal in electronic broadcasting than do reflective assessments. . . . It emphasizes character and depresses the significance of programs of action. Image, not policy, becomes the central concern of both candidates and citizens. (1990:123–24)

The *agent provocateur* of Abscam was normalized, celebrated, and presented in a TV special! But in that infamous investigation, which publicly introduced videotapes as evidence in a court of law and then as grist for the bump and grind of our popular culture, there remained the courtroom format where an individual accused of a crime could attempt a defense, including challenging the government's right to such intrusive acts. A further step was taken with Azscam.

Azscam marks a turning point in mass-mediated justice and social control. Despite the county attorney's insistence in a newspaper article that his office was merely complying with the Arizona Public Records Law, there is every reason to doubt that such unprecedented cooperation with the news media accompanied the availability of video evidence. As the motion for dismissal of charges against one of the defendants stated,

> On a national level, no prosecutorial team has ever attempted wholesale distribution of trial evidence. Not in any of the more publicized serial killings, nor even in the Kennedy or Martin Luther King assassinations. In Arizona, the Don Bolles homicide [a journalist murdered in 1976] and the Phoenix Suns' drug scandal pale by comparison to the volume of raw evidence that spewed from the media day after day, week after week. (State of Arizona v. Ronald G. Tapp, Motion to Dismiss—Pretrial Publicity, Superior Court of Arizona, July 30, 1991).

This was a prime case of persecution without prosecution as the journalists, the county attorney, the *agent provocateur*, and the citizens of Arizona were joined through dominant news formats. The legal formats were severely compromised, but few seemed to notice or care. We are not aware of a single piece by a journalist that has reflected on what this action means for the democratic process and social justice. As one TV producer explained when he was asked if this piece of the story would be followed up, "while the public should be interested in this, they just don't give a shit" (author's field notes).

The mass media, and especially TV, were integral features of the entire operation; the outcome was certainly consistent with an intention to entrap people, publicly expose them on videotape, and then get them to plea bargain, and resign. The presumption seems to have been that the publicity effect would exact a toll, and it did. An effort to stifle pretrial publicity, especially release of videotapes, was quashed before it began, as the prosecutors quickly dispensed these materials to get them on the air and in the minds of Arizona citizens. The subsequent appeal to stop what was then in full momentum was not supported, with the ruling that the information was already out. The mass media formats that promote dramatic action packed visuals were certainly consistent with the entire operation. It was regarded as made-for-TV evidence, even if it may not have been perfect for courtroom evidence.

The implications for expanding social control by FASC abound. Historically, a key issue for control has been whether and to what extent the state and FASC should directly control the information technologies and their content. As video technology becomes more available, the visual will become more relevant in social life. Video on TV appears to be real, and good enough, largely because of the way audiences have been socialized to accept the typical TV narrative as self-contained. The key issue, of course, is one of context: just as hindsight on the Gulf War videos of Patriot missiles missing but appearing to hit targets (see Chapter 9) clarifies the importance of placing what we see in a context of understanding, so too does the Azscam TV coverage; in the postmodern age when images (cf. Baudrillard 1983) are traded for reality in context, FASC and others join in editing reality. When laypeople are invited to contribute videotaped news reports to TV stations, and when military strategists take the lead from the Desert Storm infotainment brigade and wrap war as action into the evening news formats, we can rest assured—albeit not peacefully!—that video reality, in the context of TV formats, has been mastered and is challenging other epistemologies of everyday life.

When the assumption that seeing-is-believing is integrated into the FASC arsenal of consensus and control, then we are likely to see even more state expansion into video control. The boundaries of this debate become more porous when good FASC are produced as good TV news, and when public discourse about complex issues involving government entrapment, the scope of state control efforts, and culpability are viewed through an electronic entertainment perspective. In such situations, the boundaries between freedom and control are dissipated through images and formats of control; charisma, programming, and instant replays shadow reflection, ambiguity, and creativity: "But the significance (danger) of electronic broadcasting may not stem solely from state control. The threat may also stem from the evocative biases of television" (Couch 1990:125).

Social order is a communicated order and the social worlds we experience will reflexively show this logic. The challenge is to understand how media logic can no longer be seen merely as content, or as an independent or dependent variable, but becomes a feature of discourse and meaning in our age. A re-created journalism and reflective observers must work hard to decode the "text without context" apparent in Azscam (Denzin & Lincoln 1994). Only in this way can we gain a more adequate conceptual hold on "what's happening here." If we do not, then more consequences may befall us, similar to those discussed in Chapter 7.

NOTE

1.   The one state legislator who demanded a trial was found innocent of three of four charges, including bribery. However, she was found guilty of conspiracy to commit bribery and was sentenced to four years in prison. Perhaps this was due to the tremendous publicity the case received, including the prosecutor's posttrial plea on radio talk shows urging citizens to demand a stiff sentence. Another defendant, who was regarded as the key intermediary, was tried, found guilty, and received a sentence of ten years.

Policy and the Ecology of Communication: 7
"The Missing Children Problem"

The combination of information technology and communication formats is most apparent and significant when brought to bear on news reports, especially those receiving so much coverage and emphasis that a major social problem is defined, and concerted social action is required. This chapter examines how the work of *moral entrepreneurs* or *claims-makers* about the 'missing children problem' not only used TV formats in carrying out their mission, but because of the significant impact of TV messages, also enlisted a host of other public media operating within the ecology of communication. As with previous chapters, the reader is invited to adapt the activity model (Chapter 4, Figure 4.1) to how public issues are raised today, as a feature of mass mediated claims-making.

The past decade has given rise to an accelerated concern for the welfare of children, particularly regarding child abuse and exploitation (Best & Horiuchi 1985). We suggest that the mass media images and formats are central to contemporary formulations of this social problem, but that the media, particularly television, operate interactively to contextualize issues in a way that has not previously been articulated by proponents of this perspective (cf. Blumer 1969; Spector & Kitsuse 1973, 1977). It is this interactional context between various media images and a social issue that will be delineated with the missing children problem (cf. Johnson 1985; Pfohl 1977) in the first part of the chapter.

THE MASS MEDIA, SOCIAL PROBLEMS, AND SOCIAL ISSUES

The TV message is universal, and is adapted to all cultures and countries. The networks are now transnational and can permit themselves the luxury of leaving aside the individual cultures in which they operate not only because the subjects they deal with and which their films abundantly feed off are elementary (mostly sex and violence), but also because they cancel determinants of time and space. . . . The raw material of the mass media is information; this is very hard to preserve because . . . it can be stolen without being moved. (Ferrarotti 1988:98)

In his concern with the future of history, Ferrarotti implores us to examine the forces transcending tradition. In particular he is concerned with the internal contradictions of technico-scientific developments that are taking on lives of their own, less as means to ends, than as the goals toward which no one in particular is leading us, a kind of perfection without aims. As we saw in the two previous chapters, gonzo justice is popular with formal agents of state control; that they should prefer it is less puzzling than that the public should accept it! What fears, emotions, and daily outlook on life might underlie citizens supporting authoritarian tactics to stop evil? What sense of evil do the various publics have, and what is the source of this public perception of fear and danger? Such questions lead us to examine the nature and look of crises within the ecology of communication. After a brief overview of the fundamentals of crisis generation in our media age, we look at one example, the missing children problem. The comments to follow will briefly set forth the nature of communication formats, show how the policy process incorporates such formats, and what impact this incorporation has had on claims-makers, audiences, issues, and outcomes.

The social policy process does not just involve a communication process; it is a communication process attempting to define the time, place and manner of a situation. Social policy is an attempt to socially construct reality first by *presenting a claim* that a set of interactions, events and circumstances is a problem that can be resolved and improved, and second by *proposing some change*. Most important, of course, is that both components are joined together through a communication strategy to convince the significant audience(s) of the nature and extent of the problem. It is this feature that joins social policy to mass communication policy, and suggests that social policy cannot be separated from the effective environment, including the relationships in the ecology of communication.

GENERAL EFFECTS ON SOCIAL POLICY

What we know is related to the source and communication context from which that knowledge is obtained. The content of knowledge is often less important than the style of knowledge, or how it is packaged, including what it is related to that makes it familiar to us. Social policy is also embedded in a communicative context, which is shaped increasingly by media logic. Mass communication formats have altered the process of constructing, defining, implementing, and evaluating social policy. The way we communicate, what we anticipate, and the symbolic frameworks that make messages recognizable and intelligible have changed the nature of social policy. Advocates of the status quo, policy changes, and assessments of previous policies have incorporated communication formats into their messages; they do not just use the media, but rather they decide what to focus on, how to do this, and when to do it based on communication formats.

IT and mass media formats are implicated in constructing activities, scenarios, and events as well as the strategies used to promote them and evaluate them. Any mass-mediated issue is made familiar and credible in two ways: first, through the place—homes, and the times—institutionalized news at dinner time, for example; second, through joining it artfully to another context or issue with which we are familiar, usually because it has also been presented to us within the same ecology of communication context. The mass media continue to be a major source for *setting agendas*. While the media are not the sole factor, it is very difficult to conceive of issues and problems that have received public support without the aid of mass media.

While it is hardly surprising that social agendas are set by the mass media, it is not so apparent how they are set. This is usually done by relating something that may not be so familiar to an audience to something the audience is presumed to know about. Stated differently, those topics and policies are more likely to be covered and broadcast if they can be treated as a new angle to old and very familiar themes and myths.

A related point concerns the sense of urgency and immediacy in which social issues and policy are cast. Media formats set the temporal and spatial character of topics and issues that affect policy messages and pursuits. The missing children issue provides a good example. The claim that thousands of children were being abducted and that the problem was quickly growing more serious intensified the message of urgency. Thus, legislation was enacted, special enforcement prosecution teams were established, and attention was focused again on crime as individual failing rather than a result of societal conditions.

Leaders and policymakers are very sensitive to mass media presentations about problems and issues, for several reasons. Leaders want to remain leaders and so they seek to present themselves as responsive to their publics. Increasingly in the modern age, a long-term leader is a successful follower of media policies and perceived shifts in the political wind. Generally, such leaders presume that if an issue has been legitimated by the media it has also been given serious attention by constituents, and is therefore safe to support. For example, in the missing children example, leaders throughout the United States followed the dominant media theme of rampant crime and children at risk, and pledged their tearful support to all efforts to make our country safe by getting tough on crime. Thus, leaders can show that they are being responsive to public concerns. Of course, exceptions occur if the decision-makers identify the issue with their enemies; in some cases, as demonstrated by President Nixon, they will work against such presentations and policies, and will try to promote their own messages. For example, in some recently released presidential papers, Nixon ordered one of his staff members to improve their own media image. On December 1, 1969, he wrote: "When I think of the millions of dollars that go into one lousy 30-second television spot advertising a deodorant, it seems to me unbelievable that we don't do a better job in seeing that Presidential appearances [on TV] always have the very best professional advice" (Oudes 1989:46).

Another reason why media messages are so important for policymakers is that they often learn about issues from news sources. If they can locate support of a particular issue within their own agenda for action, the two can be blended and the candidate's position can be strengthened. Thus, media legitimacy takes on a double significance.

Given the competition for news attention, any issue that is to be legitimated by extensive media coverage must satisfy the format criteria. That is, the issue must be presented as something new, devastating, having immediate impacts, and a crisis, but this must be done in a familiar way. In other work, I have argued that there are distinctive features of such crisis reporting and emphasis (Altheide 1987); it is exciting and engulfing. What parent can turn away from reports of abducted children? The formats for crisis consist of the following:

1. A specific event that can be depicted visually is selected.
2. This event is contrasted with the status quo, indicating a shift.
3. The event and/or the change it is claimed to represent is argued to be consequential for a large number of people, perhaps 10 percent of a population.
4. Immediate victims are shown and are often interviewed expressing grief or sorrow.
5. Blame is placed.
6. A metaphor such as a wave is graphically presented to give symbolic meaning to the whole issue.
7. Prior crises of a similar sort seldom are assessed for their eventual impact. Each crisis is presented as new, without a historical context.

We want to stress that the criteria and definition of a crisis or serious problem requiring a social policy are mass mediated. If such an issue cannot be cast in the appropriate media formats, it will not receive much attention. And any event that does qualify as a mediated crisis will have a short life span and will fade when it is no longer new, perhaps because another crisis has been negotiated and presented successfully by its advocates.

The major problems we face do not qualify as crises in the traditional sense conveyed by the media. Consider a few examples: AIDS, environmental pollution, ozone depletion, nuclear armaments and world peace, hunger, deprivation, political domination, estrangement, global exploitation. There are many more, of course, but the important point is that few of these will receive sustained and significant publication. Even the ones that do receive some sustained coverage (not necessarily high-quality coverage, however) will receive such attention, e. g., AIDS, as long as the disease is defined as being a major threat to all populations and life-styles.

Of great significance is the temporal implication of how issues qualify as communicable problems. Standard media formats prefer a very narrow time frame, something immediate, happening now, with effects that can now be known, and with almost instant impacts. Thus, issues and concerns that have a different temporal character (e.g., ozone depletion), or issues and problems that are understood to be cyclical, rhythmical, and not in linear order will not be so appealing.

The moral entrepreneurs and advocates of change play to these criteria as the nature of advocacy changes. Leaders and others react in terms of the formats and the visual signatures. The individuals and organizations who compete for public attention and legitimacy for their favorite issue do so within a communicative context. They select issues, plan their presentations, and stress the impact in order to be consistent with mass communication requirements.

Indeed, it is the skill of advocates to blend formats and mold issues to already existing and popular entertainment styles that gives many issues an opportunity to become a focus for social policy. It is hardly surprising in our communicative environment that rock music concerts have been able to integrate global attention on hunger, peace, and environmental concerns. Issues become entertaining in the hands of skilled guitar players and the voices of popular singers.

Political processes are now informed by these formats as leaders and the led reflect media consciousness. Perhaps the best example is the selling and promotion of national politics in the United States, which includes many elements increasingly found throughout the world. President Reagan's re-election in 1984 was not a surprise, nor was his staff's skill at playing to the media. The explicit use of media techniques was more pronounced during the election of Reagan's successor, George Bush. What was surprising was the staff's willingness to explicitly state their willingness to focus on TV formats and learn from them. One of the clearest statements about the adoption of such media formats was presented by former Presidential aide, Michael Deaver, who in an opinion piece in the *Washington Post*, "Sound-Bite Campaigning: TV Made Us Do It," stated quite matter-of-factly:

My own contribution to campaign innovation resulted from observing the medium as we prepared for the 1976 presidential race. I noted how the people who run television news were reducing a candidate's thoughtful and specific speech on an issue, say, an upturn in the economy, to a 10-second sound-bite, which was then followed on the screen by an effective visual of someone, usually in the Midwest, "whose life remains untouched by the prosperity claimed by President Ford," as the voice-over told us. *The point is that rather than inventing the effective visual or the 30-second sound bite, we simply adapted an existing TV news technique that was already widely used. . . .* So, in our morning issues conference, a meeting much like those held in the editorial offices of newspapers and television networks and stations all over the country, I decided to "lead" with the housing story. But rather than have White House Press Secretary Larry Speakes hold up charts or issue a press release, and thereby bury the story in the business segment, we took the president to a construction site. There, wearing a hard hat and standing in front of homes under construction, he announced the housing start numbers and what that meant to the American people and the national economy. Naturally, the story played big on the evening news. (30 October 1988; emphasis added)

FINDING THE MISSING CHILDREN ISSUE

General and specific issues are a result of claims-making. The theoretical relevance of mass media in the claims-making process is consonant with the missing children issue (Blumer 1971; Spector & Kitsuse 1973, 1977), although initial formulations about the role of these media must be recast to be consistent with more recent findings about the impact of mass media formats on non–mass media situations (Altheide & Snow 1979; Altheide 1985).

The fate of a claim may depend heavily on the channels through which it is pressed, the strategies used to achieve visibility of the imputed condition, and the auxiliary personnel who play a part in the process (Spector & Kitsuse 1977:145). When we consider that numerous entrepreneurs are competing for media assistance in transforming their claims (problems) into a legitimate social issue, it is not enough to imply that the media play a role. Rather, we need to understand what is the mass media's role, particularly in regard to other societal information claims and counterclaims about a social problem.

THE ROLE OF THE MASS MEDIA

The missing children issue has been publicized and televised as entertainment and news. Entertainment and news programming share a format and logic (cf. Altheide 1985). With the former, Cantor (1980) and Gitlin (1980) have shown that scheduling, assumptions about the audience, and ideological factors find their way into programming decisions. And Snow (1983) suggests that producers' conceptions of "ideal norms" inform entertainment decisions.

Organizational and practical considerations also inform news content. What becomes newsworthy depends upon the format that is inherent to the specific medium. Incorporating many features of entertainment production, news formats are reflective of the newsmakers need for dramatic action-packed visuals, which address a thematic unity (Altheide 1985). The look of the news is subject to the filming, editing, cutting, and producing that have become organizationally determined (Epstein 1973; Altheide 1976, 1985; Gans 1979; Graber 1984a; Tuchman 1978; Molotch & Lester 1974). This selective nature and its subsequent dependence upon sensationalism can manufacture crime waves by suddenly focusing on previously ignored offenses (Fishman 1980; Bortner 1984; Cavender 1984).

While the specific effects on various audiences, including decision-makers, continue to be investigated, a plethora of research has demonstrated a variety of direct and indirect effects of mass-mediated information (cf. McQuail 1983). The manner in which a social problem is conceptualized and presented will affect the creation and proliferation of the phenomenon and is crucial to how the public will perceive it (Sutherland 1950; Becker 1963). For example, TV programming cultivates fear and a belief in the dangerousness of life that can contribute to the exploitation of people (Gerbner & Gross 1976). These images, along with specific messages may not predict exactly what options people will take, but they are suggestive of the kinds of things people will consider and think about. Graber (1984a) and Shaw and McCombs (1977) call attention to the agenda-setting power of the media whereby "media audiences accept guidance from the media of their choice in determining what information is most important and worthy of attention" (Graber 1984a:111–12). "In such cases, the public is very defenseless, because it lacks independent data from outside the media—'extra' media data'—with which to control the picture offered by the media" (Rosengren, Arvidsson, & Sturesson 1978:131; cf. DeFleur & Ball-Rokeach 1975; McQuail 1983; Ball-Rokeach, Rokeach, & Grube 1984).

Conceptualizing the impact of mass media messages about social problems on audience members has recently been expanded to show the effects on extramedia institutions and situations. The cultural relevance of the mass media includes the adaptation by other institutions (e.g., political, religious, and sports) of communication formats, including scheduling, pacing, rhythm, and syntax (Altheide & Snow 1979). For example, TV cartoon characters and movie heroes are routinely adapted to commercials and fast-food products. In this sense, the viewing context is extended to shopping malls and restaurants. Such institutional transfer has considerable implications for clarifying the role of the mass media in the construction of social problems.

The scope and breadth of claims-making across various media entail further examination of the mass media's role in the transformation of missing children as personal tragedies into a major social problem. We will further suggest that an informational context enabled viewers and readers to see evidence of mass-mediated reports in nonmedia settings (e.g., grocery stores and airports). Moreover, at least some of the pervasive messages of crime, fear, and danger implicit in this informational context were tied to previous claims-making activities about child abuse (cf. Nelson 1984).

THE CAREER OF A SOCIAL PROBLEM

Widely publicized claims about the nature and extent of missing children have been offered by selected parents, moral entrepreneurs, and government agencies. However, it has been the claims about the extent of the problem rather than its nature that have commanded attention. Indeed, Gentry's (1986) account of the evolution of the Missing Children's Act of 1982 and the Missing Children's Assistance Act of 1983 indicates that much of the initial effort was directed toward body counts rather than solutions. While evidence was available that very few missing children were attributable to strangers and/or "trolls" (i.e., sexual perverts), this was largely overlooked in the initial congressional hearings in favor of testimony by network producers and aggrieved parents, such as John Walsh, who presented accounts that went beyond the data. Consistent with other research on the moral career of social problems, the focus of these hearings was on political legitimation rather than validation of information (better information was not forthcoming until 1990). Senator Paula Hawkins, a supporter of the Missing Children's Assistant Act, stated:"President Reagan and you and I ran on the slogan of family, home, neighborhood, peace, and freedom. This [Act] strengthens all aspects of that pledge" (U. S. Senate 1982:59).

The missing children issue subsists on mass media reports of the frequently quoted figure that 1.5 million children vanish, disappear, or are abducted each year, with implications that stranger or troll-type abductions are the greatest concern. The docudrama Adam even quoted that estimate. Since 1979 the number quoted has ranged from fifty thousand to as high as three million (cf. Gentry 1986). The origin of the 1.5 million statistic has been traced to a Louisville study that was cited by the U.S. Department of Health and Family Services in a 1979 report. The 1.5 million figure was calculated by multiplying the Louisville figure in order to apply it to the rest of the country, then multiplying it again to estimate the number of cases not reported by the police (Scardino 1985:22).[1] If accurate, the sheer magnitude of this estimate, in the face of pervasive parental concerns for the safety of their children (Best & Horiuchi 1985), could cause legitimate public concern, and would certainly be appealing to any politician seeking to establish him-/herself as a protector of family members.

The initial claims-makers' definition of the nature of the problem was honored by politicians who were sensitive to such a "valence" issue (Gentry 1986). The advocates suggested that the problem was far worse than any data indicated. They argued that the lack of systematic tracking was partly responsible for counterclaims offered by the FBI and others that there were very few actual cases (e.g., thirty-five in 1981, forty-nine in 1982, sixty-seven in 1983). Mindful of the importance of on-line databases for bureaucratic accounting, claims-makers argued that the FBI's National Crime Information Center (NCIC) was inadequate because the rap sheets, social security numbers, and other identification symbols pertained to adults and not children. The Missing Children Act of 1982 mandated changes in coding procedures and criteria so that information like dental and medical records, scars, and other identifiers be added about a missing child upon the request of legal guardians.

Notwithstanding the lack of systematic research on the topic, decision-makers proposed sweeping policy changes, and only later did it become apparent that the extent of the problem remained unclear. How the nature of the problem could be clearly understood without an awareness of the range and extent of cases was apparently never an issue. For example, the "Report and Recommendations of the United States Attorney General's Advisory Board on Missing Children," (U. S. Department of Justice 1986), advocates far-reaching local, state, and federal policy changes, including mandatory reporting, less stringent privacy guidelines, increased control of juveniles by governmental agencies, and changes in judicial procedures. Preceding these recommendations is the following statement:

> If future public policy is to be grounded in fact, the actual numbers and types of children who are out of parental custody are needed. The national incidence study [due in 1988] will greatly enhance our capacity to make informed and responsible decisions about responding to the problem of missing and abducted children. (p. 12)

The official report of the Office of Juvenile Justice and Delinquency Prevention, "Missing, Abducted, Runaway, and Throwaway Children in America," did not appear until 1990. In stressing that "stereotypical kidnappings" may involve only two hundred to three hundred children, one of the commission's major conclusions was:

> What has in the past been called the missing children problem is in reality a set of at least five very different, distinct problems. Each of these problems needs

to be researched, analyzed, and treated separately. (Finkelhor, Hotaling, & Sellak 1990:4).

Understanding the problem was secondary to establishing the legitimacy of and organization to deal with the problem. The latter was accomplished by establishing the National Center for Missing and Exploited Children. Once the institutionalization of the problem had been accomplished, moral expert entrepreneurs could provide routine news sources for the mass media. Other facts and more informed interpretations that could only come from careful research and analysis were not regarded as essential to their work.

The creative work of moral entrepreneurs to define and publicize missing children as a social problem to legislators as well as mass media personnel is apparent:

> Parents, schools, child-serving agencies, and professionals of all disciplines are justifiably worried about the nature, scope, and resolution of problems surrounding America's missing children. Milk cartons with pictures of missing children, repetitive television public service announcements, and front page horror stories of exploited children bring a sense of fear, concern, and anxiety into many families and communities across the Nation. (U. S. Department of Justice 1986:3)

Mass media audiences throughout the United States have been barraged by entertainment shows, docudramas, and news reports of missing and killed children. Mass media portrayals tend to focus on the tragedy and suffering of individual children and parents. Once the horror is established, claims about the magnitude of the problem may be included within the script. The missing children issue cannot be seen as the sole creation of the media, but like child abuse in general, the media can be viewed as playing a major role in its creation and proliferation (cf. Nelson 1984). Johnson argues that "the publication of emotionally provocative mass media accounts [or 'horror stories'] about violence to children" has played an important role in the political, social and institutional successes of the child maltreatment movement (1989:7).

The moral entrepreneurs can always point to real horror stories about the kidnapping and harm of children. Public attention regarding the missing children issue can be traced to various media accounts of the Atlanta child murders, the stranger abduction and murder of Adam Walsh in Florida in 1981, and subsequent TV docudramas—television movies based on a true story (Best & Horiuchi 1985:493). Perhaps the missing children creation was best summed up by Adam's parents, the Walshes:

> "The movie has broken so much ground," summed up [Mr.] Walsh, 38. "It proved Linda's [the producer of Adam] contention—that the American public

is willing to deal with serious subject matter. You just have to talk their language." Reve Walsh, 31, added, "Television is the American language." "It's a sad commentary," said [Mr.] Walsh, "that people need a prime-time television show—not a documentary, not a PBS show but an entertainment form—to form their priorities. . . . "The Walshes talk and . . . people have labeled this [the problem of missing children] a national epidemic. (*Los Angeles Times*, 15 March 1984)

This same article further suggests that the docudrama *Adam* raised the consciousness of the country about the thousands of children who are kidnapped, abused, and/or killed each year, noting that it succeeded in (1) locating eleven out of fifty-five missing children whose photos were aired during the docudrama (although it was not emphasized that these children had been taken by parents involved in custodial disputes, and not strangers); (2) establishing the exigency for five local TV stations' weekly features on missing children, which they credit with finding two more children soon after their inception; (3) triggering the Reagan administration's funding of $1.5 million for the National Center for Missing and Exploited Children; (4) soliciting $87,000 in viewer contributions to the Adam Walsh Child Resource Center; and (5) persuading the FBI to open its computer services to local agencies for the use of locating missing children. The public response has not been passive.

In addition to flooding hot lines with reports of seeing missing children—sometimes leading to the rescue of the wrong children from their legitimate parents—thousands of concerned parents have taken numerous defensive actions, often at considerable expense, to protect their children. Some of these defensive steps include fingerprinting and videotaping their children, installing dental identification implants, and purchasing insurance to cover the cost of private detective work in the event their children disappear (Gentry 1986).

While the above suggests that the remaining stages suggested by Blumer (mobilization with regard to the problem, the formation of an official plan of action, and transforming the original plan in implementation) have occurred to various degrees, it is clear that the Walshes were the ultimate missing children claims-makers (Gentry 1986). Specifically, they succeeded in defining it as a legitimate political issue. They prevailed in creating the Adam Walsh Child Resource Center in Florida, and through expert testimony at congressional subcommittee hearings, the Walshes enhanced the establishment of the National Center for Missing and Exploited Children. Another indication of institutionalization beyond mass media attention is the development of annual conferences. The first National Conference on Missing and Exploited Children occurred in Chicago during the week of March 2–5, 1986.

COUNTERCLAIMS

These major historical events in the career of the missing children issue signify the completion of Blumer's proposed evolution, but as Spector and Kitsuse (1977) suggest, the natural history of a social problem evolves into an additional stage where contradiction, debate, and rejection of existing claims and procedures by new claims-makers will challenge the legitimacy of established claims and institutions. For example, a number of journalists now question the figures, noting in particular that most missing children are not abducted by strangers at all, but are more likely to be, first, runaways who tend to reappear, and second, children involved in custodial disputes between divorced or separated parents. As two *Denver Post* reporters who won a Pulitzer Prize for their work wrote: "The bottom line is clear. There are not tens of thousands of children snatched away each year to be beaten, tortured, or murdered, the common perception of many parents" (Griego & Kilzer 1985).

Some critics proclaimed that the figures for stranger abductions may very well be below one hundred! And whatever the figure for missing children, as many as 95 percent of them may be runaways, not abductions. Columnist Ellen Goodman (1985) wrote:

> Now, just now, we hear that there are not 50,000 children a year abducted by strangers. Child Find in New York has altered their estimate to 600 such kidnappings, and the FBI says 67 were reported in 1984.

Partly because closer scrutiny of the data has resulted in counterclaims carried by the mass media, at least one congressional subcommittee has conducted hearings to reexamine the nature and extent of the problem.

The ecology of communication, and in particular, the way in which different information technologies were folded together in defining a serious event played a central role in shaping this issue. In view of the counterclaimants' evidence about the problematic nature of the definition of what constitutes a missing child and how many there are, it seems to be rather astounding that so much attention, effort, and money have been directed at this issue. Further, when we consider that agencies like the National Center for Missing and Exploited Children have also greatly reduced their estimates of the number of missing children, and concede that "only a tiny fraction" are abducted by strangers, it is clear that not all of the evidence is equally problematic or subject to the ontological posturing of claimants and counterclaimants.[2] The claims-makers' success in the face of other evidence suggests that a broader interactive informational context was operating to validate, sustain, and legitimate claims about the problem. For example, what occurred to lead the private and public sector to place missing children photos on billions of pieces of mail and on posters in grocery stores and airports, to feature public service announcements on TV, and to transform milk cartons into pleas for lost youth?

THE INFORMATIONAL CONTEXT OF SOCIAL PROBLEMS

The emphasis here is not just on the news bias but on the ecology of communication in which the activity (and perspective) is embedded of finding and solving a social problem. This ecology is not just media environment, but is part of our effective reality and a feature of our normal surroundings. Under such circumstances, media logic merges with cultural logic. The mass media transmit images of reality through entertainment and news formats, which define, select, organize, interpret, and present information on the basis of media logic, which is carried over into seemingly nonviewing situations. This is part of the context for gonzo justice discussed previously. For example, images beyond the TV are arranged, recognized, and interpreted to be like the ones seen on TV (cf. Altheide & Snow 1991). A feature of media logic is the establishment of an interactive informational context, or a familiar and consonant pattern of symbolic meanings that define and organize experience from one situation to another. In this context, an environment is constructed that symbolically frames claims and counterclaims; the veracity and impact of a message is contingent on its recognition and familiarity. Audience members interact with this context as well as other mass media reports.

We suggest that an informational context pervading the effective environment also blended with the missing children issue through interactive media formats. Interaction occurred in at least three ways: (1) emergent communication formats (e.g., TV news programs, invited audience members to become more involved in the problem by calling specific telephone numbers); (2) TV news reports, docudramas, and prime-time situation comedies and dramas repeated and essentially reinforced the symbolic messages; (3) other media (e.g., milk cartons, posters, and bulk mail) proclaimed the problem and invited citizens' assistance in its resolution. They were each different, yet reinforcing about the specific problem, but more importantly, their density and frequency of appearance provided an exclamation point to the media significance and therefore the social significance of the problem. Urgency was seen and heard throughout the day and evening.

Mass media imagery of missing children thereby cut across private and public order as individual members of a mass TV audience encountered similar images in familiar interaction settings at the grocery store, as well in examining their daily mail. The nature and scope of this imagery reinforced a crisis definition of the problem, and interactively joined public and private discourse by labeling all varieties of absent children as missing, and by implication abducted. When the major sources of public information about such cases were cast in docudramas about kidnapped and killed children (e.g., *Adam, The Atlanta Child Murders*) and news formats flashed photos of children over the caption Missing, the distinctions were blurred in favor of an image of strangers abducting children.

In short, the emergence of the missing children problem is consistent with claims-making activities via the mass media. An additional concept, the interactive informational context, has been proposed to theoretically clarify why claims about missing children may be sustained against counterclaims. Such considerations can be empirically addressed by posing questions about audience members' involvements with information and claims. Accordingly, what were the various sources of information on this issue? Relatedly, if media portrayals can contribute to the definition of a problem, can the media defuse perceptions of a problem by providing additional information?

DESIGN OF INQUIRY

Noah Fritz and I (Fritz & Altheide 1987) empirically examined three key propositions:

1. The current messages about missing children promote fear by not distinguishing between children abducted by strangers, runaways, and children taken by noncustodial parents.
2. Respondents derive consonant information about the missing children issue from conventional mass media sources as well as other sources (e.g., in grocery stores).
3. A different message, i.e., a counterclaim, about the complexity of the issue will elicit different opinions and perceptions about missing children.

Related key questions include:

- To what source do most people attribute their knowledge about missing children?
- What social characteristics account for high levels of fear, and how does additional information affect these perceptions?
- Finally, does the notion of an interactive informational context enrich our theoretical understanding about the role of the mass media in the emergence and proliferation of a social problem?

The impact of television and other media was analyzed by administering a self-report questionnaire before and after a stimulus. The questionnaire addressed the source of knowledge and the degree of concern for the issue, and tested for the influence of the additional information on viewers' perceptions. The experimental stimulus was a two-part, twenty-minute videotape originally broadcast on August 8 and 9, 1985, by a public broadcasting station, KAET-TV in Phoenix. The respondents were shown this videotape in October 1985. This tape, *Child Find,* illustrated the complexity of the issue, noting the counterclaims that there are far fewer than 1.5 million missing children and that 95 percent of those missing are actually runaways. In addition to raising questions about the numeric and conceptual nature of the missing children issue, the tape addressed the role the media have played in this complex issue.

DATA

The data for analysis were collected by administering a fixed-choice and open-ended questionnaire to one denominational church forum and two upper-level college courses in a large southwestern metropolis. Efforts to reduce demand effects included pre- and posttest discussions of the issue (cf. Orne 1962). The implementation of these tests gives an indication of the initial measure of concern and its subsequent change (Hagan 1982). Respondents in the survey were 96 adults aged 17 to 64. The average age was 23.2 years old, and 54 percent were females and 46 percent males. Ten percent were parents or grandparents of children 12 years old or younger; and 9 percent had siblings of that age. All of the respondents had graduated from high school, while 27 percent had completed college or graduate school.

VARIABLES

The dependent variable is a seven-item "concern" scale that taps several dimensions of the missing children issue, including perceived seriousness of the problem and likelihood of stranger abduction. Higher scores indicate greater levels of concern and perceived seriousness of the problem. To investigate a related dimension, the respondents were asked what types of missing children prevention products they would purchase. This was used as a measure of the extent to which they feared that their child (supposing they had one) could be abducted.

The media effects were derived from four items designed to elicit respondents' assessments of media influence, media accuracy, and rank ordering of sources contributing to one's understanding about missing children. Another measure of media effects asked the respondents to estimate the percentage of missing children that are runaways, noncustodial-parent abductions, and stranger abductions. This item assessed the content and relevance of a range of media sources, including network and local TV news, docudramas, milk cartons, and word of mouth. In addition, subjects were asked to write how they felt about the missing children issue.

Control variables examined include relationship to a child below the age of twelve (sibling, parent, or grandparent), gender, age, exposure to docudramas about missing children, and frequency of television viewing. Other control variables were not employed because the selection design did not offer enough divergence on these items.

RESULTS

The preceding propositions were examined by analyzing and comparing frequency distributions, percentages, and t-tests before and after respondents viewed the videotape. Results from the frequency and percentage distributions offer support for the proposition that most respondents were very concerned about missing children, tending to see them as abductions. In the pretest, 61 percent of the respondents believed that the missing children issue was a serious problem, and 68 percent felt it was a national crisis. Only 7.3 percent saw the 1.5 million missing children statistic as a fallacy. Nearly 73 percent expressed a moderate or greater level of fear about abduction by a stranger and 37 percent perceived that a child had at least a fifty-fifty chance of being abducted. Only 21.9 percent felt that most missing children are runaways, while 58 percent indicated that there has been a drastic increase in the last two years in the percentage of children abducted. Relatedly, at least 74 percent of all persons surveyed indicated some degree of concern (i.e., scored 21 or higher on the scale measuring the dependent variable). These data suggest that the subjects were definitely concerned about missing children.

The second proposition was that additional information would alter perceptions of the issue. Comparing percentages before and after the stimulus illustrates the shift in opinions and perceptions regarding the missing children issue. Of the 61 percent who initially indicated that the missing children issue was a serious problem, only 33.3 percent maintained this view upon viewing the more complex message. Similarly, those who initially perceived the abduction of children by strangers as a crisis (68 percent) altered their perceptions, so that only 31.3 percent chose this option after seeing the tape. Following the viewing, 39.6 percent questioned the 1.5 million figure (vs. 7.3 percent earlier). Twenty-eight percent rerated their level of fear that a child is in danger of being stranger abducted as moderate or above (vs. 72.9 percent before). After viewing the tape, only 14.5 percent indicated that the chances of a child being abducted by a stranger was fifty-fifty or better, compared to 37 percent who chose this option prior to the viewing. While 74 percent of the cohort reflected a concern over the issue by scoring 21 or above on the perceived seriousness scale during the pretest, only 28 percent of the respondents held this same level of concern during the posttest.

Further evidence supporting this proposition can be seen with data comparing respondents' perceptions about the proportion of missing children who were runaways, before (Time-1) and after (Time-2) viewing the tape. At Time-1, the majority of the respondents (63.3 percent) estimated that less than one-fourth of missing children were runaways, while at Time-2, the majority (84.0 percent) believed that more than three-fourths of missing children were runaways.

t-tests comparing the mean scores on the concern scale for the entire sample before and after the stimulus strongly suggest that a difference between the means exists other than by chance, with a *t*-value of 15.00 and significant at the $p < .001$ level. This demonstrates that the new message had a significant effect on the audience. Similarly, *t*-tests were employed to determine the differences between the means when controlling for various demographic characteristics: gender, age, parent or sibling of a child, amount of television viewing, and whether or not the respondent had viewed any docudramas regarding missing children.

Regardless of the control variable, each subgroup changed significantly from Time-1 to Time-2. That is, for example, whether or not respondents were male or female, they experienced a reduction in their level of concern about missing children after viewing the video. Particularly noteworthy was the video's impact in reducing fear about missing children for those who had viewed a docudrama (e.g., *Adam*). At Time-1, those respondents who had viewed any of the three docudramas mentioned had significantly higher mean scores than those who did not. However, at Time-2, the difference between the mean scores disappeared. When both groups were examined separately, the results suggest that they both experienced significant degrees of change in the means from Time-1 to Time-2. This finding implies that the stimulus potentially affected both groups, even though the docudrama viewers had greater fear initially.

The relevance of an interactive informational context is suggested by the various sources of information. The data indicate that the mass media, particularly television, play an important role in the public's understanding of the missing children phenomenon (proposition 3). Seventy-six percent of the individuals suggested that the mass media had greater than moderate influence on their knowledge about the missing children issue, although slightly more than one-third of the respondents (35.4 percent) indicated that the media portray an inaccurate account of the phenomenon.

Lastly, the difference between the means for respondents who were considered frequent TV watchers (ten hours or more/week) and infrequent TV watchers (less than ten) was not significant at $p < .05$. Both groups were significantly different from Time-1 to Time 2. These data suggest two things: (1) TV was not the sole source of information on this topic; (2) a coherent message can change one's perceptions, at least over a short period.

Written comments after viewing the video indicated that some respondents reflected on their media experience with this issue and did not like it:

No. 29:   "I'm torked off! Why does the media always have to create a story!"

No. 11:   "The media has traditionally misinterpreted facts, which is why I don't watch TV. The missing children 'epidemic' was created by mass media. Why aren't there more programs on parenting or family counseling to prevent the tragedies of runaways, throwaways, instead of focus on the one or two children that were killed vs. the millions who are unhappy in their home situations?"

No. 7:   "Somewhat disgusted that the whole truth isn't told. Good news can certainly be misperceived by the unsuspecting public. Related to the missing children issue seems to be the recent focus on abusive child-care centers—the same fear and paranoia is there."

When we asked respondents to rank their sources of information, local TV news out-ranked the second source three to one, although the other sources, including milk cartons and posters, were clearly supportive. The prominence of the top two sources would support the *Los Angeles Times*'s contention that "'Adam' Points to TV Power," although it is also clear that respondents were familiar with a range of media (e.g., bulk mail ads).

The role of TV news in this study does not, however, operate uniformly and without qualification. While many of our respondents did show measurable change in understanding and awareness of the complexities of the missing children issue after exposure to a more extended treatment of the issue, many respondents remained concerned. For example, 29 percent of those who defined the missing children issue as "serious or very serious" before the documentary maintained this definition after viewing it. And 92 percent of those persons who indicated that they would purchase a fingerprinting kit for their children at Time-1 would also do so at Time-2. A few illustrative comments follow:

No. 24: "The media always tends to inflate problems beyond certain limits. One must realize this when viewing any broadcast. However, I do feel that the problem of missing children is a clear and present threat to our society . . . as it has always been. This problem did not suddenly spring up. Rather, it has/and always will be with us for a time to come. . . . The media has simply sensationalized it."

No. 37: "I believe it is a very big issue, that should not be taken lightly. I think that the media has done a great job on making missing children an important issue, that used to only affect the parents and organizations that dealt with the problem. Now more people will believe that it can happen to their children, no matter what the upbringing or conditions may be."

No. 39: "I feel the media has exaggerated it, but I feel the fear it has produced is good. Maybe this fear will make people more careful about watching their children. Also children will be more afraid of strangers. Hopefully, this will stop or at least cut down on the number of children who really are abducted."

No. 59: "I feel it is a very serious problem. I strongly disagree with the people who feel the media is distorting the facts or statistics about missing children. . . . A lot of these cases go unreported. As long as the media keep informing the public on the seriousness of this crisis and people continue to help each other, hopefully, we can get closer to a solution for this problem."

For these people, the one-time viewing of counterclaims about the missing children issue was not enough to offset months of mediated imagery on TV, posters, and mail about fear in general and the plight of thousands of children in particular.

CONCLUSION

Events and issues are marked by information technologies and communication formats. The impact of the mass media on the missing children issue was examined in order to further clarify the relevance of mass media for the social construction of social problems. The mass media contribute the most to the claims-making process when an audience member can interact with imagery in a variety of viewing and nonviewing situations. Such an informational context frames an issue. The construction of news messages becomes joined with claims-making perspectives when mass media are conceptualized as active contributors to the definition, selection, organization, and presentation of an issue. Further, when TV news reports cast the missing children issue within a visual format that is essentially duplicated in nonviewing situations such as grocery stores, airports, and reading bulk mail, then an informational context is also created for defining, organizing, and learning about an issue.

We are suggesting, then, that it is information in the context of other experiences, fears, and understandings that makes claims or counterclaims plausible and legitimate as social problems. Legislators tried to keep up with the documentaries and made-for-TV movies, and hurriedly passed "enabling" legislation in the mid 1980s to "take action" even though more reliable information, which challenged these early assumptions, did not become available until 1990 (Finkelhor et al. 1990) and did not support such steps! The initial concerns of the claims-makers are consonant with other cultural myths, which tend to be explicitly or implicitly reported via the mass media and are more likely to be sustained through the development of an expansive informational context. Thus, the missing children problem was tied to our effective communication environment: in the United States, considerable attention was paid to missing children, who, according to some moral entrepreneurs, were being kidnapped and molested by the thousands. It was the way in which this alleged problem was related to an already accepted fear that crime was rampant in the United States. Accordingly, the issue was cast in this way: children were in imminent danger of being abducted by marauding trolls and perverts. In fact, very few children were abducted by strangers, but the majority of children who were missing for short periods of time were runaways, throwaways, and "lost," often fleeing horrible home conditions. But since these children did not fit the prevailing myths about crime, little attention was focused on this story, and consequently little has been done to provide shelters and assistance to those who do run away. However, we now have even stronger and more punitive laws to regulate the trolls, few in number though they may be! Most significantly, the public perception that crime was rampant and the most fearful impediment to an orderly and safe life was reinforced.

Our reformulation of the role of the mass media in the emergence of social problems clarifies how the mass media are relevant for claims-making and counterclaims-making in the career of an issue. Numerous topics, fears, and concerns qualify as urban legends, but few emerge to become social problems. Such emergence entails a broad consensus about the definition, legitimacy, and urgency of an issue. The important research query for placing the missing children issue in a theoretic context is: *What is the process by which it becomes a social problem?* While it is clear that the missing children issue may be defined as an urban legend, its emergence as a social problem depended extensively on claims-making activity and the impact of the mass media on this process. The emergence of missing children as a social problem appears to have evolved because of the ability of claims-makers to employ the agenda setting and formative nature of the media in constructing an informational context compatible with their respective claims.

When deep-seated concerns about one's children are one of a handful of issues lobbied for via extensive news media reports, then the fear becomes more pronounced, and alarm can spread as fellow citizens symbolically demonstrate concern by putting posters in windows and featuring photos of absent children on milk cartons. The claims-makers, via mass media formats, may provide an artful interpretation and description of the nature and extent of a problem, particularly if there has been a local victim. When these views are reified through non–mass media contexts, such as grocery stores, then any counterclaims will be less effective if they pass only through the mass media because the essential message is reinforced and demonstrated wherever one turns. Moreover, there are good organizational reasons for TV news operations to not systematically consider the counterclaims, because this would amount to a negation of an earlier claim, or a qualification that the prior media blitz about the magnitude of the problem was not quite correct, not so cut-and-dried. To do so would require that the mass media reflexively assess their prior performance, and would imply that reports about other issues might also be less than accurate. Numerous studies of news production demonstrate that this is unlikely to occur (cf. Epstein 1973; Altheide 1976; Tuchman 1978).

We are beyond the time when ideas were developed, worked out in policy statements, then negotiated with key political players, and finally reworked so that the public could be informed through various communication media. It is increasingly the case today that social policies are brokered according to the range of conventional interest groups, but also in terms of the communication formats and their attendant temporal frameworks (cf. Dobash & Dobash 1992). Issues are selected, cast in certain ways, associated with certain groups, and marketed along nonsubstantive lines: the communication forms. Thus, we are in a period when a taken-for-granted test of competence of a social actor is the ability to know what problems, issues, and serious social policy considerations look like and sound like. Until the media gatekeepers permit new formats that will foster more expansive and inclusive issues for consideration and public debate, the social policies that are hardly important will continue to grow while the less dramatic, less visual, and nonlinear concerns will compete, at best, on entertainment grounds and immediately apparent relevance; thus, the here and now and future are products of the media formats that we have come to rely on for encapsulated imagery of significance. There is, however, some place for optimism as journalists and other chroniclers of the political process have shown more awareness of the media processes in political campaigns. For example, during the 1988 U.S. presidential campaign, journalists made a number of references to the way that speeches and events were oriented to obtain thirty-second sound bites. This is hardly enough, but it does suggest that reflexivity has been enhanced. Hopefully, audience members will also become more aware of the way in which formats are guiding substance.

More specifically, with the missing children problem, we conclude that the mass media do play a critical role in the emergence of social problems, albeit a more complicated one than previously set forth. The mass media formats not only convey messages, but also images, which can be recast in other situations (e.g., grocery stores), which are nevertheless mediated. More than information transmitters, media logic and formats promote and delineate the publication of "social practices ordered across space and time . . . continually recreated by them via the very means whereby they express themselves" (Giddens 1984:2). The evidence suggests that people's perceptions can reflect the media messages that they receive. These results offer a different view than media nonresponsibility, and imply that some disquieting images and concerns could be reduced if media formats would accommodate the complex nature of social problems. Greater accuracy and conscientious conceptualization of social problems and their reportage by mass media workers can apparently reduce fear and eliminate the inappropriate emergence of urban legends as social problems.

A related issue concerns the taken-for-granted knowledge and experience that audience members may apply to new claims by entrepreneurs. The gonzo approaches noted in Chapters 5 and 6 did not occur in a vacuum of experience, but were built on a plethora of claims and visually interesting reports night after night about problems and issues. Perhaps we need to begin considering the cumulative impact of one mass-mediated issue on others. For example, we can ask whether the missing children issue would have been so readily validated, both publicly and privately, if previous claims about crime in the streets had not been reified. It seems hardly coincidental that routine family problems that produce runaway children and custodial disputes resulting in parental kidnappings have not been the focus of the media blitz. Indeed, the missing children issue was popularly attributed to strangers and "trolls," not unlike the stereotypical caricaturization of criminals who rob and rape.

NOTES

1. The method for calculating this figure and its generalizability are problematic. In light of the juvenile population—47.9 million below the age of fourteen—the percentage of kids missing each year would be 3 percent. Stated differently, one out of every 33 youths would be missing each year. Nicolas von Hoffman calculates, based on the 1.5 million figure, that "[i]n a decade, that means that 15 million people have gone through the doughnut hole into anti-world" (1985:10).

Comparing the figure of 1.5 million missing children to other highly reported crime statistics further challenges its validity. In 1984, only slightly more than one million auto thefts were reported by the Uniform Crime Reports (U.S. Department of Justice 1985:33). Additionally, there were only 820 juvenile murder victims—age fourteen or younger, or about one out of every fifty-eight thousand kids. Of these, only 17.6 percent of the murders were committed by strangers. These comparisons suggest an enormous divergence between the upper and lower limits of the quoted figures regarding missing children and the more systematic reporting by the FBI regarding child murders and kidnappings, thus warranting closer analysis.

2.   Please note that this assertion is an implicit critique of Woolgar and Pawluch (1985), who reduce social constructionist accounts of social problems to "ontological gerrymandering" or "selected relativism," whereby the truth status of some portion of the argument is called into question, while other portions of the argument are not questioned. Key to our analysis, like numerous examples cited by Woolgar and Pawluch, is that assertions of relativity, stability and fluidity (i.e., sociohistorical change) can be sustained with evidence, and moreover that not all evidence is of a positivistic or objectivist character. A basic assumption of the social constructionist perspective is that all sense making is symbolically based. When researchers utilizing this perspective claim that things have not changed (or changed) from time 1 to time 2, but that the accounts have changed, the following is implied: the symbolic meanings used to make sense of things at time 1 would have revealed little change if also used at time 2; however, other criteria, definitions, etc., were implicated and/or invoked at time 2, thus registering a change. The critical issue for a researcher or anyone who makes a claim (e.g., John Walsh), is the source, character, and assessment of their evidence. As most people of common sense and science are aware, all findings and conclusions reflect their origins.

The Ecology of Communication and TV Coverage of Terrorism in the United States and Great Britain 8

February 26, 1993. The lives of New Yorkers and Americans would never be quite the same, because this was the day that a terrorist bomb blasted the World Trade Towers, financial and symbolic capital of American commerce and independence. While there had been other incidents before that involving dissidents, this attack, slow to penetrate some Americans' consciousness in its significance, marked the migration of terrorism from "them" and "over there" to "us" and "here."

IT and the mass media are central players in all terrorist activities. The ecology of communication has numerous consequences. Lest we be misunderstood by anyone, we want to stress a critical point in our perspective: The news media do not cause terrorism, nor is access to the news media the only motivation for terrorists. Terrorists existed before modern IT and TV news, but we suggest that their approach and operations differed in ways that were consistent with their effective environment. It is the way in which changing IT and formats have been joined with our effective environments that has altered the approach to terrorism. *The ecology of communication within which the news media operate is one of the most significant features of terrorists' effective environment.* The temporal/spatial dimensions of our effective environment, as we have stressed, have changed because of electronic media and information technology; we witness in our homes events that occur in other places; at news time, we experience in our homes activities that occur other times; and the length, duration, and rhythm of these activities—other important elements of temporality—are altered to fit the formats associated with IT and TV news. All of these are considerations for terrorists. This means that their plans, tactics, and activities are influenced by their knowledge and use of IT and news formats. As suggested by Figure 4.1 in Chapter 4, the activity of news work has implications for the activity of terrorism. This includes knowledge of the immediacy with which it is possible to get pictures of an event in one part of the world to viewers in another part of the world. We have stressed that news sources are particularly important as we rely on routine forms of knowing, such as newscasts, for guidelines and informal criteria about significant events. The mass media increasingly *are the public agenda*. When importance and crises begin to look like the kinds of stories presented on TV news, for most people it is but a small step toward the practical conclusion that whatever is not on TV news reports is not likely to be highly relevant for public life, and certainly not of major importance. Given the penchant of TV formats for exciting and dramatic visuals, it is not surprising that much of our local (e.g., crime), national (e.g., disasters), and international (e.g., armed conflicts) news media stress events involving drama, action, conflict, and often violence. Indeed, having an issue or concern that lacks these characteristics is practically a formula for being ignored.

Groups who engage in what are referred to as terrorist activities usually operate outside the legitimate news channels. Their terrorist activities are intended to communicate symbolic messages even as they inflict pain and suffering on innocent victims. While terrorists have not always been mainly oriented to sending a message and making the news, in modern times this is the case.

A number of examples of the relationship between IT, formats, and the temporal and spatial characteristics of terrorist activity are contained in Paletz and Schmid's (1992) edited volume on the use and perspectives of the terrorists, government, press, public, victims, and researchers. In ten chapters on various facets of mass-mediated terrorism and its effects, Paletz and Schmid integrate materials from a series of several conferences in Europe pertaining to terrorism. Their chapters frame significant research with ongoing issues. Materials drawn from researchers, journalists, victims, and selected terrorists themselves illustrate the multiple meanings associated with the media and how all of these major actors are joined through an ecology of communication. An interesting implication of recent innovative studies about the relevance of IT and formats of control for terrorism and society is that the state's efforts to stop terrorists invariably tend to produce the same blocked and highly surveillance oriented society for all citizens. In this sense success at producing a blocked society may be the terrorists' most important victory (Bonanate 1979). Control itself then takes on a harsher look in our computer/media age. As the previous chapters indicated, state authorities are quick to assume the mantle of righteousness and use the latest IT as well as TV news formats to achieve their always justified ends. It is for this reason that we include the role of IT and formats of control, which are so important in understanding the recent directions taken by terrorists, and public perceptions and misinformation about some of the most compelling issues. This includes the terrorists themselves, as well as the official government agencies, whose emphasis and reactions produce a blocked society, which becomes more controlled, regimented and repressed as agents of control seek to protect citizens from terrorists.

As suggested in Chapter 1, which charted the evolution from information-to marketing and surveillance via dominant formats of new ITs, one of the unanticipated consequences of strong government action toward terrorism is control itself. In our desire to understand and improve the prospects for peace and coexistence in a conflictual world, it is useful to assess the way the news media, and particularly TV news, operate to bring us messages about local, national, and international issues. In this chapter, we focus on an analysis of the nature and foundation of TV coverage of terrorism in the United States and Great Britain. Attention will be directed to the interaction between TV news formats and symbolic messages. In pursuit of this aim we suggest that (1) news formats significantly define and limit the range of symbolic expression and focus of attention, and (2) much of the news media coverage about terrorism promotes the symbolic legitimacy of established leaders.

MEDIATED VIOLENCE

The last two decades have seen a significant increase in public attention to acts of terrorism, or the use of force and violence against nonmilitary targets. While definitions of terrorism remain problematic, most include a reference to attacks on the public places often frequented by unarmed civilians. Paletz, Ayanian, and Fozzard define terrorism as "politically motivated violence that strikes at symbols and figures of authority in society, seeking to achieve the goals of the perpetrators through intimidation" (1982:145). Often the symbols include hijackings of aircraft, trains, and buses, and the taking of civilians as hostages. The "victims" of such attacks are usually intended to be a mere vehicle for making another point: for establishing a symbolic victory or for asserting an identity as a viable force (cf. Schmid & de Graaf 1982:176ff.). The mass media are often the implicit or explicit rationale for such acts; getting the message out is important for those individuals committed to a cause, particularly when TV coverage can transform a specific incident into a global drama. Given the widespread recognition that the mass media, and especially TV, prefer action-packed events ripe for good visual reportage, the media formats are explicitly played to by more and more groups who lack access and legitimacy to get their messages across through other channels. In this sense, terrorists are good communicators; they understand the media (Schmid & de Graaf 1982:170ff.). But getting access to media attention is not synonymous with getting good press. Indeed, recent work suggests that the disproportionate amount of mass media attention to terrorist tactics and their aftermath rather than precipitating social conditions, goals and objectives has provided *TV attention but not legitimacy* (Paletz et al. 1982:151ff.). The shape, organization, and impact of such messages remains unclear, particularly when government officials draw on a substantial symbolic arsenal to condemn such actions.

SYMBOLS AND MEDIA FORMATS

Acts of terrorism take place in a symbolic context through which leaders and constituents define, interpret, and "understand" the nature and consequences of political behavior. It is these symbols that make political actions meaningful. According to Edelman:

> Meaning is basically different from information and incompatible with it. Meaning is associated with order—with a patterned cognitive structure that permits anticipation of future developments so that perceptions are expected and not surprising. (1971:23)

But symbols are neither neutral nor up for grabs in the political realm. Because state leaders and others increasingly understand that political communication to constituents must be redundant, or reinforce basic premises, the rule of thumb for effective politics is to incorporate any challenge to state legitimacy within the prevailing symbolic system. As Edelman has stressed:

> The politically significant observation in every example is that the symbolic or ritualized conflict enables specific groups in conflict over instrumental rewards to use their respective bargaining resources free from interference by mass publics who may be affected. (1971:23)

Thus, leadership can assume greater stature, more legitimacy, and perhaps even more political currency as a result of having the symbolic coin challenged. It is the mission and the challenge that is highlighted and *not the adequacy* of the leadership.

Edelman notes:

> If a political leader symbolizes ability to cope, his followers perceive his specific acts, redundantly, as evidence of that ability and may be oblivious both of information calling that meaning into question and of the frequent impossibility of proving either his competence or his incompetence. Put another way, symbols make messages assimilable by reducing their originality, the degree to which they complicate cognitions, and the degree to which they lessen ability to predict. (1971:34)

This line of reasoning carries some implications for the nature of communication engaged in by terrorists, on the one hand, and by the political leaders who respond to them, on the other hand. The former's actions are intended for an *audience* that is politically responsible for the victims, or the target of the attack (e.g., a railroad or a building). However, the political leaders who may publicly—and officially—as well as unofficially respond to them, address *two audiences*: (1) the terrorists themselves, and (2) more fundamentally, their own constituents and rival political factions. Indeed, it is not uncommon for "purposes of negotiation" for state leaders to be more truthful and open in their responses to hostage situations with the terrorists than with their own constituents, including family members of hostages. For example, in responding to criticism from family members of hostages who were being held by "Arab terrorists," President Reagan replied several times in September 1985 that many things were being done that even the families could not be told. But what is most important for our purposes is that these messages are broadcast through the major news media.

Previous chapters have illustrated the relevance of IT and media formats in a given cultural context, and how activities change and incorporate the ecology of communication. We have stressed how the time, place, and manner of more and more activities, including getting the news and watching the news reflect this part of the effective environment. Accordingly, the nature and use of political language, e.g., a news conference, will be used insofar as format features are satisfied. For example, TV news "tells time" with visuals, particularly videotape. This means that all other things being equal, the report with the most relevant visuals available will get the most air time (cf. Altheide 1985). On U. S. TV networks, without such visuals there is little likelihood that an event will be selected for coverage, or that it will receive more than a few seconds.

A COMPARATIVE LOOK AT TERRORISM ON TELEVISION

More researchers are actually beginning to examine the coverage of terrorism, and are finding that it is fairly diverse and that the formats of TV reporting have something to do with it. This emphasis does not deny the role ideology may contribute to the definition, selection, and coverage of certain acts of terrorism (e.g., the IRA bombing of a building) nor that legitimate states may also be involved in acts of terrorism (e.g., the hand of the French government in sinking a Greenpeace vessel on July 10, 1985). Rather, the attention to format suggests that even explicit ideological statements must be organized and presented through media formats, and that such formats do contribute to the shape, texture, and emphasis of certain coverage, which cannot be easily accounted for by ideology. A variation of this point has been made by Schlesinger et al., who essentially argue that there is more diversity of coverage than would be expected under the *dominant-ideology thesis*, which holds that the production of media messages reflects and is consistent with superordinate values, interests, and objectives:

> These distinctions [in types of news format] were prompted by our discovery
> . . . that presentations of terrorism on British television were a good deal more
> diverse and complex than simpler assumptions about television's relation to
> the state and to dominant ideology predict. (1983:32)

But does format (as part of the IT and ecology of communication) operate similarly across cultures, with varying communication contexts, organization, and orientation? Ideally, this question should be examined by looking at how the same event was handled by media with different formats within and between societies.

RESEARCH DESIGN AND DATA

This question was addressed in an exploratory comparative study of the coverage by U.S. and U.K. media of the same incidents—two IRA bombings in London—in order to illustrate the relevance of different formats for presenting information about this act. Data for BBC and ITV coverage of the incidents were extrapolated from the materials in Schlesinger et al. (1983), while the data for the U.S. TV networks—ABC, CBS, NBC—were obtained from the Vanderbilt University Television News Index, CBS Index, and CBS transcripts.

Data were collected and coded on the following dimensions: news format, quotations, length (time, when available), visuals (when available), topics of focus, action, and other sources of information cited. Lengthy excerpts from several of these newscasts are included in order to enable the reader to follow the complex interaction between ideology, symbols, and news format. What unfolds is illuminating about the nature and consequences of terrorism in contemporary life, as well as its theoretical relevance for mediation in our contemporary effective environment. By examining the formats within similar ITs and coverage by U.S. and British TV of a specific terrorist act, the role of the ecology of communication in shaping the symbolic messages can be illuminated further. Specifically, four aspects of terrorists' behavior reported in newscasts—*precipitating social conditions, goals, objectives, and tactics*—were examined to see if they were equally suited to prevailing news formats (Paletz et al. 1982:151ff.), and whether an additional emphasis must be considered: the way leaders are able to tap such incidents for further legitimacy.

For purposes of this comparative study on TV news coverage of terrorism, it was useful to draw on analytical distinctions for each of the three elements noted below. These analytical tools will then help develop two ideal types of news formats—*event* and *topic*. The former is usually found in regular evening newscasts, while the latter is more typical of documentaries, although numerous exceptions do occur. [The overlap in these formats is apparent, and the British researchers (Schlesinger et al. 1983:36ff.) distinguish between a news bulletin, news magazine, current affairs, and documentary.]

The analytical concepts borrowed from previous work are as follow (cf. Schlesinger et al. 1983; Altheide 1985):

1. *Open-closed* refers to the source of information and range of perspectives permitted into the report. Event reports tend to be closed, mainly using official views, while the topic type provides "spaces in which the core assumptions of the official perspective can be interrogated and contexted and in which other perspectives can be presented and examined" (Schlesinger et al. 1983:32).

2. *Tight-loose* refers to the internal organization of the report itself. If only one definition or slant on a happening is permitted, then the report is tight; if several angles are set forth and/or permitted to emerge in the course of the report, then the report is loose. Event reports tend to be tight, while topic reports tend to be a bit more loose. The former, more typical of regular news reports, tend to be organized around one central theme or angle, with little ambiguity; loose structuring, more common with certain documentaries, invites comparisons, different points of view, and does not avoid ambiguities or uncertainties.

3. *Scanning time–object time*, an additional element, must be considered in our attempt to clarify format features of TV news coverage about terrorism. In addition to noting the apparent overlap in tight-loose and open-closed formats, it is also important to add that these formats differ in mode of representation. Schlesinger et al.'s (1983:36ff.) distinction between "production techniques" for a news bulletin—"visual clips, brief interviews"—and a documentary—"film report"—is not as precise as we would prefer. Elements of both may be found in a report in a regular evening newscast, as well as in a documentary. What is critical is the role of the imagery in the thematic emphasis of the report. And imagery on television is based on the premise that real life events and objects that exist in at least three dimensions— *object time*—can be communicated in only two dimensions—*scanning time* (Altheide 1985:48). The former is more explicit, while the latter is more implicit, relying on the audience's ability to contextualize and fill in what is presented as information in order to make sense of the report, and thereby see the connection between an interpretation and visual evidence.

Scanning time is associated with the event type. On the one hand, it is time transformed through format into space as a visual representation on a TV screen. On the other hand, it is an artistic and technologically mediated interpretation of object time, or the context, circumstances, and actual physical layout of the actors, action, and objects contained within it. Not only is scanning time consistent with conventional news briefs, but object time is more compatible with the topic type, generally found in documentaries, extended interviews, and, in brief, any effort to try to put a specific event (or visual coverage of it) into some kind of broader context or framework beyond the temporal confines of a handful of information bits lasting ten to twenty seconds.

An ideal type of news format can be constructed by combining the previous distinctions between open-closed and tight-loose formats with scanning time—object time. It may be schematized as follows:

Ideal Type News Formats

Event		Topic
Closed	Official perspective	Open
Tight	Thematic emphasis	Loose
Scanning	Temporal order	Object
Regular newscast	Program type	Documentary

This scheme will be applied to variations in coverage about terrorism.

THE INCIDENT

On July 20, 1982, two bombs exploded in London in Hyde Park and Regents Park, ultimately killing ten people, injuring some fifty more, as well as killing ten horses. The IRA claimed responsibility. This incident dominated British TV newscasts and newspaper coverage for several days, and also received considerable play in U.S. media.

THE BRITISH COVERAGE OF THE INCIDENT

Schlesinger et al. (1983) provide some excerpts from various event and topic reports to illustrate the various combinations of formats noted above. For example, they found that when the bombings of Irish terrorists resulted in death or injury to British military or civilians—especially in London—TV reports tended to be somewhat negative toward the Irish, the political motives of the terrorists were not extensively discussed, and British government officials were often consulted for comments. However, in programs with an interview format—closer to the topic type—conflicting and opposing views were discussed, often by an interviewee who was politically representative of and/or sympathetic to the terrorists. Both of these are intelligible within the format considerations entailed in the ecology of communication.

First, in regular newscasts, the negative comments tended to focus on the destructiveness and suffering of the terrorists acts. After noting that producers for these shows draw an agenda from a wider range of social, political, and economic questions (compared to the earlier news report), the researchers add:

> They rely less on studio presentations of those speaking for various legitimate views and opinions [and] more on sequential reports of the material that the producer has managed to put together on a subject. (Schlesinger et al. 1983:41)

However, this is done with visuals, as illustrated by the report about an IRA blast in 1982 that killed nine people:

> The news bulletin established the two locations with aerial shots and a map of Central London. The newsreader warned the audience that there were going to be "horrible pictures." There were scenes of devastation at the bandstand and in Park Lane, of covered-up bodies and of dead horses, of the emergency services at work. The bulletin, therefore, established the dreadful effects of the bombing, the loss of both human and animal life, the disruption of everyday life and the destruction of property. (p. 43)

The BBC's evening news on July, 1982 began:

> IRA bombers return to London. Their target—British soldiers—but civilians die too. At the bandstand in Regent's Park six people are killed at an army concert and three more die in Knightsbridge as the household cavalry ride past to change the guard. Injuries are terrible. Nearly fifty people are taken to hospital. (cited in Schlesinger et al. 1983:42)

The emphasis in most of these reports was on *tactics*, but a commentary did touch on *goals*:

> When it comes to shaking the British public, the IRA work on the principle that ˙ one bomb in London or another major English city is worth several in Belfast or Londonderry. *Publicity is their aim rather than outright military success with any one bomb* and for that reason even soldiers engaged on ceremonial duties are satisfactory targets, though civilian bystanders are also likely to die. (cited in Schlesinger et al. 1983:43; emphasis added)

The broadcast also carried condemnations from Margaret Thatcher: "These callous and cowardly crimes have been committed by evil and brutal men who know nothing of democracy" (cited in Schlesinger et al. 1983:43–44). In brief, these reports were quite compatible with the ideal type of the event report generally found in regular newscasts.

The incident was also dealt with in another TV production, "Nationwide." Produced daily, this show has a news magazine format, a bit closer to the topic type. Following a review of the death toll and previous campaigns by the IRA, the studio presenter (Frank Bough) added: "Eight dead; many more injured. We're asking, Is this the start of a new terror campaign and what can be done to keep the bombers out of Britain?" Next came a report about security forces working against the IRA, followed by some background information about upcoming assembly elections in Northern Ireland. Out of this context followed an interview with David McKittrick, London Bureau chief of the *Irish Times.* Even though the thrust of the interview was consistent with "the official premise of irrationality and inhumanity," an alternative position was set forth during the interview. For example, following interviewer Bough's point that such bombings are "totally counterproductive," McKittrick replied:

Well you have to remember that the Provisionals look at things in a very different way from the way you and I would. One big factor for them is that when they set off a bomb like this in London whatever the damage it might do, as we would see it, to their cause, the fact is that it is tremendous for the morale of their volunteers, the low down guys back home. They see it as a blow struck at the soft underbelly of the enemy. The other general factor is that I gather at the moment that there was some criticism in the ranks for the fact that the IRA didn't do very much during the Falklands campaign when it might have been thought that they had an opportunity to strike at the heart of Britain. (cited in Schlesinger et al. 1983:44–45)

Despite the strong continuities that exist between the questions asked and the content of the event reports on the regular newscast, there are some subtle differences that are consonant with a movement away from a tight, closed, and scanning time format. As stated by Schlesinger et al.:

The *Nationwide* example illustrates our thesis that as one shifts from hard news to current affairs the scope for articulating alternative views increases, and that this is, in part, a function of the form of the programme. (p. 46)

The news coverage of the incident continued for several days, including a report about Sefton, a horse injured in the blast. Using the horse as a symbol of the British will to survive, one commentary included the following:

Nineteen year old Sefton, his jugular vein severed in the blast, became a symbol of the nation's outrage and compassion. The cavalry vets managed to staunch his wounds and save his life, and by the end of August he was running free again in the grounds of the Royal Army Veterinary Corps hospital at Melton Mowbray. Gifts, sweets and telegrams and cards poured into the cavalry from all over Europe and the progress of Sefton's recovery became the subject of almost nightly bulletins on the TV and radio. (cited in Schlesinger et al. 1983:48–49)

Clearly these reports share information, but in different ways, with varying emphases. The report about Sefton represents the most redundant, resonant, symbolic message; it is perhaps more affective than cognitive. The initial reports about the incident itself were tied to visuals; in a sense, the audience was given a report about the visuals, albeit surrounded in the symbolism of tactics, and characteristics of the actors (e.g., "bombers," "callous men"). And the only data suggesting a context for the incident were found with "Nationwide," which did provide some context and ambiguity beyond mere tactics, directed toward an understanding of other goals. Similar points were apparent in the American coverage.

THE AMERICAN NETWORKS' COVERAGE OF THE INCIDENT

The three U.S. networks provided fairly extensive coverage of the bombings. All had videotape, narrated by a reporter on the scene. For example, ABC devoted nearly six minutes; CBS allotted four minutes and twenty seconds; and NBC provided the least coverage with three minutes and thirty seconds, although it also included a commentary (one minute and twenty seconds) by Roger Mudd, who reminded the audience that the contemporary leaders, Sean McBride and Menachem Begin were also regarded at one time as terrorists. This more analytical assessment appears to be related to a more general finding that foreign journalists seem to be more detached and more likely to accord a modicum of recognition, if not legitimacy, to the perpetrators (cf. Schlesinger et al. 1983). This comment was far less passionate than Margaret Thatcher's statement prior to this incident:

The world is daily assaulted by those who seek to impose their views upon us through violence and fear. Terrorism is an attack upon the whole community. . . . If [the terrorist] can destroy our trust in a well-ordered society, if he can spread consternation and provoke retaliation—then he is on the way to achieving his ends. (Schlesinger et al. 1983:11)

The tone of this statement is more in keeping with a comment by CBS News's Bill Moyers on February 1, 1982, about the rescue of General Dozier from his Italian abductors:

This time the battle had gone not to terrorists but to society. . . . We need such victories, for terrorists aim to wear down the morale of democratic societies. Murder by murder, they would win with slow, numbing fear what they cannot win with votes or logic. It's hard enough making this great, unwieldy Western experiment in self-government work. It won't work unless people can believe their governments are able to protect them from marauders.

Transcripts of CBS's coverage of the bombing illustrate the way different news formats may address precipitating social conditions, goals, objectives, and tactics. Even though there were no documentaries per se offered on the broader issue as a result of these bombings, there were instances compatible with the topic type.

Information was presented in a variety of ways. The evening newscast can be contrasted with the more open format of the morning news shows, which provided opportunities for interviews.

On July 20, 1982, the "CBS Evening News with Dan Rather" opened with a report about the bombings. The transcript of the four minute and twenty second report is presented below:

RATHER: Good evening. This is the CBS EVENING NEWS, Dan Rather reporting. The unofficial truce between Britain and the IRA ended brutally on this bright, clear summer day in London. Bombs went off in two of London's most famous parks. When the carnage was complete, eight British soldiers were dead, more than 50 soldiers, spectators, and tourists wounded. Martha Teichner reports.
MARTHA TEICHNER: The first bomb, planted in a car, was detonated by remote control just as the Queen's horse guards passed through Hyde Park on their way to Buckingham Palace for the changing of the guard. Two guardsmen died; at least 24 people were injured by the blast and by flying nails taped to the explosive.
MAN 1:   The guards were just standing there bewildered just shouting, "Bastards! They're bastards." Just looking at the—this carnage of horses and mess and excreta that was everywhere.
TEICHNER: Seven horses were killed, or were so badly mutilated, they had to be shot. Debris was blown through the park into the streets of London's fashionable and crowded Knightsbridge. The sidewalk was covered with broken glass. Less than two hours later, the second bomb went off in Regents Park to the north, hitting another military target. The bandstand where the army's Royal Greenjackets had been playing was blown to bits. Musical instruments were strewn hundreds of feet away. Six of the musicians died, at least 29 people were injured, most of them seriously.
MAN 2:   Well, bodies and torsos everywhere.
QUESTION: How many of them your friends?
MAN 2:   They're all my friends. I've been working with 'em for ten years.
TEICHNER: The injured from both bombings were taken to several hospitals where striking health workers dropped their pickets and went back to work.

Surviving Greenjackets, who are often assigned to Northern Ireland, left one hospital, faces covered to avoid recognition by terrorists. CBS News Engineer Dave De Hann had just parked his car about 100 yards from where the first bomb went off.

DAVE DE HANN: As I was locking the car door, the guards all passed me. And I went round to my boot to put a few things into the briefcase from my boot. When the explosion went, I quickly shut the boot up, looked down the road, and there was three guardsmen on three horses running towards me in a panic fashion.

TEICHNER: This is De Hann's car. For hours, it kept all of Knightsbridge in suspense as police tried to determine if it contained yet another bomb. Hundreds of office workers were evacuated from buildings across the street as a robot was sent to look for the device. First, it switched on the tail lights, then, it fired shots into the front and the back. (shots) When De Hann returned to claim the remains, the police said, "Sorry, but we had to blow it up."

DE HANN: Well, I've been told this is a total write-off.

TEICHNER: Scotland Yard said the bomb attacks were the work of the IRA and that members of Parliament had been warned of such a possibility.

GILBERT KELLAND (Assistant Commissioner): Because it's just prior to the recess that's coming up and it was thought proper to warn people in public life—a general reminder to be on the alert.

TEICHNER: The bombings occurred when Britain could not have been more vulnerable, members of Parliament already outraged at serious lapses of security. Those lapses include what may be a major spy scandal involving Britain's Intelligence Communications Headquarters at Cheltenham. One man has already been charged with passing secrets to another country. But in her statement to the House of Commons this afternoon, Prime Minister Margaret Thatcher refused to say whether others might be involved. All this, of course, comes on the heels of two other security scandals; one in which a 31-year-old man made a mockery of Palace security by dropping in for an early morning chat with the Queen in her bedroom. How he did it is still being investigated. And then there's the Queen's personal bodyguard who suddenly resigned after admitting a long term affair with a male prostitute. Why the bodyguard's affair did not surface during supposedly stringent security checks is also being investigated. But all seemed secure at the Palace late today as the Queen and Prince Phillip received thousands of guests for another in a series of garden parties. But unusually thorough searches of handbags and briefcases were another reminder of today's turmoil, all of which has most of London wondering what next.

CBS's coverage was quite consistent with the event type commonly found in regular newscasts, except that more time than usual was devoted to this incident. The emphasis in this report on the visual scenes led to a focus on the IRA's tactics, and the aftermath. The explicit visuals, the comments from bystanders, and the fact that horses were killed provided a scenario that could be unambiguously reported to the audience. Moreover, Teichner's final statement about Britain's vulnerability in the face of other scandals and security problems cast the event as a crisis issue, with "most of London wondering what next."

The focus shifted a bit on the "CBS Morning News" of July 21, 1982. Following Connie Chung's opening statement, "Yesterday was a day of carnage in London; the deadly bombings that shattered the ceremonial routine connected with the British royal family," Martha Teichner reported, "Prince Phillip was at the barracks to review the injured Horse Guards," and then updated the casualty count, noting that civilians were hit "indiscriminately as well." She concluded with a voice-over videotape of horsemen:

> Britain is determined not to allow IRA terrorism to destroy the pageantry, the tradition that exposes its soldiers to risk. Today, the Horse Guards left the barracks and rode to Buckingham Palace for the Changing of the Guard along almost the same route where the bombers were waiting yesterday, as if nothing had happened.

Connie Chung then continued the overview of the day's top stories by reporting that an Armenian liberation group claimed responsibility for "a rash of bombings [that] also hit Paris, including one last night that injured at least fifteen people at a popular Left Bank cafe just across the Seine from Notre Dame Cathedral."

Several minutes later in the morning newscast, Bill Kurtis in Dublin interviewed John Hume, leader of the Social Democratic and Labour Party in Northern Ireland. Kurtis introduced Hume with, "Like most of the Catholic minority there, he favors reunification with the Irish Republic, but he utterly rejects the violence of the Irish Republican Army, like those bloody bombings yesterday in London." Notwithstanding this qualifier to paint Hume as one opposed to violence and the IRA, the resulting discussion did focus more on the *goals* of the IRA, as well as some of the *background* of the issue.

After noting that "it's very difficult to give a rational explanation for what they're doing," Hume added:

> So it's very difficult to give a rational explanation for what they're doing. Clearly they see it as a means of letting the world know that they're in existence and letting the world know that their approach to a solution to the Irish problem is continuing.

Hume again stated how the Irish people felt revulsion and shame for this act, but when asked by Kurtis to further explain a new proposal for a system of government in Ireland, added:

> Well, the British government . . . has brought forward proposals for a new system of government for Northern Ireland. It's a rather complicated set of

proposals, and its a set of proposals which has been opposed by all of the political parties in Northern Ireland, and by all editorial opinion within Northern Ireland, including ourselves, that we don't think it will work and we think it's a mistaken adventure by the British Secretary of State Mr. Prior. Of course, it is also opposed by the extremist people. It would be opposed as well by the provisional IRA. . . . What they in fact do [by acts of violence] is intensify the divisions, and what yesterday's atrocities does is intensify this—or—strengthen those in British politics who have no sympathy for Ireland or for an Irish solution to the problem.

Hume rejected Kurtis's claim that the first group to accept the proposal will be put in the British camp and suffer from it.

HUME: Well, no, I don't think so. I think that . . . in Northern Ireland, sadly to say, we're used to this sort of atrocity; we've had 2,200 people killed in the past twelve years. And atrocities happen here weekly. They don't get published any more. And I might add, by the way, that one of the reasons why these atrocities are committed by paramilitary extremists is that the . . . media give them attention when these atrocities take place. The daily hard-working slog of trying to peacefully resolve the Irish problem by political means doesn't get the same amount of attention.
KURTIS: Well, it's rather hard to ignore the kind of—the size of bombings in London—
HUME: Oh, exactly, yes. Yes.
KURTIS: And certainly the media has to look at that. But what is your solution? What would work to solve the Irish problem, if anything?
HUME: Well, first of all I think you have to recognize the problem first, and the problem is really not simply a matter of relations between Catholic and Protestant within Northern Ireland. It's a matter as well of relations between both parts of Ireland; it's also a matter of relations between Britain and Ireland. And therefore a solution must be found in the context of Anglo-Irish relations, and in a cooperative effort by both British and Irish governments working together to build a new unity within Ireland and a new agreement between Britain and Ireland. It's this sort of agreement within Ireland that gives a positive protection to the different sections of the Irish people, and a positive role to each section in molding our future.

Finally, in response to Kurtis's query whether the provisional IRA and IRA are different, Hume adds,

No, they're the same people, really, at the moment. The provisional IRA are the only IRA that are active at the minute in a campaign of violence. There are, of course, on the other side, on the Protestant Loyalist side, there are paramilitary organizations as well, who engage in campaigns of sectarian murder.

A critical point about these comments for our interest in format is the way the situation has been broadened to include more ambiguity. Despite the clear intent of Hume to condemn the bombings as terrorist acts, his attempt to put the incident in a social and historical context of frustration, mistrust, and hate flows from the relatively open, loose, and object temporal format. Granted the issue is not totally surrounded the way it may be in a lengthy documentary; nevertheless, emphasis moves beyond tactics and aftermath to include goals and background factors that figure in any context.

Indeed, the power of the entertainment format that has been applied in somewhat different ways in the United States and the United Kingdom is further suggested when it is recalled that such issues emerged from a discussion with a man who is obviously an adversary of the IRA! But the relative openness and an effort to attempt to explain a complex issue—and why virtually no political faction supported the British plan at that time—served to add at least part of another dimension. Note, too, that the topic was an issue rather than visuals of an incident, or rather, the aftermath of an incident—a bomb blast.

The previous discussion takes on more significance when compared to a report configured by an event-type report found in conventional news coverage. On the "CBS Evening News" of the same day, July 21, 1982, the report again conformed to our ideal type. Dan Rather noted that a hunt was in progress for the IRA terrorists. Quoting Margaret Thatcher—"Our anger at those who did this is total"—Rather added that the survivors "were trying desperately to convey the image that nothing had changed, when it had." A cut was then made to Martha Teichner, who, essentially, repeated an embellished version of her initial "CBS Morning News" report that preceded Bill Kurtis's interview with John Hume. Teichner's voice-over videotape of cavalrymen riding stated again that Prince Philip had visited the barracks of the injured cavalrymen, and that the cavalry had again ridden toward Buckingham Palace. The aftermath of the tactic was reintroduced by noting, "Now the total is nine dead in both bombings, more than fifty injured." Then a cavalryman spoke:

> You'd have to be there to see it. Carnage: a horse trying to get up and not understanding why he can't stand on three legs; and an officer that had been married three weeks and was lying there dead; a trooper in my troop who'd been married four weeks and was lying there dead.

After noting that Margaret Thatcher had visited the army musicians who were injured (a voice-over of videotape with applauding cavalrymen), Teichner closed with:

> Crowds applauded the cavalry as they arrived at Buckingham Palace for the changing of the guard. Their commanding officer said today, "It will take more than a cowardly attack like yesterday to stop us doing our duty."

As noted above, this report is quite redundant; the visuals and the narrative focus on the tactics and aftermath, and in the process tell the story about courageous—and moral—victims and cowardly attackers. The focus on the incident is both directed by the visuals and also directs further attention to the human costs. This coverage is not caused by the visuals, but they do provide the occasion to transform a single incident into a meaningful report, albeit a very incomplete one. Indeed, CBS's final report about this incident described the cavalrymen riding to their post at Buckingham Palace, and Teichner concluded:

> The widow of one of the dead cavalrymen came to watch, clutching her younger sister, and crying as the Guards came closer to the place where the bomb went off. As they passed, she was heard to choke out the words, "Well done, boys" ("CBS Morning News," 22 July 1983)

CONCLUSIONS

The effective environment informs all relevant social activities, including covering the news and engaging in newsworthy activities. Common to both activities is an awareness of communication-related dimensions. Cultures produce different news because they operate with different effective environments. This chapter has addressed what might happen if effective environments become more similar, specifically in regard to IT and formats. TV coverage of terrorists illustrates this relationship and how the ecology of communication links IT formats and logic with events. How an event is framed and discussed on television, for example, depends on the format of the program; views and images of the world come to us through IT and the formats selected for organizational and presentational purposes. Obviously, other contexts contribute as well, including the commercial interest of television, and an interest in "grabbing" and "holding" the largest possible audience. This chapter is important for the argument of this book because the materials presented indicate that common IT and formats contribute to the production of similar kinds of messages despite cultural differences. The mass media provide publics with important information about events and their meaning for our lives. Ironically, perhaps, we need to be aware of the role such media play in editing and distorting the information we receive when visual imagery on TV can give an impression that what is being seen is what is most significant, particularly when these reports involve terrorism. This chapter has argued that we can enhance our understanding about such reports by examining how the communication process itself is organized around formats—the rules for selecting, organizing, and presenting information.

Two ideal typical formats emerged by combining prior work (Schlesinger et al. 1983; Altheide 1985): The event type of report characteristic of regular newscasts consisted of a format made up of closed official perspective, tight thematic emphasis, and a scanning temporal order that utilizes two dimensions of an event through visual depictions. Its analytical opposite, the topic type, often associated with documentaries, consisted of an open official perspective, loose thematic emphasis, and object temporal order through which context and an incident are reflexively examined.

Comparing selected coverage of the same incident in the United Kingdom and the United States indicated that the focus of reports on IRA bombings varied consistently with the type of format. While all variations were not available with this particular incident, it was apparent that, with few exceptions, on the one hand, *event-type reports* blended to focus on terrorism as *tactics* and aftermath, and to a lesser extent on *objectives*. On the other hand, *object-type* reports more compatible with the documentaries tended to emphasize *goals, objectives*, and to some extent, *precipitating social conditions*. In this sense, we tentatively conclude that *reports cast in the event mold are more ideologically constrained than are reports compatible with the topic form* (cf. Schlesinger et al. 1983). Moreover, we have found that these different types of report may occur throughout the various news programs, e.g., reports closer to a topic format may occur within the evening newscast and conversely.

The symbolic capture of the issue by government leaders was also apparent in several instances. One-line statements by leaders are more readily carried in the event type, particularly when the tactics and not the context are featured. In addition to the one-liners, implicit statements are also made via enemy themes and metaphors that make it hard to take the enemy as a significant other (cf. Edelman 1971:115). This seems to come with the visual territory of the event type as it is presently cast in TV news.

The world and events may differ "really," but the effective environments that provide the IT, formats, and "ways of seeing and knowing" significantly structure and contribute to what we see and know. While more work is needed to compare messages across formats, these findings support additional efforts to delineate the interaction of ideology and symbols via organizational formats. Until we begin to view temporal and spatial organizing principles in social life as important elements of social order, our various studies—including those involving mass media—will focus mainly on content and decision-making processes involving editing, which may be accounted for by politics, economics, ideology, and even bureaucracy. Generic to all of these, ecology of communication and formats of control offer yet another conceptual tool for discovering and understanding the way in which media of communication also contribute to the nature and process of much more than the explicit communication message or product; format guides and shapes experience, expectations, appearances, and interaction with other media. When the popular culture industry transforms a news event into a plaything or toy by dramatizing and entertainmentizing complex events as made-for-TV movies, the terrorist identity and persona live on, are known and feared like Godzilla, King Kong, or Frankenstein. The reality changes, and the next time we see a news report about a terrorist incident, the audience has images and even faces to place on characters and fill in the events. This is the process of the social construction of reality through IT, and formats of control. As the next chapter suggests, the interaction effects of various media can have deadly consequences.

Postjournalism: The Gulf War in Perspective

9

Access was not really the issue . . . greater openness would not necessarily have produced better coverage.

—Michael Massing

INTRODUCTION

The ecology of communication is nowhere more significant than in the role it plays in defining situations and in constituting the actual conduct and interpretations of events. The ultimate event in my lifetime where technologies of information, communication formats, and the conduct of a series of actions have interacted with tremendous consequences is the Persian Gulf War in 1991. A major focus of this chapter is how social reality on several levels was informed by the interaction between ways of knowing, ways of acting, and evaluating.

A French television journalist described his experience in covering the 1991 Persian Gulf War:

> I started to work on the 2nd of August. We wanted to go to Kuwait. . . . Of course, nobody went to Kuwait. I reached Dubai on the third of August. . . . I stopped my coverage just before the ground attack, around the 15 of February. I spent around three months in the area. The most important thing I remember . . . is that in Saudi Arabia, we saw absolutely nothing . . . that was one of the reasons I came back, I got fed up. (author's field notes)

This sentiment was frequently expressed by journalists we talked with in the United States, United Kingdom, France, and Italy. Ironically, even though journalists were generally unable to do their work, the Gulf War nevertheless received the most intensive news coverage of any single event in U.S. history! An explanation of how this occurred will include an overview of how *media logic* has altered the relationship between news organizations and sources; how military officials learned to better orchestrate information from coverage of prior wars; and how a new kind of *war programming* has emerged.

179

This chapter takes a somewhat different approach to the issues of access and control in the news media. It is important to stress how access to the media takes on a different meaning today. Access, while still relevant, is not the problem it once was, especially as channels and outlets have expanded. We are in a situation beyond access; the bigger problem is not access but rather, what is necessary to gain it, and what happens to your material? Our answers include the potentially disquieting contention that the Gulf War was perfect television, and that treating the government sources in the usual postmortem of such events as cunning propagandists and manipulators may obscure some other developments in journalism.

Historically, access has been part of the ecology of communications and control. Previous chapters presented numerous examples how IT interacts with communication formats to alter many institutional practices and expectations, on the one hand, while adding entirely new ones on the other hand. Several of the previous chapters illustrate how this ecology limits and defines certain activity in various ways, including restricting access to information sources and channels. One way views and interests could be controlled in a media-technological age was to control access to media channels. This was basic throughout history, including controlling and regulating who had knowledge-access via technologies and skills for using various media, including language, speech, and writing. These were all features of control and order, and their codes and logics defined the hierarchy of order and legitimacy in a society. Social power, communication, discourse, and control have historically been joined. Yet, throughout history, the relevance of various forms of control has changed. As availability and access to various dimensions of life increases, then its relevance diminishes (Couch 1984). The intellectual challenge is to recognize new moments in the *reflexive process* of the ecology of communication in order to develop more comprehensive paradigms and perspectives for adequately interpreting events. This means being sensitized to finding even other barriers and limitations, impediments that interfere with the capacity to contribute to meaning and dialogue. This is essential for defining the situation, for sharing in the definition of situations, and for exploring the consequences. It is the nature of access, then, that must be articulated within an understanding about the ecology of communication.

AN APPROACH

In keeping with our approach throughout this work, a guiding premise is that how an event is communicatively organized is very important for what is communicated. First, we will give an overview of the logic of TV news and suggest how this played a key role in setting the stage for the production of the Gulf War as a program. Second, an overview of the nature (rather than only the content) of news coverage of two events, the U.S. invasions of Grenada and Panama, will be presented in order to establish a kind of baseline for comparing the production of the Gulf War. Previous work on other Middle East conflicts, e.g., the Iranian hostage crisis, and several related analyses of news coverage of terrorism also inform our approach (cf. Altheide 1985). As we discuss in more detail below, the news coverage of the Gulf War has been exhaustively investigated, and we will not duplicate that effort here, but instead will present materials from the Gulf War coverage to illustrate the *production logic*, including what was special about this war as a kind of television program (cf. Morrison 1992; Taylor 1992). We will also address this analysis to clarify this new genre of coverage that has been nurtured by information technology, global communications, and an increasingly convergent set of perspectives among world leaders and news organizations about the nature, relevance, and role of the mass media in our time.

In order to further draw out some of the theoretical implications of previous work, we will not repeat what was obvious from this coverage, and what numerous other critics noted, namely that "all the truth was not reported," and that this was due to various pressures and influences on the news media, e.g., corporate control, overly compliant news sources and officials, and journalistic dislocation. Rather, our approach is to reverse angle, so to speak, and focus on the news media perspectives and orientation because our studies of the mass media's impact on culture suggest that media logic and communication formats dominate the ordering of events. Our approach is to view the Gulf War in terms of news media work, perspectives, logic, and formats.

MEDIA LOGIC AND POSTJOURNALISM

What most Americans, and most of the world, know about the Gulf War and the combatants is related to the dominant information sources they use. (Of course, perception is active and people interactively interpret information. Moreover, people have many beliefs and assumptions about how the world works that are not derived directly from any mass media source.) This suggests that the sources and the media that carry them are major players in any information game. We now know unequivocally that these media are not passive, neutral, and inconsequential for shaping the messages. While this understanding does not negate the importance of some event—in all its ambiguity and uncertainty—for news content, it does strongly suggest that news messages are not merely reflections of some event, but rather that some complex relationships are at work.

In general, as we have argued, *media logic consists of a form of communication, the process through which media present and transmit information.* These elements work together within the confines of what we have termed media logic, or the general guiding assumptions and principles that govern the interaction between audience members, a medium (technology), and a subject or topic. Since media answer or solve this relationship in various ways, each medium has its own format. Indeed, research indicates that within a particular medium (e.g., television), there are also distinctive genres that can be identified by format differences. Elements of this form include the various media and the formats used by these media. Format consists of how material is organized, the style in which it is presented, the focus or emphasis on a particular characteristic of behavior, and the grammar of media communication. Format becomes a framework or a perspective that is used to present as well as interpret phenomena. A key element of this perspective is *format control*, or how the content is defined, selected, organized and presented. Material is continually selected in the modern (and postmodern) age on the basis of what can be done with it, whether it has the necessary requirements for the medium, and its purpose (e.g., commercialism, entertainment). These are key questions, and are central to issues about access now, but especially in the future as more countries communicatively converge around similar formats and modes of information processing.

This relevance of format in modern newswork for all news is considerable, as well as the perspective and activities of news sources that have learned the news formats as a key to news access. It is the rise of format-driven planning and orchestration that has helped produce our postjournalism era. As we stated elsewhere:

> In a media world, organized journalism is dead; we are postjournalists for two general reasons. First, journalistic practices, techniques and approaches are now geared to media formats rather than merely directing their craft at topics; second, the topics, organizations, and issues that journalists report about are themselves products of media—journalistic formats and criteria. In a sense, it is as though journalists, and especially TV journalists, are reporting on another entity down the hall from the newsroom. Public life subscribes to the media logics and formats that have been spawned in our age of electronic information; the politicians and others who are covered use the same criteria the journalists do, and often more skillfully! (Altheide & Snow 1991:x–xxi)

A key element that has helped create the postjournalism era is also central to any discussion about access to media outlets. We refer to sources and the way in which their position has changed with respect to news organizations.

Numerous studies on the perspective, tasks, and interaction of sources and news agents have shown that sources have learned the discourse, formats, and logic of newswork, and have incorporated them into their own planning and construction of events (cf. Ericson, et al, 1989; Schlesinger et al. 1983; Paletz & Schmid 1992).

The formats for the selection, organization, and presentation of mass-mediated information are ever expanding and becoming more sophisticated. *A key feature of this format for TV news reports is the nature and extent of visual information that is required, and increasingly provided by prospective news sources.* Television "tells time," or allocates time according to the news item's capacity to generate and be presented with visuals, particularly entertaining videotape representing action, drama, emotion, and conflict. Our work, along with others, has shown the power of this perspective in accounting for the expanded use of TV and other news channels by law enforcement, by criminal courts, in undercover police procedures, in the process for defining a range of social problems including missing children, domestic violence, child abuse and molestation, drug wars, and gonzo justice. It is no longer the case that the state is the sole agent as a source for managing information and seeking to influence information; rather, the format knowledge, skills, discourse, and techniques for getting our story out is widespread and embracing. Social issues, events, and their subtexts of morality, punishment, and control can no longer be separated from the frameworks employed by journalists and others who work on them. More than ideology, postjournalism cuts to the core of the very appearance of information and knowledge. It is for these reasons that our work for more than a decade has focused on how communication is organized, and especially, what information must look like in order to be sanctioned as newsworthy. This approach, while still mindful of the content of information, shifts considerably toward the more generic form and shape of information. We find coverage of recent wars a useful place to continue the investigation about the form or information.

A significant literature on the logic and perspective of the work of TV news, production indicates that a significant element of any prospective news item is its visual representation and potential, which are a key element of TV formats. Formats are metacommunication features of any information, or message. One example is the shape and size of a television screen; a related one is the volume and channel controls on electronic media. Regardless of what one wants to see or hear, these devices and their accompanying logic must be encountered. It turns out that the techno*logical* features of a medium can spill over into other constraints and requirements of a particular medium, including production-*logical* and purpose-*logical* formats. For example, the cultural context in which TV news is organized and used—including its commercial features—is an important part of the news code or the news formula. Similarly, the related concern of how to attract an audience in order to gain more advertising revenue has implications for entertainment, dramatic visuals, and emotional resonance with an audience. We are speaking here about some core elements of entertainment and good programming. Of course, there are others, but these are among the most important.

These considerations are central to understanding the nature of recent news coverage about peace as well as conflict, since such topics are interpreted within the organizational world of newswork in different ways. What is selected for coverage and how it will be presented is largely contingent on what can be "done with it" in terms of the prevailing format and logic. In a sense then, news events are not selected so much as they are recognized as a likely news item. Conflict, drama, action, and especially war are newsworthy for a number of reasons, but they have special relevance to TV news because of their potential for dramatic visuals (e.g., explosions, bombs, people running, and a range of emotional reactions of people).

From the perspective we are offering, TV content is a production through and through; it begins with and is guided by certain news codes and format criteria. Those occurrences or "happenings" that are most compatible with TV news formats are then most likely to be sought out for inclusion. Quite often, since newsworkers also solicit certain news sources that can provide "the kind of events we need," the sources themselves are highly selective (cf. Ericson, 1989, 1991).

THE DISAPPEARING EVENT

Examining some of the news coverage of the recent Gulf War and contrasting it with coverage of other conflicts and events illustrates some of the points about temporality, control, and formats, and how sources and journalists share perspectives. The Gulf War was a television war but it was done through accepted formats of news, sports, and press conferences. And just as a plethora of research has demonstrated how the nature of this coverage has altered events (e.g., politics and sports), so too has it changed "wars as news events" (cf. Altheide & Snow 1991). It was reported on March 28, 1991, in the *Arizona Republic* that National Football League (NFL) Films "is putting together highlights of the Persian Gulf War for a documentary co-produced by the Pentagon." A spokesman for NFL Films stated, "I don't want to say that war is the same as football, but our talent as film makers can very easily be transferred to this sort of venture." After the article noted that the production "will include footage of bombing missions and ground assaults on the Iraqi army," and that viewers "should expect booming narration and orchestral music with the declassified military footage," the NFL Films spokesman added, "Football is obviously the military's sport of choice. . . . President Bush even called it his 'Super Bowl'."

Information was put together in ways required by TV formats in particular, and news information in general. More was involved than the war simply being a media event, as discussed by Dayan and Katz (1992); this was not a mere broadcasting of history as they suggest, but rather, from a different perspective, history was being constructed through media logic. Citizens throughout the world became TV-war-viewers, and incorporated their viewing activities into what Robert Snow (1983) has referred to as the routine order or "temporal ecology" of everyday life. Not only did it interfere with other activities, but people called television stations wanting even more information. CNN's ratings soared by several hundred percent, and newspapers became a secondary source of information for many people. Some print and radio journalists were quite critical of the coverage. The director of information for France's most popular TV station TF1 explained:

> "The same problem with pictures of the war existed for the other channels. There was not enough pictures, but people were very interested. People watched, and the press was very jealous. We had experts each day . . . military experts. That's not enough for the press. Everything we could do was . . . wrong." (author's field notes)

The Gulf War and the major conflict-managed events that preceded it pose major problems for journalists, but especially scholars and other critics. The Gulf War news coverage, and especially that of television, was a production in its own right. The Gulf War may be the first news *program* rather than a conventional *news* program. It was not regular news reporting, or regular special reporting; rather, the coverage was planned months in advance of the actual start of the war in order to have "up to the minute," if not "live" coverage, but it would be different from anything that had ever been telecast. The nature of the news coverage about the Gulf War was not simply due to journalists being duped or misled; most realized that they were part of a massive propaganda and disinformation campaign, even prior to the bombing of Baghdad. Still, the war was covered, usually on the sources terms, because they supplied the visually dominated reports on which TV news formats thrive. News organizations covered the war even when they knew they were being misled systematically; putting on the newscast and grabbing the audience was more important than "getting it right," because there were other considerations. As Meyrowitz (1991) noted, "TV's hyper-selectivity of stories tends to present events without the context and perspective needed to make rational sense of them. . . . In the recent coverage of the Gulf War . . . we heard more about the siren-interrupted sleep of the correspondents than about the history and context of the conflict." The main idea was to "get it," to be "part of it." The journalists were even smaller components of this production than regular newscasts. The same French journalist cited above explained,

> "When you work in Lebanon, you know what you do. If you are on the West side you work with the Syrians. It is clear. If you work with the Christians [you work with someone else]. It was just a small piece of truth. During this war, nobody knows what the truth [is], nobody knows what we saw. . . . [W]e have so many things, so many pictures, we don't have the possibility to check, to be sure, of anything." (author's field notes)

Our work to date makes it clear that the French journalist was not alone. Network correspondents from the United States, the United Kingdom, Italy, and likely, other countries as well knew they were part of a massive propaganda effort, a practiced disinformation campaign right from beginning of the coverage. For example, during a conference I attended of the Royal Television Society in Manchester in November, 1991—some two months before the Gulf War began—a top British correspondent, Nik Gowing, made the following comments as part of a videotape presentation to the audience:

> Since the airlift of American forces to Saudi Arabia began within hours of Saddam Hussein's invasion of Kuwait, military and political planners seized on the television image as a vital tool in their strategy. . . . [notes that the early images were of military preparedness, putting massive forces into Saudi Arabia]; television images that were beamed into Saddam Hussein's bunker had achieved their aim of halting any planned military advance but the military reality was different. There was less hardware in the desert than claimed and fewer troops and personnel. We now know there was less of a military capability than these images suggested [notes the overworked transport systems, lack of spare parts, and no reliable inventory] but despite this confusion sources say that television images have achieved what President Bush and his strategists wanted—the impression that the anti-Saddam allies would sacrifice no effort or resources to stop Iraq's aggression. For Iraq, too, Western media coverage has clearly been a vital tool as Saddam weighs his options . . . it's known that foreign news reports are a major source of his intelligence; television is therefore a medium of transmission, not just of images of hostages, and of statements, ultimatums and information, but also for disinformation. In other words [there is] the potential for both sides to manipulate facts and intentions in order to deceive the potential enemy . . . [people are then quoted; conflicting messages noted] ; as the world sleepwalks into war, broadcasters are having to decide how far they compromise and succumb to the news management of war. Do they report without question or do they expose the inconsistency and thereby possibly undermine allied strategy?

Still it was covered, night after explosive night. And like many other events, the TV coverage informed newspaper and news magazine accounts as well. The distortions, propaganda, and manipulations have been widely noted by others. One piece that summarizes much of this criticism and adds its own analytical critique is by Kellner:

> In this article, I shall analyze some of the ways that the mainstream media served as a mouthpiece and amplifier for U.S. foreign policy in the crisis in the Gulf. I will argue that the range of policy discussion in the mainstream media during the pre-war crisis period was woefully restricted and that the media thus failed to serve their public interest requirements of providing a diverse range of opinion on issues of public importance. In particular, they failed to inform the public concerning what was at stake in the Gulf crisis, what the consequences of war would be, and who would primarily benefit from a Gulf War. In retrospect, I would argue that the uncritical coverage of Bush Administration and Pentagon policy worked to make war practically inevitable and helped to promote and legitimate the eventual military attempt at solving the crisis. (1991:2)

We concur with the thrust of this and other studies and criticisms (cf. Greenberg & Grant 1993). Indeed, our extensive data from TV news reports in several countries take the critique a step further: exploring how it was possible that such essentially single-minded coverage could have occurred. What was the "it" that was covered, then? What was it that a worldwide audience watched in real time and in videotape replays? What does this kind of coverage tell us about the nature of TV in the face of peace and conflict, and the nature of journalism more generally?

THE LOOK OF WAR

A general thesis of this work is that war looks like good television. That is, if it is done right, meaning right for television. As stressed above, the key is what is visual, and what qualifies and seems more likely to be selected for visual news coverage? No wonder that social conflict is a staple of TV news (cf. Cohen, Adoni, & Bantz 1990). In a sense, conflict is potentially better television than peace, which might also be very newsworthy (e.g., the reconciliation of East and West Germany). Indeed, the reaction of TV journalists to the fall of the Berlin Wall was much less involved than the coverage of the Gulf War. The director of information for France's TF1 explained: "(We) had a crisis cabinet; working 24 hours a day; people (journalists) liked it. People did not want to take time off. People were proud to be with the channel" (author's field notes). I asked if they did anything different in covering the Berlin Wall and related events. The Berlin Wall was very important to the French, more so than for the American people, but the war was very spectacular. The implication is that nothing like a crisis cabinet was formed. The Berlin Wall did not have the same meaning as the war.

But some wars are also more interesting than others if they are more relevant to TV coverage, including the all important visuals. On our road to clarifying whether there is something about peace that runs counter to TV formats, and therefore is likely to not qualify for rather extensive coverage, the remainder of this Chapter will look at how some recent wars and conflicts involving the United States were covered by television in particular. We will examine briefly some relevant aspects of the Grenada and Panama invasions as television events, followed by the most recent Persian Gulf War.

The Gulf War coverage grew out of a television tradition, including the Vietnam War, and the more recent military conflicts, including the Iranian hostage crisis, the Falkland Islands War, and the invasions of Grenada and Panama. Some very raw numbers for Grenada and Panama provide a shadowy overview of the relative amount of time given to these events by one American network, compared to the Gulf War.

- Grenada. For the two-week period October 24 to November 7, 1983, ABC News devoted approximately 115 minutes (less than two hours) of its regular newscast to Grenada.
- Panama. For the two-week period December 20, 1989, to January 4, 1990, ABC News devoted approximately 111 minutes of its regular newscast to the invasion of Panama. Several of these newscasts were preempted by NFL football games!
- Persian Gulf War. For the two-week period January 16 to February 1, 1991, ABC News virtually revamped its regular evening newscast around the Gulf War, and devoted 406 minutes, nearly seven hours to its coverage. As the Vanderbilt University Television News Archive Index noted, "The Persian Gulf War, which virtually began on January 16 during the evening news time period, often altered the half-hour format of the weekday news broadcasts. A few times the evening news program was preempted by, or simply extended into, special reporting on the war. At other times, the evening news was expanded into one hour coverage, sometimes with the second half hour preempted by the local affiliates." Indeed, ABC News presented its regular half-hour newscast on only two days (January 30 and 31) during the two-week period!

The Gulf War coverage differed from the two American invasions, the Grenada excursion in October 25, 1983, and the invasion of Panama in

December 20, 1989. These two came on rather suddenly. In the Gulf War, the major TV news networks had advance warning to plan better, had more lead time and preparation, and did not have to rely on press pools exclusively for coverage, since they had months to prepare. But there were also some other major differences between these conflicts. These included ideology, planning and preparation, duration, destruction, and media antagonism/adversarial/partnership relationships. Very salient for Grenada and Panama TV coverage were the networks' lack of access to preparation and combat zones. Indeed, there was a clear hostility toward the press in general, and an explicit attempt to keep them uninformed. After all, these were surprise attacks, albeit the word was out days, if not weeks in advance. Moreover, the news coverage was discouraged and forbidden in the case of Grenada and Panama, as journalists were prevented from having initial access to the general theater of war. In a few instances with Grenada, U.S. armed forces directly prevented craft bearing journalists to proceed to the island, threatening to destroy them! At the other extreme, the Persian Gulf War, journalists and TV cameras were welcomed and deployed in controlled and regulated press pools, but the important point is that they were a major part of the staging of the operation. Indeed, the military/government(s) involved in operations Desert Shield and Desert Storm went to some lengths to assist the major networks in obtaining appropriate video materials.

GRENADA

Grenada was the worst defeat for the U.S. press, especially TV news, because they were not allowed to accompany the invasion and had a tough time landing visuals. They still presented visual reports, but they were simply not of the fighting, but ranged from simulations of forces, graphics of maps (with voice-over), radio reports in which the words were put on the screen, to a few interviews.

On October 25, 1983, CBS News allocated seven minutes and fifty seconds to the coverage of the Grenada invasion itself, with another four minutes and forty seconds focusing on Reagan's rationale and the State Department's activities. The first report is what concerns us. It was separated into eight segments or parts, in which there was a clear division in attention (e.g., via shifts to different locales and different reporters). The thematic emphasis of the initial reports was informed by the bombing several days earlier of a marine barracks in Lebanon:

> Americans are dying again in military actions in foreign countries. Some died in Beirut and some were killed today in a military operation that began today in Grenada after events in island last week led to a U.S. invasion.

The U.S. now has a strong military and used it, but hopefully will not have to stay long in Grenada.

There are reinforcements if necessary.

We need to have some justification in being there, and have some not only in American civilians being there, but also due to the buildup of Cuban and Soviet interests there.

U.S. officials promise that we won't be there longer than necessary, but still, lives may be lost.

There was some negative reaction globally. (CBS News, 25 October 1983)

These points were illustrated with graphics (e.g., slides), radio transcripts, words on the screen from film provided by a student in Grenada, Defense Department (DOD) file film of various weapon systems, DOD film of military aircraft on the island of Barbados, ships; file tape of Grenada's beaches. Since journalists were not given direct access to the very brief encounter, which was over in a matter of days, a good deal of press attention was given to visual topics that were more accessible, including critics' comments, which included many from the Soviet Union as well as allies led by the vociferous Margaret Thatcher. It was not until October 27 that the U.S. military permitted fifteen journalists and their escorts to enter Grenada (Mungham 1987:301). But it was the unloading of bodies at Dover Air Force base that provided some of the most memorable video footage. The following is from our data about the coverage from October 29, and November 1. The importance of *actuals* or tape of a recent event is noted.

October 29: Segment 1

At Dover AFB, ceremony for men killed in Beirut bombing—the mood was very different there: "flag draped coffins resting on floor of hangar, 14 marines and 1 sailor killed at Beirut bombing and one captain killed in Grenada"

A few families traveled here for brief service—the chiefs of the services most affected led the mourning—"come home to our beloved U.S." (Navy)—"as I wept inside I asked, Lord, where do we get such men?" (Marines)

After 20 minute ceremony, chiefs offered condolences to each of the families and father spoke and said they were proud to have their son be a marine and the son wrote many times and said we needed to be there, there will be many more ceremonies here as this base becomes a waystation for those who fell in Lebanon and Grenada

e. *Actuals*: anchor with graphic flag and heart-shaped locket; to zoom out showing caskets and soldiers standing at attention; families sitting in chairs, couple being escorted to seat by uniformed man; close up of hanging flag with zoom out showing caskets and soldiers at attention; couple, man has arm around woman, look sad; family; caskets; chiefs giving speeches at podium; band playing "Halls of Montezuma"; service chiefs shaking hands, saluting crowd lined up; father speaking at podium with marine behind him; marines in dress uniform walking in single file with rifles raised; anchor solo

November 1: Segment 1

a. 23 killed in Grenada and Lebanon honored at Dover AFB in Delaware at largest service yet for men killed in service of their country

Army spokesman: "They join a long line of compatriots"

ONE OF COMPATRIOTS (use of one dead to exemplify others) buried in Ohio, first "of at least 4 Ohio sons to come home this way" (shows casket being carried by pall bearers)

19, been in marines 1 year

Mother says he "was American all the way, we talked about what Communism is and he didn't want that in America," Mark Cole was good at football, average academically, knew everybody, Principal says he'll be remembered as boy "with quick smile, pleasant personality" (audio bad, hard to hear)

"Brotherhood of marines" Marc liked (audio hard to hear)—last photos he sent parents days before he and others were killed

Father: "He knew he had to be there, those people could not survive without it"

Helped parents build their modest home, put his name and *Mom* in cement

Ceremony in Baptist church, eulogized as a Christian first, family has "rationalized" as God's will, not military or political miscalculation, mother says "people should be proud of country and stand behind president"

Actuals: dress-uniformed marines carrying in casket to church, labeled W. Milton, Ohio

Close-up of photo of Mark Cole in Dress uniform

Close-up of interview with mother

W. Milton high school, pictures of football team, showing Marc, interview with high school principal,

PHOTOS sent home by Marc , of marines in group, marine looking through binoculars on stand, marine near building, close-up of marine in uniform with helmet

Actual of interview with father

Actuals of family's home, close-up of where Marc carved his name and the word *Mom* in wet cement

Actual of parents walking ; church, inside of church, close-up of woman crying, pastor eulogizing; marines carrying flag draped casket at burial; marines raising rifles; Delaware labeled, "voice of Sandy Cole"; soldier playing Taps; photos son had sent home

PANAMA

Panama was different: despite the lack of complete access, a lot of visuals were available. This was mainly because the networks had more extensive visual files about Panama and Noriega, and also because they had more time to prepare them. Compared to the other events we have studied, the coverage of the Panama invasion used more graphics (including photos, logos, and maps) per news report.

The entire newscast on December 20, 1989, was devoted to the invasion of Panama. A key reason for this was that press pools had been established, there had been speculation for weeks that an invasion would take place, and alleged attacks of Americans living in Panama had been widely publicized during the weeks preceding the invasion. More importantly, there was a coherently orchestrated effort to depict Panama's leader, Manuel Noriega, as the drug-devil incarnate, complete with pre- and postinvasion raves about his heterosexual and homosexual activity, voodoo, scarred complexion—"pineapple face"—and his drug running and dealing, which was said to be affecting the United States. In short, few informed people were surprised when George Bush ordered the invasion of Panama to arrest and "bring to justice" his former CIA colleague. When Operation Just Cause was planned and then launched, the electronic and print press was primed, had been working on press pool arrangements for some time with the Pentagon, and was ready to work.

The invasion of Panama occurred in a context of other major events in Eastern Europe, especially Rumania. Our findings concur with those of Morrison (1992:73ff.) that news reports often featured comparatively more tape of actual fighting in several of the Eastern European countries, because the reporters were less restricted. We present only those materials from ABC's coverage pertaining to Panama here, followed by summaries of some five segments of actual footage of the attack, fire and smoke, soldiers. The early segments dealt with the invasion itself.

> The general message is that the invasion of Panama has been invaded, but news people have been kept away from action.
> Bush thinks he had good reasons for invasion.
> Noriega may be a bad guy but the U.S. went along with him before.
> Rumanian demonstration shows increasing tension where soldiers demonstrated along with crowd. In Lithuania there was a rare split in Communist Party. To say the least, a very strong message of world unrest, told by a calm Jennings who appears to have the world at his fingertips, yet uses "we" terms as if he is sitting right in viewers' living room.

The main focus was on Manuel Noriega, who had been demonized by extensive press prior to the invasion. Some of this tape was provided by the Defense Department. Also included in our summary presentations are comments about numerous graphics, maps, and visuals of President Bush, other White House officials, and some congressmen who challenged the decision, and some discussion of who might follow Noriega into office (Note: As we collected some of these data we wrote in our notes, "CBS basically completed in one newscast for Panama, what they did for several months with Iraq!")

In sum, the entire broadcast essentially dealt with Panama, with the largest amount of the coverage focusing on "the attack." ABC anchor Jennings carefully articulates words when he talks about casualties (as if to show concern). Beginning with actual videotape of helicopters instead of the usual anchor shot suggests the importance and action of what is to follow. This initial coverage of Panama used far more actual videotape of fighting than the Grenada invasion, although the coverage of both supplemented *actuals* with graphics and file materials. Our research team got the distinct impression that this invasion compared to the Grenada invasion was not questioned as much by news people and others. One change that did occur was the coverage of death; in the Gulf War we saw little even though there was a lot; in Panama, as with Grenada, despite the low number of American casualties, they received a good deal of coverage partly because the wars were short, but partly because the visual opportunities at Dover Air Force Base were too good not to emphasize. A portion of the CBS news transcript on Christmas Day gives the tone of this coverage during the invasion of Panama:

> RATHER: The bodies of two more U.S. soldiers killed in Panama were returned today to Dover Air Force Base in Delaware. The Pentagon says officially 23 U.S. servicemen have been killed in action and 303 wounded in the invasion. Correspondent Bruce Morton looks at this Christmas Day as it was observed by some Americans who fought in Panama, and by the American families who cherish them. (Church service; congregation singing "Joy to the World")
> BRUCE MORTON: All over the country today Americans prayed for their soldiers in Panama.

Before proceeding to a discussion of the Gulf War coverage, it may be helpful to reflect on a few key comparisons in the coverage of Grenada and Panama. There are some troubling points to be considered in trying to assess the nature of the news coverage of these conflicts. In a manner that was consistent with some of the practices carried out by the British government during the Falkland Islands War, journalists' access was severely limited. Also, like the Falkland experience, the press was increasingly aware of how its access was being limited to certain events, yet it was still able to cover the events. Indeed, the press became more determined than ever to present even censored materials on regular newscasts and numerous specials. We will see that this was particularly true during the Gulf War. Another consideration is that despite the limits on videotape—the most important visual tool for the networks—the press relied heavily on graphics, still photos, and simulations, seemingly in inverse relationship to the availability of videotape: that is, the less tape was available the more graphics and simulations were used. With Grenada, compared to the Gulf War, the networks were a bit caught off guard, since it happened so quickly. With the former, the networks really had to freelance—sometimes, literally using freelance ham radio operators on Grenada or Barbados. We shall see that in the case of the Gulf War, there was ample warning and preparation for the events, which were being planned in August, although the actual attack took place on January 16, 1991. It should also be noted that there were reflective and critical pieces broadcast about both ventures within a year or less of their completion.

There is another curious feature of the coverage of these conflicts. Conflict is quite normal to news operations, and indeed, many would argue that newsworthiness or news values are implied by the notions of conflict, deviance, and even war. What is also important is the copresence of network criticism of an event, particularly governmental action, and the extent to which the access opportunities are open or closed. Stated differently, if news access is limited, if news agencies are not part of the action, so to speak, it appears that they are more likely to be somewhat critical of the overall operation. No causal connection is made here, because networks' access does not guarantee that they will engage in favorable, promotive reports of the government pursuing those aims. Indeed, analyses of news coverage of the Falkland Islands War (cf. Glasgow University Media Group 1985; Morrison & Tumber 1988; Mercer 1987), Grenada (cf. Mungham 1987), as well as other conflicts suggest that the political context in which journalists often find themselves treated as administration adversaries should not be overlooked. However, not letting something be public, and keeping it secret clearly implies control, so there must be some sharing or openness, at least of a strategic nature, to partly offset the negative features of coverage.

Another element of this rather crude equation is that the work of the networks changes if visuals, particularly the all-important videotape, are not available. Recall that a central feature of the TV news format—especially the regularly scheduled evening news report—is that time and importance are "marked" with videotape, especially dramatic, action tape—thus the interest in combat footage (or Superbowl highlights). From this perspective, what journalists need is exciting videotape for the evening newscast; their work entails access to visuals. That defines air time, importance, and to a remarkable degree, good work. If access and tape are not forthcoming, as was the case in Grenada, then we have a peculiar situation. Some coverage must follow since, after all, one's country is involved, and viewers are interested in this sort of thing—in part because of the constant hype of conflict and violence that pervades news and entertainment programming. Also, the other news organizations are likely to cover the war. There is archival file and graphic material to use, as was done with Grenada and Panama in particular.

THE GULF WAR

Following the invasion of Kuwait by Saddam Hussein's forces in August, complex negotiations, military posturing, planning, and extensive media work took place before NATO (primarily the United States) directed its fire on Baghdad on January 16, 1991. This nearly five months of preparation was put to good use by the networks, particularly in view of what they had learned about Pentagon and Defense Department distaste for their presence during the Grenada and Panama invasions. They knew that the notion of the press pool would be invoked for the Gulf War coverage, and it was, despite the journalists' protests. During a congressional hearing on the control of the press by the Pentagon, the dean of American journalism, Walter Cronkite, stated,

"With an arrogance foreign to the democratic system, the U.S. military in Saudi Arabia is trampling on the American people's right to know," Cronkite told the committee. . . . "Because of these onerous and unnecessary rules, the American people are not being permitted to see and hear the full story of what their military forces are doing in an action that will reverberate long into the nation's future." Cronkite took aim at the Pentagon's pool system, which dispatches limited numbers of reporters accompanied by military escorts to units chosen by the military. "The press should be free to go where it wants, when it wants," Cronkite said. "We have a pre-censorship now, with the military deciding what will be reported and when" Cronkite said. "I'd rather have a post-censorship."
    Cronkite said such a system of free reporting with censorship before publication worked well during World War II and could be equally workable in the Persian Gulf despite advances in television technology that enable live coverage. "It doesn't really matter whether we report it this minute or this hour or this day even . . . as long as we can report it in due time." (*Mideast Media, Peacenet*, electronic bulletin board, 26 February 1991)

The American networks took several steps to provide entertaining coverage for their viewers, including special news programs for children! First, they developed additional simulations and beefed up their computer graphics. Being uncertain of what they would get in terms of "hot" visuals, the extensive graphics they developed using the sophistication of computer software programs went over very well, indeed. Recall that when the bombing of Libya took place in 1986 in retaliation for that government's suspected complicity in aiding those who bombed a disco in Athens, resulting in injury to some American troops stationed there, TV showed this event by using computer-generated cartoonlike caricatures of planes on bombing runs, with a soundtrack of Kenny Loggins's "Highway to the Danger Zone," the theme song for the hit movie, *Top Gun*. (Air Force pilots were reported to psyche up for combat by listening to rock music through their own earphones in the cockpits of their jets.)

Second, the networks lined up military experts to discuss tactics and weapons. These people became quasi-co-anchors, since they were on the air so much between August and the end of the Gulf War in March. While we will return to this point a bit later, it is critical to stress the significance this had for coverage; anchor sets were constructed as space was made for the military experts who were given equal—if not greater—voice and credibility than the journalists! One postwar observer, Danny Schechter noted how the use of these experts further joined source and journalist:

> The Pentagon's chief in-house briefer, General Thomas Kelly, would later joke with Johnny Carson about how easy it was to control the press conferences. He drew laughs when describing how the briefers met beforehand to strategize and plan who to call and who to ignore. The "troublemakers" were put in the back, out of camera range. When Kelly retired after the war he was promptly hired by NBC News. ABC's military consultant Anthony Cordesman previously worked at a conservative think tank and for Arizona Senator McCain, an ultra-right wing Vietnam POW. . . . Now Cordesman is back in McCain's office—jumping back from the center of media power into politics. (1992:30)

Moreover, the network anchors learned the military discourse and lingo from these men, while the military experts became ever more skilled at speaking to video of weapons, and at the timing and rhythm of exchanges with the anchors as well as other reporters. Similar adjustments occurred in other countries including France and Italy.

Another thing the networks did in preparing for their Gulf War coverage was to dig into their extensive visual files. Now computerized in sophisticated filing systems, these materials could be retrieved, copied, edited, and updated by being inserted into historical reports and situation reports, which were being laid out in advance of the actual conflict.

Our presentation of the TV coverage of the Gulf War will be described in several stages: (1) The invasion of Kuwait, negotiations and planning, (2) the air war, (3) ground war, (4) settlement, (5) postwar.

INVASION OF KUWAIT, NEGOTIATIONS, AND PLANNING

The emphasis of most of this coverage was on the history and common features of Arab unity—especially problems with Israel, accounting for the previous U.S. support of Saddam Hussein's government, the demonization of Hussein (including accounts of his untrustworthiness), and the close U.S. ties to the Emir of Kuwait. In addition, considerable attention was focused on the nature and extent of military support to Saudi Arabia, diplomatic excursions to line up the United Nations coalition, and the massive movement of troops, particularly from the United States. Television was the star as leaders challenged each other via satellite hookups, and even aired videos of their adversaries on television! We noted elsewhere:

> During these tense times, several U.S. network newsanchor persons raced for "on the scene" reports, including CBS's Dan Rather's "scoop" interview with Iraq's leader Saddam Hussein. Ted Koppel was there for *Nightline* reports, and thousands of video-cameras were sent to GI's so that they could record their experiences. Bush complained that he did not have the same access to the Arab people as Hussein did to U.S. news watchers, although Bush would accept Hussein's invitation to give an eight minute taped statement to the Iraqi people; Hussein would request equal time; and comedian Jay Leno would opine during the 1990 Emmy Awards (for television) that the war was being fought through television! Indeed! Organized journalism covered it all. (Altheide & Snow 1991:253)

Domestically, while there was considerable public discussion about various options to the situation, the news media—and especially TV—as documented by analyses by FAIR, a media watchdog organization—gave little attention to alternative views:

> A new FAIR survey shows that nightly network news programs largely ignored public efforts to oppose the Bush administration's military policies in the Persian Gulf. FAIR examined five months of TV coverage of the Gulf crisis, from the first commitment of U.S. troops on August 8, 1990, until January 3, 1991. Of a total 2855 minutes devoted to the Gulf crisis—nearly two full days of coverage—only 29 minutes, roughly one percent, dealt with popular opposition to the U.S. military build-up in the Gulf.
> FAIR executive director Jeff Cohen commented (January 16): "Now that a war is actually starting, the networks are finally noticing the anti-war movement, but the coverage is often no more than a blur of street action—from mass marches to the flag-burnings of the fringe. Missing from the news are coherent statements from national peace leaders explaining their positions." (*Mideast Media*, Peacenet, electronic bulletin board, 16 January 1991)

The relevance of TV news formats for ideology has been established in previous work and will not be repeated here, except to note that despite the intent of various interest groups to propagandize and promote their positions, a key feature of the message is the way it is packaged. In a style reminiscent of the way Manuel Noriega was demonized to help justify the invasion of Panama, known as Operation Just Cause, the Iraqi situation was given the video persona of wicked Saddam Hussein, compared to Hitler, outlaws, terrorists, with the most lasting nickname, the "Butcher of Bagh-

dad." Such imagery appears to have contributed to the discourse and vocabularies of motive that helped frame the impending war. The media dimension was considerable.

In our media age, public relations (PR) firms have adopted the TV news
formats penchant for visuals and dramatic sound bites and have shaped
them to their interests. Public relations firms have become partners with
interest groups on topics ranging from Mothers Against Drunk Driving
(MADD), various children's and domestic violence groups, a host of medical
interest groups promoting support to combat muscular dystrophy, and more
recently, the phenomenally successful public relations campaign of AIDS
advocates. A related approach to access is for sources to provide *video news
releases* (VNRs) of packaged messages that meet the temporal and visual
requirements of news formats. This was done by Citizens for a Free Kuwait to
enlist American and congressional support for intervening against Iraq. With
primary funding from this committee, for some $11.5 million, which in-
cluded a substantial donation from the royal family of Kuwait, a major PR
firm, Hill and Knowlton, orchestrated a series of atrocity stories about Hussein and the Iraqi army. The high point of their effort involved the use of a
fifteen-year-old Kuwaiti girl, Nayirah al-Sabah, to give testimony in a public
hearing to the United States Congress's Human Rights Caucus, on October
10, 1990 (*Columbia Journalism Review*, September/October 1992:27ff.).
She testified that she saw babies being removed from incubators and killed
by Iraqi soldiers. Numerous print and TV reporters presented this testimony,
and subsequent accounts of terror (also directed by Hill and Knowlton) to
the U.N. Security Council. Her comments were referred to in a public
statement by President Bush, as well as those by several senators during the
U.S. Senate debate about whether to give President Bush authority to de-
clare war, a measure that passed by five votes. By the time the House
Committee on Foreign Affairs held a hearing on the Kuwait situation, the
number of alleged incubator deaths had jumped to 312, a figure that was
also supported by Amnesty International, which later retracted it. Military
action was officially approved four days after this hearing, and Baghdad was
bombed four days later. It was not until about a year later, January 1992, that
it was revealed that Nayirah was not merely a hospital worker, but was
the daughter of Kuwait's ambassador to the United States, and related to the
royal family. Subsequent efforts by journalists and others to confirm the
alleged baby killings have consistently found that they did not take place. A
transcript from the ABC News show, "20/20" on January 17, 1992, illustrates the journalists' surprise at what had occurred. The segment "The Plan
to Sell the War" included the following comments:

DOWNS: Do you remember, when Iraq invaded Kuwait, a report that Iraqi
soldiers had yanked babies from incubators? President Bush used that story to

help marshal public opinion. But is there proof that it really happened, and did
a PR firm hype that story to help sell the war to the American people? Tonight,
a 20/20 investigation.

WALTERS: No one disputes that Kuwait's citizens were victims of Iraqi atrocities and, given what we now know about Iraq's plans to make nuclear weapons, few question that Saddam Hussein was a menace who had to be stopped.
But our focus tonight is how the idea of going to war was sold to the American
people. Was it sold with slick marketing and exaggerated claims? And if it
happened then, could it happen again? ABC News correspondent John Martin
has been following this story for nearly a year, and has this remarkable
account.

After a rather lengthy report was presented that covered the testimony, the
way politicians used it in promoting their definition of Hussein and Iraq, and
comments by detractors who could not substantiate the slaughter, Barbara
Walters and Hugh Downs had this closing exchange:

WALTERS: Well, what does this do to the credibility of Kuwait? After all,
they're going to have relations with us, they may need us in the future.
MARTIN: It threatens the credibility, and the government is very concerned,
the ambassador is very concerned. He told me that they are scouring the
country, more or less, for witnesses to all these atrocities, and will try to make
a complete case for it in the coming weeks.
WALTERS: As they said, absolutely fascinating, and in the emotionalism of
war, the kinds of things we may never know.

For students of the media, culture and social change, this was more than
merely "absolutely fascinating." It was the continuation of a trend to incorporate news values, technology, and formats into the process for defining a
situation in a credible manner. Similar to the way in which network reporters, anchorpersons, politicians, and even Pentagon briefers are selected, the
PR firm used focus groups, did coaching for delivery on camera, studied
tapes, and emphasized key slogans and expressions for the final products
that would be delivered to congressional committees, but more importantly,
to millions of viewers throughout the world.

Moreover, many informed journalists and commentators either realized
the distortions at the outset, or were quickly convinced by reading the
plethora of press criticism that quickly appeared (cf. *Extra*, 16 January 1991,
26 February 1991). The thrust of many of the well-documented comments is
that the news coverage was strongly oriented to the views of military and
governmental sources; that virtually no attention was given to nonmilitary
options until just weeks before the first missiles were fired; that the nation-
alistic, jingoistic, and ultrapatriotic coverage was not only reflective of the
military's orientation especially regarding the hardware and state of the art

weaponry, but that the military experts (often retired) graced national news desks to provide additional background.

As President Bush's deadline approached, more attention was given to the now infamous meeting between U.S. Ambassador April Glaspie and Saddam Hussein before Iraq invaded Kuwait. This meeting came to symbolize the ambivalent U.S. position toward Hussein, and the way in which he was permitted to do his own bidding without official censure, largely because he had been our ally against Iran. On the other hand, notorious lack of attention was obvious when the major American TV networks did not broadcast live the U.S. Senate debate about a declaration of war. (It should be noted that these same networks gave extensive coverage to nomination proceedings for Supreme Court Justice Clarence Thomas, particularly following the electrifying charges by Anita Hill). The focus of most of the coverage was on strategy and the general impact of such a war, with little hard-hitting TV reportage about the likely ravages of war, until around November, but that subsided until a few weeks before U.S. Cruise missiles found their Baghdad targets on January 16.

THE AIR WAR

The visual emphasis took over during the most destructive part of the war. Featured as a kind of surreal music video, the day and night reports referred to sorties, missiles, high-tech accuracy, military targets, Western industrial dominance, and efforts to protect civilians. The meaning of the war was communicated as live videotape mingled with file tape, photos, computer simulations of last week's, today's, tonight's, and earlier scenarios for future attacks. Some exceptional accounts of damage and destruction to civilians were carried partly due to compelling videotape provided by Iraq and other countries' news services. With these exceptions, speed and antiseptic neutralizing without blood was the point; there was little tape available for this, especially since the movement of many journalists was restricted. We became accustomed to military experts serving as coanchors on the news sets, as war coverage became divested of political discourse in favor of discussions of tactics, weaponry, and the military frame. An endless elaboration of battles complemented and were interspersed with the terrific videos of victory, and viewers became accustomed to three-dimensional maps, instant replays with commentary, and forecasts for the pending action. Network anchors in the U.S. and abroad quickly became accustomed to this format and integrated it into their vocabulary and language.

But the coverage of the earliest hours of the war was via radio by CNN's correspondents, who gave eyewitness accounts of the bombing of Baghdad.

This became the model for worldwide planning, execution, and expectations of coverage. This was the first complete satellite war, which permitted the beaming of military signals and television transmissions throughout the world. CNN became a primary source of information for the militaries in this conflict, the politicians, and worldwide audiences. With its instant replays, commentaries by retired generals who stressed tactics, and correspondents who gushed with amazement and chagrin that they could not keep up with the pictures being received by audiences thousands of miles away from the battle scene, even the CIA tuned in:

> William Webster, newly retired head of the CIA, said . . . that he used to tell the White House to turn on Cable News Network for updates on Iraqi "SCUD" missile shots. "I used to get the call when the sensors detected a Scud going up in the air with its probable destination," Webster said. "And I would push the button to (national-security adviser) Brent Scowcroft, and I'd say, 'A Scud has just been launched from southern Iraq headed in the general direction of Dhahran or Riyadh. . . . Turn on CNN.'" (*Arizona Republic*, 27 August 1991)

CNN became the standard, and the seemingly instantaneous flow of images led the way as journalists used the film they were given and permitted to obtain by military censors; the valued TV visuals were produced and owned by the military sources, who had immediate around-the-clock coverage. The networks could not get enough dramatic visuals from gunsight cameras as missiles and "smart" bombs were tracked onto the targets and beamed into a worldwide audience connected via TV receivers. It was largely the availability of such visuals, which the networks knew would be forthcoming well in advance of the initial attacks, that led to the adjustment of formats for presenting the information. Countries around the world adjusted their news presentation to the dramatic visuals; it did not matter that months later the success of the numerous hits ascribed to the missiles and bombs were challenged. What we saw is what we got. Consider some detailed notes about CNN's role in the organization of war news from France and Italy:

> TF1, French TV, Tape 1, January 17, 1991
> Opens with anchor describing situation, nearly one minute. Compared to U.S. and Italian TV with more flashy openings, including logos, graphics, there is none of this; just start with anchor.
> Segment 1. The following segment took approximately 2:50. Approximately 18 cuts are used.
> *Actuals:* Plane landing at night, on the runway, then graphic, map of Saudi Arabia with cities, aircraft indicated, and flags of U.S., Great Britain and France. The idea seems to be to show that their forces are there, perhaps to interest viewers; the presence and actions of one's own forces are what makes the war interesting.

Tape of aircraft flying at night; then a few seconds of a camouflaged fighter; real vs. graphic? After looking at additional coverage in this report in which similar visuals are used, I realize that it is a computer simulation; this too had to be taken from CNN or elsewhere.

The French reporter talks over a graphic of CNN, a map/graphic of Baghdad, with the U.S. embassy marked, Iraqi TV, a few other places; the face of Gary Shepard, and it says so at the bottom. This lasts for about 10 seconds; the cuts are very quick, some as brief as 5 seconds; it is a collage of visuals, many of which are taken from CNN.

Next *actual* is from the USS *Wisconsin*; CNN credit is given; it shows a missile leaving the ship, then a quick cut to a computer graphic showing a missile leaving a ship and heading for Baghdad, about 5 seconds; then cut to Marlin Fitzwater speaking before a podium, then a 10 second simulation of a fighter flying, with a tank shooting at it on the ground; then an immediate cut to *actual* film of a bomb going off through bomb sights, after a plane passes over; then a battery of tape of bomber runs; the terrain looks like Vietnam, with trees; more file tape of Apache helicopters; Iraqi troops, with missile launch vehicles, Iraqi TV is given credit; SCUDs, CNN credit is given; cut to graphic/map from CNN; John Hollimann reporting from Baghdad, describing the missile attack that lasts 10 seconds, then computer graphic of missile striking a target in Baghdad, with flashes of flames; then cut to troops at airport, pilots walking; CNN credit, U.S. Pool tape. air craft taking off, landing, loaded. Return to thoughtful looking anchor.

Italian Channel 3, RAI 3, February 24, 1991, 7:00 P.M.
Topic is land war.
Opens with CNN film of battleship explosions, troops loading guns, tanks, artillery, jet fighters. Each lasts about 3–5 seconds; about 15 seconds of prisoners being taken.

About 50 seconds of visuals, with its own sound (no other voice), Then the anchor comes on. He reads in studio about the land action and introducing their reporters report, for about 35 seconds. Then the reporter, Flavio Fusi provides the voice-over of CNN film of tanks; prisoners; oil well fires, exploding gun-sight targets, a map of Kuwait and surrounding area, with American and Iraqi flags, and even one Italian flag, showing where they are.

More visuals of big guns firing at night; this lasted about 1:00; then a cut to Schwarzkopf for about five seconds; visuals of prisoners; marines leaving helicopters around Kuwait city; lots of firing; trenches; battleships firing; about another minute.

Then cut to another reporter, Fabio Cortese, from Baghdad, showing people walking, city life, presumably discussing the impact on everyday life; back to anchor for 10 seconds; then voice-over of what appears to be U.S. network film of a reporter driving across the desert, looking at soldiers, equipment, with a voice-over by an Italian. Visuals of tanks, equipment in sand; apparently allied equipment; no CNN credit is given for this.

Some of this was Italian film; an Italian reporter is shown on the scene doing a stand-up; interviews are shown with the reporter troops; reporter is shown eating with troops around a tank; shown driving through a sandstorm, it had also been raining. This lasted for about 3:30; then return to anchor. (author's field notes)

Images had access because they constituted the news reality, which, as usual, was quite different from other realities. According to one freelance reporter, John Alpert,

> the predominance of information coming to the American people were these music videos from Saudi Arabia of planes taking off in the sunset, bombs being lovingly loaded onto planes, and what happened on the other end of those bombs, we never saw. (BBC-2, 21 March 1991, "The Information War")

Then there was the Ameriva "bunker" full of civilians that was bombed. The bombing was justified by military officials because their information portrayed it as a command post, so they hit it. The numerous casualties were covered by the press, but not enough, according to some. Horrible images and photos of burnt bodies, and children at the bunker were shown in Iraq. They were sent to the West but they were not shown—images that had been passed by the Iraqi censors were not used by the American networks. The networks did discuss it, however. A partial transcript from ABC's "Nightline" illustrates how civilian deaths became a special component of death, something which had received little coverage to this point in the war. Another point to keep in mind while reading the transcript is "information management," which was acknowledged by the U.S. reporters, at the same time military spokespersons were cautioning against accepting claims from the managed Iraqi press!

NIGHTLINE—02/13/91—Ted Koppel
Voice-over (of Brig. Gen. Richard Neal, U.S. Marine press information officer in Riyadh) visuals of bombed out civilian shelter in Baghdad:
RN: It was a military target and it was struck as it was planned and as it was targeted.
Ted Koppel (voice-over as visuals continue): The Iraqis insist it was a civilian shelter.
Unidentified elderly Iraqi speaks at the shelter site: "I don't know why they hit children and . . . "
TK: But what if it was both? [What happens] when the lines between civilian and military targets are blurred during war? We'll examine that painful dilemma tonight.
(Nightline Music—Graphics—Verbal Intro)
TK: Today as the Gulf War entered its second month, what has seemed too often as a remote and bloodless battle took on a ghastly human face. There is no reason to doubt the word of U.S. military commanders who insist that what was bombed in Baghdad today was an Iraqi command and control center. But

the evidence is also overwhelming that hundreds of men, women and children had taken shelter in that building. And most of them were killed.

Sometimes in war, civilians are targeted intentionally. The Germans did that during the Second World War when they aimed their V-1 & V-2 rockets at London and then when the Luftwaffe bombed Coventry. And by grim coincidence, it was on this day 46 years ago that more than 35,000 Germans died as the result of Allied bombing raids against Dresden. But in this war, the United States & its coalition partners insist that they are doing everything humanly possible to avoid civilian casualties. What still remains unanswered, however, is what will happen if Saddam Hussein deliberately insulates his remaining strategic targets by placing them in the midst of civilian centers. Or by sheltering civilians at military targets—as may have been the case today. We begin with this report from Nightline correspondent Jeff Greenfield:

[Note—compilation of tape and narration—many voices/images are spliced together]

Brig. Gen. Richard Neal: From a military point of view . . . nothing went wrong. The target was struck as designated.

JG: Four weeks after the Gulf War began, the United States came face-to-face with the real face of war. Not the images of pinpoint hits on buildings and bridges—not the high-tech wonders that blow up only buildings—but the deaths of hundreds of civilians in the capital of the adversary. They died in a building bombed by American planes. A building described by Allied forces as a clear-cut military target—claimed by Baghdad as a civilian bomb shelter.

Unidentified Iraqi male in front of shelter (35–40 years of age): A lot of children [died], many women . . .

JG: It was the kind of horror that sent Allied spokesmen into a day-long effort to explain what had happened. And to put responsibility for the dead and injured squarely back on Saddam Hussein. This morning, at the military briefing in Riyadh . . .

RN: In fact, it was a command-and-control bunker. I can't explain if there were civilians in there, why they were in there.

ABC reporter Barry Serafin alone in Riyadh briefing room:

BS: U.S. military officials here in Riyadh fended off inquiries all day long until the regular briefing. On camera and off, they took a hard line. They had radio transmission and photos, they said, showing that the Baghdad bunker was a legitimate military target.

JG: At the White House, where the normal rules were suspended to permit on-camera coverage of press secretary Marlin Fitzwater:

MF: We all know that Saddam Hussein does not share our value in the sanctity of life. Indeed, he time and again has shown a willingness to sacrifice civilian lives and property that further his war aims.

Clip from Brit Hume, at night, in front of the White House:

BH: One idea that was considered was the release of the satellite information upon which the decision to bomb that facility was made. However the CIA, as it has in the past, vetoed that idea.

JG: In a speech by Defense Secretary Richard Cheney:

RC: There is in Iraq a city called Ur, spelled U R. It is a city of significant archaeological interest. Satellite imagery obtained just this morning indicates that there are now two MIG 21's—a combat aircraft of the Iraqi Air Force—parked right next to the pyramid.

JG: At a Pentagon briefing this afternoon:

Capt. David Harrington, U.S. Navy, Defense Intelligence Agency: The fact that it has a camouflage roof, the fact that it has a security fence around it—barbed wire.

Army Lt. Gen. Tom Kelly: Everythin' that we're seein' relative to this facility is comin' out of a controlled press in Baghdad.

ABC Pentagon reporter Bob Zelnick: So the game of damage control became one of expressing the right tone over the deaths of civilians while suggesting that Saddam Hussein had no grounds to complain because of his own SCUD attacks against civilians, suggesting even that maybe he had put Iraqis in danger by situating them in a military facility.

CNN was not without its shortcomings and detractors, particularly in the early days of the war. Its control of the technology clearly gave it power to deny access to others. Alfoso Rogo, a reporter for *El Mundo/The Guardian*, had tried to use

a telephone controlled by CNN and was not permitted; at one point he and Arnett were the only two Western journalists in Baghdad; he asked Arnett to use the telephone, and Arnett would not permit it, to limit the competition.

ARNETT: We were not serving as a link for the world press, we were CNN, and I would be similarly restrictive in the future with a foreigner, and I suspect someone else who had that competitive advantage would also be restrictive [he, the other reporter, got angry and stormed off]; if he had been in any way reasonable, I probably would have accommodated him, but, you know, if you're dying to use someone else's communications you'd better be nice about it.

Rogo stresses that it is unprofessional to claim, as CNN did, that they were the only Western journalists in Baghdad, and just wants to make the point that was not true. He draws an analogy to the way the U.S., when they play baseball, say "the world cup," when they play football, the "world match." He sarcastically suggests that maybe there has been a mistake made in geography, that maybe they don't realize that Spain is part of the Western world. (BBC-2 "The Late Show," 20 March 1991)

THE GROUND WAR

The ground war was preceded by some concern and trepidation about blood being spilled, not only for the Iraqi "others" but for the "coalition" forces as well. Massive bombing runs to soften up the opposition, especially its claims about being dug in, well reported via military spokespersons, but there was little video provided of the actual bombing runs. However, it did not matter, since Department of Defense (DOD) film of carpet bombing in Vietnam was available. Long anticipated by news analysts, the ensuing ground war had been previously scripted as part of the war narrative, as though this third stage were significant to keep in mind while presenting the air war. Without doubt, the high-tech stardom of smart bombs was compelling in its own right, but it was also given meaning and significance for what would come if it did not work—the ground war, in which machines killing machines would be substituted for more bloody bodies. What we continued to see, however, was still more graphics, maps, game plans; we were in the postmodern locker rooms of death!

Victories with little death were dealt to the world's audiences directly, bypassing journalists, who were merely bit players at televised press conferences. Indeed, the occasional journalist who challenged the frame leading a particular briefing, was cast by other reporters as conflictual and even unkind. Indeed, popular shows (e.g., "Saturday Night Live") performed skits demeaning journalists' behavior. Journalists were expected to follow the rules of access or it could be denied, and most did. Schechter's comments are instructive here.

> The few journalists who decided it was not their job to win a popularity contest nevertheless cooled their aggressive questioning at Pentagon press briefings as the winds of war boosterism started blowing through their news organizations. They began to feel isolated and out of step, especially after *Saturday Night Live* made journalists, not the generals, the target of their spoofs. According to the *New York Times*, once the Pentagon felt it had won legitimacy from such an unlikely source, it would not revise its media restrictions. The distinctions between entertainment programming and news further slipped away. (1992:30)

Comments from journalists I have interviewed from several countries are well represented in the remarks of some photojournalists who reflected on some of their war experiences, including those who relied on TV newscasts for their photos. A picture editor with the *Observer*, Tony McGrath, explained why they published a photo of the charred remains of an Iraqi soldier burned to death in his retreating vehicle.

> "I tried to find a picture that . . . would hold up the story." He says war is disgusting, terribly disgusting. . . . [W]e'd been watching eight weeks a "brilliantly sanitized war; nobody was killed, nobody was injured. We saw a lot of destruction down camera gun sights, Cruise missiles operating, but we never saw anybody die . . . [A]ll of the pictures I saw was [*sic*] of equipment, not one of a body, not one of a wounded person, not one of a captured person. I

just thought we can't allow this to pass without telling the people what happened. . . . [T]his [referring to the photo] is just one of the unfortunate people. It offends and it should." (BBC-2, "The Late Show," 20 March 1991)

SETTLEMENT

Victory was won, with several major tank battles, culminating in massive destruction and entanglements for both military and civilians along major roadways. The resulting carnage was not shown, with the exception of a few celebrated cases (noted above) in British newspapers, and later in some documentaries. The negotiations received considerable attention. Saddam Hussein was still alive and was actively pursuing Iraqi rebels in the north, who revolted with U.S. and coalition encouragement. But the political winds had shifted, and it was not in the coalition's interest to support them, so many thousands had fled, were stranded, and were being hunted down by the still sizable remnants of Hussein's vanquished forces. Since journalists were not restricted from pursuing these events, hundreds, with cameras rolling, began to chronicle the human misery. The visual scenes of the bodies of small children being buried by their distraught parents appear to have eroded Bush's position, and the U.S. and coalition forces intervened and provided food and supplies, as well as military protection for thousands of Kurds to immigrate into Turkey, where they were not wanted.

POSTWAR

Celebrations lasted longer than the war itself. Untold thousands of Iraqis and others were killed, but few members of the coalition forces were. Indeed, some facetious estimates suggested that the number of pregnancies that had occurred on board naval vessels during the war exceeded U.S. military deaths! President Bush had the highest voter approval rating of any president in modern history. Generals were pursued to serve as future presidential contenders, senators, and university presidents! Parades were held across the country, and they were extensively covered. Heroism was won by having served "in the sand."

As with previous wars, however, "midnight" came around, and with it questions about truth, purpose, and where to go from here. Disconcerting information emerged, as in previous wars, that things were not as they were seen and believed. The Patriot missiles that were celebrated for knocking out SCUDS—and we had all seen this—really did not do so well, according to a Pentagon study, hitting, by some accounts, less than 10 percent of their targets! And the size of the Iraqi army and its numerous tanks turned out to not be so large after all. Moreover, the veterans, who were only months ago celebrated as heroes to whom the nation owed a debt of gratitude, were soon coming down with a wide range of ailments, infections, and emotional distresses, attributed by some to their having been subjected to unproven antidotes for poison gas. Of course, Hussein was still alive and was soon reported to have regained control and rebuilt his armaments. He was uncooperative with U.N. inspectors attempting to locate nuclear materials and poison gas stockpiles, and was pursuing another threatening minority group—the Shiites—in the south. This time the news reports mimicked the infamous "line in the sand" of Desert Storm, by providing graphics of what we might term a "line in the air," as the U.S.-led coalition forces instituted a no-fly zone over southern Iraq. The pictures, themes, and sources had been carefully chosen, edited, and professionally presented throughout, but here we were again, facing similar problems with the "Butcher of Baghdad."

There is an issue here about journalistic control, integrity, perspective, and future in view of this discussion about access. One very significant thing that happened in the Gulf War that has not previously been noted is the way journalists accepted the guidelines and dictates of the military sources, and actually became self-controlling! Despite reports in several countries about restrictive guidelines that amounted to censorship of press activities, most journalists went along with the limits, and relied on the exciting pictures. There have been numerous reports about journalists who were turned in by other reporters for breaking the rules, for taking advantage of the military guidelines, on the justification that this was hurting all reporters.

CONCLUSION

In sum, the Gulf War was a postjournalism production. Within the conceptual parameters set forth by the ecology of communication, *the Gulf War was a television product.* The TV coverage and, indeed, a good deal of the way in which it was conducted reflect information technology, and particularly TV news formats. Information was set forth in good production terms, sources and journalists shared points of view about what constituted good work, and even though some journalists would have preferred to have more options to move about on their own, in the end it did not matter. The largest numbers of viewers in history were achieved through this kind of postjournalism broadcasting. World wide TV news operations (and the journalists they pay) should have such a horrible problem again! This coverage has emerged from a more recent history of other conflicts and the resulting negotiations, developments, and definitions set forth regarding public information.

More specifically:

1.   The history of recent conflicts and wars (e.g., Iranian hostage crisis, Falklands, Grenada, Panama) is important in understanding the approach used in the Gulf War. The challenge is to connect the information that is provided, i.e., content, with how the information is organized. i.e., by the sources, to what it looks like.

2.   The visual information was controlled on sight; domestically, the local angle was used, but there was a problem with the Dover Air Force base services for the dead, which received a good deal of visual coverage during Grenada and Panama, but not the Persian Gulf.

3.   All three wars follow a change in individual attributions of evil and wicked, from Khomeini in Iran to Noriega in Panama to Hussein in Iraq.

4.   The Gulf War was different because of the advanced technology and planning time; other wars had been featured as news reports, responding to certain facts or incidents. The Gulf War was a real TV event. *The military planners and the network people used much of the same technology and logic in planning-to-make-a-war and planning-to-cover-a-war.* Technology dominated in conducting and planning this war: satellites, lasers, fiber optics, microprocessors, video screens, computer analysis (at data stations away from the immediate action). This war occurred partly because of the way the previous two wars (Grenada and Panama) had not been covered and planned. This war introduced a new kind of programming, with a very close approximation to a major sports event (e.g., a Super Bowl).

5.   Throughout the technological world, there was advanced planning for months (from August 1990 to January, 1991). Scripts were written, scenarios were played out, sets were constructed, three-dimensional maps were developed for studio use, file (archival) film was dug up, computer graphics and simulations were constructed; DOD film was obtained; military and especially weapons experts were placed under contract by the networks; anchors learned, before and during the official war, the language and euphemisms of the military; the news was given in military discourse. It was to be a news PROGRAM.

6.   Events reflect and are partially constituted by the discourse used in thinking, planning, and conducting an event. This is partly what we mean when we speak of the frame of an event, as illustrated by a news report. It is usually news sources that help frame events, and, in some instances, frame the process of choosing events. This is why sources' use of media logic is important in order to understand the Gulf War.

7.   The Gulf War was communicated differently. Journalists were not adversaries, but were important supporters. This time the newscast was framed from the standpoint of good television and media logic. However, the production of the event and the coverage were *reflexive.* It was a massive

program dominated by the technology and logic noted earlier. The military and the president were the real producers, and they had learned a lot from those other wars. The journalists would do the rest insofar as their dominant resource—the images and likenesses—were oriented to visual materials, which were controlled and limited; they knew this would happen, but they covered it anyway, because it was good television.

Our ongoing postjournalism project reveals some rather drastic interpretations and applications for future events and for the issue of access. A key element is that events are now mass mediated, and can be joined and spliced together through media logic and formats to produce a kind of extended programming. This extends even to criticism, perhaps my very words! TV coverage of wars have helped join different segments together into a coherent event. It is all grist for the logic of programming to borrow from established formats and genres in producing *war programming*.

WAR PROGRAMMING

1.   Reportage and visual reports of the most recent war (or two).
2.   Anticipation, planning, and preparing the audiences for the impending war, including "demonizing" certain individual leaders (e.g., Noriega, Hussein).
3.   Coverage of the subsegments of the current war, using the best visuals available to capture the basic scenes and themes involving the battle lines, the home front, the media coverage, the international reaction, anticipation of the war's aftermath.
4.   Following the war, journalists' reactions and reflections on various governmental restrictions, suggestions for the future (which are seldom implemented).
5.   Journalists' and academics' diaries, biographies, exposés, critiques, and studies about the war, and increasingly the media coverage.
6.   Media reports about such studies, etc., which are often cast quite negatively and often lead to the widespread conclusion that perhaps the war was unnecessary, other options were available, and the price was too high; all of this will be useful for the coverage of the next war.
7.   For the next war, return to step 1.

The First Test

From this perspective, the "doing it" and the "reporting it" are bound together by the same information technology. While it will take numerous events over a period of years to adequately check the veracity of this perspective on the role of the media in events in our postjournalism era, an initial event that followed this coverage by about one year, the invasion of Somalia (Operation Restore Hope) provides a partial glance into the future.

Somalia Calling

In December 1992, Pentagon press releases prepared dozens of journalists to be on a Somalia beach, with lights ablaze to capture the U.S. Seals and Marines who landed there at night. My analysis of the TV coverage of this invasion, subsequent follow-up requests for interviews, and then discussions and further reflection about the appropriate role of the news media—and the IT—on which it is based, illustrate some of the complexities. At one point during Ted Koppel's stand-up analysis of the invasion, ABC cut to Camp Pendleton, with reporter Judy Miller. A military vehicle—a humvee—is parked behind her. She notes that the marines have been watching the landing on TV; when she notes that one Marine jokingly stated that it looks like the media have them pinned down, Koppel added that "I think it is about the only hostile force they met so far, and it wasn't all that hostile. There was actually a fairly reasonable meeting of the media and the military." Koppel and undoubtedly other media types as well were anticipating a wave of criticism of their actions.

Just before I wrote the above lines, I was called by a local TV station to do an interview on the media angle; the caller stated that a lot of people are upset! Since I am known as a media critic, it was assumed, as I found out at the start of my interview (later in the day), that I would "trash" the media for being irresponsible and for interfering with a military operation. When I stressed just the opposite, that the media were doing what was expected of them by the Pentagon agents who planned the assault to look good on TV, the reporter expressed some dismay.

The networks covered Somalia by the script written and produced by the Pentagon. As our other work has noted, Somalia is but the latest in a long line of events that have been planned and executed through media logic, including the use of formats for news presentation (cf. Altheide & Snow 1991). What has changed in recent years, however, is that sources such as the Pentagon and White House now routinely include this logic within their own planning (cf. Ericson et al. 1989)

Notwithstanding public outrage at the spectacle of marines hitting the beach and finding themselves pinned down by camera lights, the media were not any more irresponsible in this event than they were in the coverage of the Gulf War and its predecessors, the invasions of Panama and Grenada. As Ed Tuner, the vice-president of CNN stated, "No one should have been surprised that there was a crowd of journalists on the beach because they were told what time and where, and encouraged to be there in briefings at the Pentagon and the State Department. . . . In effect, it was a photo op" (*Arizona Republic*, cited from the *Washington Post*, 10 December 1992). Turner went on to say that he did not think viewers understood the situation.

The key point about the Somalia coverage, like the Gulf War, was the availability and quality of dramatic visuals, the staple of network TV news formats. Just as in the Gulf War we saw Patriot missile hits that were not hits, in Somalia we saw a beach invasion that was not a beach invasion. Given the cost of satellite feeds, only the visuals that will connect easily with the network news formats, which in turn help build prime time ratings, will receive this attention. Hopefully—but not likely—the extensive coverage of Somalia will provide a large enough space to include some material about the history of this situation and the role the superpowers, and especially the United States, played in creating this deadly situation. And media criticisms were part of this coverage.

Schorr's (1993:20–22) observation that the changing nature of TV news has posed a major challenge to journalists resonates with earlier arguments about what we termed the "postjournalism era." What had begun as a severe limitation on journalists in Grenada had been normalized over a six-year period. In reflecting on the way in which TV news of war has been shaped more by television the medium, Schorr remarked:

> In the Gulf War, the censors did a pretty good job of controlling coverage. On the landing on that beach in Somalia, television made a mockery of the best-laid plans of mice and managers. In the next war involving Americans, news management may be defeated by all the latest wrinkles in minicams, portable dishes and cellular phones. (1993:21)

As we have noted (Altheide & Snow 1991), there are profound implications for news coverage in a postjournalism era in which the activity of news making incorporates the information technology and formats of television as a medium. Commenting on the future of journalism, Schorr noted:

> I have this sense that somehow journalism has to separate itself from the media. I'm not sure how it is going to happen. But reporters have to somehow draw back from being part of the great performance and say there are responsibilities that we have. (1993:22)

Conclusion:
Our Communicative Future ⎯⎯⎯⎯⎯⎯⎯⎯⎯⎯⎯ 10

Social power resides in the ability to define a social situation. The capacity to define and sustain definitions of situations for self and others is the capacity to construct social reality. Toffler and others advise that in any attempt to understand social change "it helps to figure out who commands access to which of the basic tools of power" (1990:6). With power as one of the central questions, the previous chapters set forth an approach and a conceptual mapping to aid in understanding contemporary views about knowledge as power vis-à-vis information technology and the organizational contexts and frameworks in which it operates. The study of social life in all disciplines can be viewed as a mapping and clarification of the process through which criteria for defining a situation emerge, are sustained, reinforced, and changed, and the consequences of such changes. What we have termed the ecology of communication is the center of this process. The elements of the ecology of communication include information technology, communication formats, and an activity, which provides the substantive material to fill out the temporal/spatial dimensions of IT and formats. The basic argument is that the involvement of information technologies and communication formats with activities shapes and changes those activities. Moreover, one cannot adequately understand those activities without considering the underlying communicative foundation that silently guides symbolic interaction. Just as the dimensions and contours of a baseball field can influence how the game will be played, information technology can alter the experience of playing and viewing the game. And just as baseball players take the playing field for granted over a period of time, participants in everyday life develop routines to incorporate information technology and communication formats in daily activities. To continue with the spatial and temporal metaphors from previous chapters, it is suggested that the playing fields of everyday activities are more uniform because they are tied increasingly to communication IT and formats:

> Electronically mediated communication to some degree supplements existing forms of sociability but to another extent substitutes for them. New and unrecognizable modes of community are in the process of formation and it is difficult to discern exactly how these will contribute to or detract from postmodern politics. (Poster 1990:154)

Because we reject technological determinism, as well as the poststructuralist position(s) that social life essentially is best conceived of as texts, our aim has been to offer yet another way to conceptualize some of the main elements, contributors, and moments in this process. We want to understand something about the process and interaction that is becoming more common to numerous activities. When more activities are informed by a handful of information technology and communication formats, then these considerations are significant in their own right for social life. More activities may be said to be guided by a nondiscursive or even taken-for-granted logic and perspective; the look and operation of culture move into the time/place of the more dominant communication forms:

> A basic assumption in the approach adopted here is that the application of the technologies and associated institutional and organizational changes will be governed by a range of factors, including political and economic considerations, which may or may not be related to individual or societal perceptions of communication needs. (Halloran 1986:47).

We are less certain than Halloran and others (cf. Traber 1986) about the intentions, implementation, acceptance, and consequences of information technology for social activities. We see more emergence, negotiation, resistance, and even "IT sabotage." One reason for this is that the grounds, character, and parameters of the culture stream and the effective environment have changed drastically. Power is not "done" the same throughout history; the context and conditions of its realization and application change. Toffler's distinction between the character of power is useful for a concluding statement:

> Knowledge, violence, and wealth, and the relationship among them, define power in society. Francis Bacon equated knowledge with power, but he did not focus on its quality or on its crucial links to the other main sources of social power. Nor could anyone until now foresee today's revolutionary changes in the relationships among these three. (1990:16)

A central thesis of this book is that more social activities are influenced by knowledge considerations than wealth and force. The world is more uniform today because the information technology and formats employed in defining, focusing, organizing, and arranging tasks and activities is quite similar, bearing the mark of the common electronic circuitry and rationale of efficiency and control. Of course, all are implicated in most activities throughout history, but the relative significance has changed. This is particularly true with modern information technology, which underlies and shapes a good deal of knowledge bases and criteria in the postindustrial world. We do not deny the historical and continuing contribution of wealth and force in terms of the origin, nature, and relevance of activities, but we do stress the relatively newer significance of information technology. Rather, the cultural and organizational contexts in which information technology have been developed and applied bear the strongest print of force and particularly wealth, while specific activities that essentially define the work and focus of these organizations have been more influenced by information technology. For example, several chapters illustrated the ecology of communication and the dominance of information technology by looking at news and public information, law enforcement, and state control, as well as warfare. Clearly, these were not developed or originated with the electronic technology on which we focus; the idea of news, crime, law, and national interests held forth when every nation goes to war are tethered to clear historical contexts, events, and memories involving the use of force and wealth to exercise control and domination. That these activities are now ensconced in formal and bureaucratic organizations adds to the relevant contexts of our time. It remains an open question how changing IT influences the way organizations do business and negotiate control and legitimacy of their activities for their audiences. This makes the activities different in kind, if not quality and impact. Moreover, the information technology itself becomes a standard and a kind of template, a series of parameters that increasingly are common and shared by many organizations.

A brief discussion of the relative merits of the role of force, wealth, and knowledge in any activity is bound to be simplistic and therefore distorting, but it is worth attempting for purposes of illustrating differences in information technology. If the three terms are placed in a spatial dimension, we could suggest that each has its own space, even though they commonly overlap. Any activity could be said to be a feature of this spatial arrangement. For example, scholars have noted that the activities surrounding formal education in Europe occurred in the space of organized religion, the Church. Its doctrine reflected cosmology, theology, and organization, including hierarchy and student-teacher relationships (cf. Aries 1972). And Weber (1963) instructs how capitalism and economic considerations emerged from a religious context; work and worship shared similar space, values, motivation, ideology and indicators of success. Even science flourished in this shared, but still somewhat distinctive space. Force was used to maintain, broadcast, and export this ideology, which was also sustained by explicit and implicit criteria and modes of wealth. The favored religion of the day was also the one with the largest armies behind it, which in turn required a lot of wealth. And the knowledge that came from this production context—the monasteries, schools, armed forces, and corporations— Marxist scholars inform us, reflected this foundation. Indeed, new modes of transportation, communication, and ultimately surveillance were inexorably tied to new technologies, including those that spawned the electronic types, channels, and formats noted throughout this work.

Yet, the development of movable print, the Gutenberg Bible, and its trans-ference to other literature was also implicated in the threat to the Church's dominance. As long as people could read, and someone had access to a printing press, other messages could be disseminated on a broader, more massive basis than word of mouth. This proved threatening over and over again, especially with Martin Luther, and with later challenges of state legit-imacy by dissenters who had access to print. Ultimately, all political units had to contend, incorporate, and even combat and censor the way in which information technology was used. New activities, perspectives, awareness, and approaches were developed as the communication forum, knowledge construction, and dissemination process became more rationalized, mecha-nized, routinized, and ultimately more accessible.

Controlling information did not originate with the state and information technology, but as organizations were established to produce information for a political/ideological purpose the problem became more "pressing" (Couch 1984). As more organizations and activities became intertwined with information technology—from literacy to hearing (radio) to viewing (movies, TV, videos) to information processing (record keeping and compu-terization)—many of those activities also changed while also becoming more similar because of what they shared. Indeed, the availability of the knowledge to operate information technology machines and formats, as well as having access to them, contributed to the capacity (the desire was probably always present!) to resist and even challenge the information mo-nopoly and control of activities strongly tied to the role of wealth and force. The ownership and control of such technologies were, at least initially, the province of a few, but with expansion throughout the market, creative inven-tion and application of some serious technologies to those in the "fun" market, and "convenience" market, skills and familiarity were acquired as part of a common-sense understanding and routine social competence (e.g., dialing a telephone, logging onto a computer, and programming a VCR).

The logic and technology were more pervasive, and at the end of the line (sometimes literally) were other knowledge/opportunities/awareness that were far less bounded by space and time, physical sentries, and status eligibility requirements. It was not an open society by any means, but it was becoming more sievelike. Communication skills, or rather access to the information technology, formats, and general principles underlying the communication process (especially in the context of formal organizations), became the key. We know this best as various forms of media, including the mass media. Activities have changed, new ones have been spawned, and others are emerging, and with these changes follow adjustments in the various organizations since it is the activities of life and any social setting that essentially define and set the social significance of an organization.

The project is the continuation of a broader concern with social power and the reflexive relationship between the nature of social activities and the communication process through which they are produced and accomplished. The major focus is on selected social routines and activities to see how individuals, often working in the context of formal bureaucratic organizations, have constructed certain typifications from their effective environment. The task is to understand how communication itself is organized, and what role the elements of an organization—including IT and formats—may play in the activities and substantive matters in which they are manifested. This is a modest effort to continue to develop a research program into the communicative foundations of social activities. For example, it has been asserted for at least two decades (cf. Epstein 1973; Altheide 1976) that news as a product is reflexive of the production process of news including the cultural context, technology, and formats that were invented to manage news work. News, it was argued, is a kind of "machine" that "creates reality" for practical purposes. With modifications, this view essentially has been adopted by scholars, as well as practicing journalists. For example, Schorr observed that visuals dominate TV news, which has consequences because of "TV reality":

> However, the picture is far from being the whole reality and that's the trouble. But images now tend to replace reality, or create their own reality. We are spellbound by pictures of the assault on the parliament in Moscow. . . . So we end up reacting to pictures that show you what pictures can show, and not knowing those things which pictures can't show, and that is a new reality. It is a reality of what is on television. (1993:20)

While this book has included some materials about TV news and social issues, the emphasis has been on other activities in order to illustrate a common foundation in our changing communicative culture. When activities seemingly as diverse as news making, dispute resolution, testing, marketing, surveillance, making war, and social problems construction involve common information technology and formats, then the culture stream is flowing through a common and swifter channel. The activity changes and will reflect the information technology and its formats. More is involved, however, than the mere claim that activities occur in a context or that activities are embedded. Of course they are, but it is the systematic way in which the communication process underlying social interaction and the organization of activities is itself organized and can shape action that concerns us. Communication has been more organized and structured through IT and formats, which comprise part of the culture stream that is also carving the channel for future action and activities. The cultural stream has become a torrent that requires different navigational skills. While the intents and purposes of human actors will continue to occupy students seeking to unravel the origins, criteria, nature, and consequences of various definitions and activities, the contribution of IT and communication formats should also be included in any thoroughgoing investigation of an activity.

This project remains incomplete because we did not begin with an all-encompassing and preinformation technology paradigm. This work should not be read as concluding with "here's another instance of the power of X," or "nothing is really new in social life, just the same old power configurations of dominance over subordinates." Both of these may be true, but our focus is on the cultural ground and logic through which our future will be constituted. The continuing claims and counterclaims about reality and truth, we are suggesting, will take place in the IT arena we have set forth; the criteria, grammar, syntax, style, and approach will be developed from these new threads. The approach is to seek some common features that can be helpful in understanding the change and organization of a range of activities. Technological and format considerations are implicated in the organization of communication and the activities that incorporate them. But, as we have stressed, this is not a deterministic model by any reach, since these parameters are merely that: human actors engaging in activities will configure and shape further IT and formats—indeed, new formats may be invented—in pursuing their own projects. Our assumptions are that every moment is neither random nor context free, and that the culture stream of previous additions and innovations—in the sense of IT and formats—may be applied and incorporated into old activities, and thereby change them, while in other instances, new activities may be created.

As noted throughout, we have drawn on a wide range of ideas and work covering the intellectual landscape from social science to communication, cultural studies, and interpretive studies. The challenge of our task has been to build on previous efforts at articulating the role and significance of formats and media logic, and apply these to other cultural domains and activities. The technological form suggested by the more generic notion of information technology is adapted in a nondeterministic framework compatible with the rich tradition of media, cultural, and interpretive studies. The inherent control bias of IT appears consistently to pervade and essentially dominate corresponding activities. This general view also has been suggested by Carey and others:

> This capacity of the new electrical technology . . . enhanced the capacity of imperial powers to bring satellite areas within the orbit of their control. No amount of rhetoric could varnish or reverse the pattern of technological control . . . ; only the workmanship of politics and scholarship, the consistent attempt to maintain another counterculture, offered any viability. (1989:135)

Most of the control issues involve temporal rather than spatial dimensions. As Carey suggests:

> When the ecological niche of space was filled . . . as an arena of commerce and control, attention was shifted to filling time, now defined as an aspect of space, a continuation of space in another dimension. As the spatial frontier was closed, time became the new frontier. (1989:227)

Temporal adjustments take a cultural toll. They are not inherently bad or good, but they are deviations from the culture stream, the stock of knowledge, and the sense of a natural flow of events.

Adjustments to duration, location, rhythm, etc., are accomplished with IT and accompanying media-specific formats for users to recognize and use. For example, computer screens are now part of the culture stream of postindustrial life, but they are a peculiar space, different from that of a TV screen, with distinctive rules for access, sequence, depth, duration, style, and change. They are a time-space that permits symbolic manipulations incompatible with virtually any other medium. But their accomplishment entails peculiar knowledge, information packaging and appearance, and matching-person interfacing and interaction. The personal adjustments are profound. Postindustrial culture has not come to grips with the routine disparity that exists in our capacity to see that which we have virtually no control over; the stressful, desensitizing consequences, for example, of witnessing routinely the death of thousands of human beings in a part of the globe as close as our living rooms, yet very remote politically and economically, remains to be investigated. In suggesting how the temporal consequences of the computer were prefigured by the telegraph, Carey noted how time, control, and technology are implicated:

> The penetration of time, the use of time as a mechanism of control, the opening of time to commerce and politics has been radically extended by advances in computer technology. Time has been redefined as an ecological niche to be filled down to the microsecond, nanosecond . . . down to a level at which time can be pictured but not experienced. (1989:228)

We are in the midst of massive social changes in a number of arenas in social life. The most profound changes involve how information technology and formats of communication have altered a wide range of social activities and perspectives. Individual evaluation, surveillance and control, dispute resolution, criminal justice sanctioning, diplomacy, claims-making and social problem creation, and making war are done differently because of IT and new communication formats. It is the mix of a number of logics that is significant, especially since the proportions are not equal: The basic argument is *How we do things, and how we think about things, is influenced by what we do in order to accomplish them.* Increasingly, we must attend to and be familiar with a host of information technology requirements and formats before we can accomplish even the most mundane tasks, and certainly the most important ones in our lives. Contemporary life occurs through the interaction of organizations, purpose, information, and communication logics. These three, when placed in our historical contexts, form an ecological net that defines, selects, organizes, presents, and influences the outcome of an expanding array of activities.

What is critical for our future is not just that our lives are organized, but how they are organized. What is the broader cultural context, and the most relevant effective environment, and how do these inform what people take into account in defining a situation? Even deviance and resistance reflect an ecology of communication. One cannot successfully cheat on an examination unless the proper logic, format, and procedures are known and followed: embezzlers, cheats, and frauds, in this scheme, are the most successful at conforming to rules and expectations. This is possible because an expanding array of activities have a similar look, e.g., people voluntarily put money-freeing personal identification numbers into "false" automatic teller machines. Eligibility, performance, and resistance can look even more alike within the limited purview of data-based information technology. The ultimate "irony of security" (Altheide 1975) is that nearly everyone knows the pathway through the effective environment.

Future studies may investigate the ecology of communication in several ways. One modest suggestion is to consider the metacommunication and essentially contingent embeddedness of all activities within an ecology of communication. First, we can track how certain activities have changed as a result of new information technology and the adaptation of different communication formats. Examples include public information, e.g., press conferences, news reports, organizational PR proclamations, testing, and bar codes. [The latter was examined by using an information base (NEXIS) that essentially did not exist ten years ago. Thus, this book reflects the ecology of communication.] Second, how do specific activities (with attendant formats and information technologies) connect temporally and experientially to others? Can we conceive of primary, secondary, etc., pattern overlaps involving career paths, including individual cases of deviance, as well as social issues? Third, new activities or additional features of prior established activities may be analyzed through documentary materials. What is the manner or style of the activity, what is the temporal perspective, and above all, what is different from another period? This approach is also another way to focus on a unit of study besides the individual or a situation. The impact of an expanded effective communication environment should be visible in the perspective, discourse, and emphasis of participants in their routines. The interaction of activity, information technology, and formats increasingly defines our symbolic spaces through which the past, present, and especially the future are being forged. Only by recognizing and developing a discourse about what was previously nondiscursive can we see the next dimension of control and claim it as a feature of our mundane and scholarly effective environment.

If it is correct that varieties of communication and information technologies influence how certain activities are organized, then it seems appropriate to push this argument as far as one can, even to attempt to integrate previous formulations of the stuff of social order and social change, as well as to reconceptualize the foundation of social order. Previous work brings us to the realization, jointly developed and shared by many others, that *social order is a communicated order.* Accordingly, any mode that influences the nature and significance and role of communication in social life is a likely candidate to enter into any theoretical discussion of social life and social change. For these reasons, we have sought to integrate the notion of the ecology of communication with a symbolic interactionist perspective that stresses the significance of social meanings in social life, including the origins of such meanings, how they are derived in specific social situations, which routines get carried over from one situation to another, and what the implications of this are for how other situations are defined.

A critical point gleaned from a plethora of research in the human sciences is that not everyone's definitions have the same significance for self and others, and that those definitions and criteria that significantly inform how numerous individuals define situations are particularly noteworthy of investigation. As noted above, in our media age a significant range of influence is cast by information technologies that, in many cases have become standardized and routinely integrated.

The materials presented in previous chapters were offered as examples of the substance of this approach, and the approach itself. When internal or communicative features of an activity are critical elements of how that activity was itself developed, understood, used, and interpreted, then those aspects must be examined and identified. The approach used to get us to that point is to combine mental experiments, by contrasting hypothetical and constitutive properties with actual empirical investigations and case studies.

A critical feature of this approach is to momentarily replace the recalcitrant Why? of all scientific investigation with What? and How? As most ethnographers and qualitative researchers are well aware, the focus on what people actually do, and how they do it is a back-door substitute for gaining further insight into motives, rationale, and so forth. In the context of this study, in which the relevance of information technology is held to be influential if not definitive, projects have been pursued by simply learning the right questions to ask of the activity, which in turn led us to seek out certain materials, which were subsequently analyzed, queried, and clarified. The key question, for example, that led to an understanding of keyboard rationality and keyboard formats was simply, What does competence and quality look like in contemporary organizations? Similarly, investigations about testing drew heavily on the solid foundations of several decades of educational research and particularly the best students of reflexivity in social life, the ethnomethodologists, as illustrated by studies of educational testing by Cicourel and his associates. The key query here is, What does intelligence look like? If it is performance of a specific task (e.g., answering some questions), then what does performance look like, how are we to recognize it? Similarly, this was the general approach used in our work on crises, which was greatly informed by our studies of the missing children issue and a host of other topics. When such events are passed through television news formats, then those aspects of the process of claims-making are likely to be at work in the missing children issue as well as in others. One then expands the query about what it looks like to How does anyone make it look that way? and What is their perspective (the producers of the information) for making it look one way rather than another?

Answers to such questions enable the researcher to get within the format driving so much public imagery today. The formula is widely known, and it has had great implications. All varieties of claims-makers are now aware of it, in different degrees, including politicians, terrorists, and claims-makers (e.g., missing children issues, domestic violence advocates, drunk driving crusaders). The sharing of such information has all but destroyed journalism and taken us into the postjournalism era, when the ecology of communication and the celebration of format-as-signature-for-content reigns supreme. As we noted in our discussion of the Gulf War (Chapter 9), a significant blending of communications technology, the doing and reporting, were inextricably linked. The public understanding of this unprecedented military operation turned on the visual information (mainly disinformation) that was provided. The connections between events, formats, and information technology were demonstrated further in the organization and conduct of Operation Restore Hope, when the United States invaded a Somalia beach defended by dozens of journalists, with cameras rolling.

These events illustrate that what is actually done in terms of specific steps and procedures to make something happen, gets us very close to a more informed version of Why? The nature of the significant explanations to the whys of our time is irremediably bound up with the information technologies that influence their shape, logic, and impacts. Consider, for example, the relevance of temporality, scheduling, sequence, visuals, speed, and data processing. When the dominant news media continue to be the main public forum for developing, pursuing, and achieving legitimacy and political resolution, then the mass media characteristics will shape and fade into the issues themselves, the people who support them, evaluate them, and react to them. The electronic visuals carry different images and loose-fitting messages that can be easily adjusted to suit our own emotional inclinations at the time of encounter. As an abundance of work has shown, when it comes to television, we do not so much watch it or look at it, as we embrace it, and interact with it.

Justice in its varied forms—criminal, political, and social—reflects the ecology of communication. Consider the nature and impact of public information about criminal proceedings. Notwithstanding the routine presence of cameras in courtrooms, and the typical inclusion of some visuals on evening newscasts (at least in the United States), it is apparent that the public still knows little about legal proceedings. One reason is that usually only the most dramatic moments are included, e.g., the time of sentencing someone accused of a brutal crime, or the sentencing of celebrities (e.g., the O. J. Simpson murder trial). This is mass-mediated justice within the ecology of communication.

The use of this ecology and its further evolution were illustrated with the pieces on Gonzo justice and Azscam. As we asked what and how judges and prosecutors could show good work in a television age, the materials virtually leaped at us. With Azscam, the concern was how to promote a policy and get convictions while minimizing prosecutorial uncertainty. The courtroom itself continues to operate with a different logic than public life. In court, its format and ecological arrangements organized around written text, language, and procedures are somewhat less influenced by the visual formats of television. It is a specialized ecology, driven by something called case law and judicial precedents rather than broader contingencies and situational influences that surround people in everyday life. One never knows for sure how a court case will turn out, especially compared to the virtual certainty that the prosecutor had in the Azscam case that most of the people would cut deals before going to court to challenge the very questionable entrapment procedures used. It is partly for this reason that most people do not know much about court proceedings or judges, except when their judgment is criticized by police spokespersons—on the news and other entertainment shows—for letting someone off on a technicality, or "handcuffing the police" by throwing out cases in which a defendant's due process rights were compromised. Many have embraced gonzo justice as a feature of information technology, thus promoting a contemporary angry moralist view as a soldier for common decency and values. All a researcher needs to do is ask the question, find the materials, and analyze their parts.

The court forum, with its ecology involving specialized knowledge, language, and skill at integrating them in the context of private and somewhat guarded understandings that some judges are better than others, poses a particular foreboding barrier to someone without this background, support, knowledge, awareness of ecological connections, and above all, money! Most people fear court, a fear that when combined with the temporal order and aggravation of dockets, proceedings, and the rest, leads most people to do whatever is necessary to avoid court, including "letting the thing drop," "sucking it up," or "taking care of it themselves." It is this subtle understanding of the ecology of communication that led thousands of people to the TV troubleshooter we discussed in Chapter 4. Without question, in our age, far more people trust mass-mediated justice than the courtroom, partly because of the information they have and partly because of the information they lack.

CODA: IMPLICATIONS OF AN ECOLOGY OF COMMUNICATION

The ecology of communication is a conception, perspective, and research program on additional dimensions of communication in our lives. An initial step is to make what was previously nondiscursive discursive. This has been one attempt. One cannot resist, challenge, or amend what cannot be conceived and recognized. The future of an ecology of communication remains uncertain, but one thing is certain: if activities and the events they help contextualize are informed by IT and formats, then our future is the space of the ecology of communication. If the culture stream suggested by Lind (1988) includes the transformative capacity of IT for change, then the relationships that we have identified between information technology, communication formats, and specific activities will endure, although their configuration may change and, indeed, be replaced and influenced by other technologies and formats. What is important, however, is that we continue to develop ways to think about, define, and name things and relationships; this aspect of concept development defines our project. The pieces of the puzzle are important, and they emerge dialectically through an awareness that, first of all, there is indeed a puzzle, and second, that the puzzle may be one thing rather than another. Because we have found other explanations and conceptualizations of our contemporary situation to be lacking in important ways, we have pursued some conceptual foundations developed in previous work. The project is never over, and the conceptualization is never good enough, but we have attempted to direct our theoretical gaze at the intersection between information technology, communication formats, and meaningful and organized activities and social projects. The studies hum the refrain from the minds of others much wiser than us that the present is big with the past, and the future is now. If our capacity to reflect on our lives and the expanding integration of information technology into more activities spurs others onto similar investigations, even to challenge our current formulations, then we will have contributed in some small way to an expanding awareness, and the necessity of making the invisible visible by calling it into scholarly discourse, and to the options and freedom for us all. This is our hope.

References

Abel, Rick. 1982. *The Politics of Informal Justice: The American Experience*. New York: Academic Press.

Altheide, David L. 1975. "The Irony of Security." *Urban Life* (July):179–98.

Altheide, David L. 1976. *Creating Reality: How TV News Distorts Events*. Beverly Hills: Sage.

Altheide, David L. 1985. *Media Power*. Beverly Hills, CA: Sage.

Altheide, David L. 1987. "Ethnographic Content Analysis." *Qualitative Sociology* 10:65–77.

Altheide, David L. 1992. "Gonzo Justice." *Symbolic Interaction* 15:69–86.

Altheide, David L. and John M. Johnson. 1980. *Bureaucratic Propaganda*. Boston, MA: Allyn & Bacon.

Altheide, David L. and Pat Lauderdale. 1987. "The Technocratic Form in the Study of Mass Media Effects." *Social Epistemology: A Journal of Knowledge, Culture, and Policy* 1:183–86.

Altheide, David L. and Robert P. Snow. 1979. *Media Logic*. Beverly Hills, CA: Sage.

Altheide, David L. and Robert P. Snow. 1991. *Media Worlds in the Postjournalism Era*. Hawthorne, NY: Aldine de Gruyter.

Aries, Philippe. 1962. *Centuries of Childhood*. New York: Vintage.

Atkinson, Paul. 1992. *Understanding Ethnographic Texts*. Newbury Park, CA: Sage.

Ball-Rokeach, Sandra, Milton M. Rokeach, and Joel W. Grube. 1984. *The Great American Values Test: Influencing Behavior and Belief Through Television*. NY: Free Press.

Barnlund, Dean. 1979. "A Transactional Model of Communication." Pp. 47–57 in *Basic Readings in Communication Theory*. 2nd ed., edited by C. Davis Mortensen. New York: Harper & Row.

Barrett, M., P. Corrigan, A. Kuhn, and U. Wolff (eds.). 1979. *Ideology and Cultural Production*. New York: St. Martin's.

Baudrillard, Jean. 1983. *Simulations*. New York: Semiotext.

Baumgartner, M. P. 1980. "On Self-Help in Modern Society." Pp. 193–208 in *The Manners and Customs of the Police*, edited by Donald Black. New York: Academic.

Becker, Howard. 1963. *Outsiders*. New York: Free Press.

Beniger, James R. 1986. *The Control Revolution: Technological and Economic Origins of the Information Society*. Cambridge, MA: Harvard University Press.

Bennett, Lance. 1983. *News: The Politics of Illusion*. New York: Longman.

Bennett, Lance and M. S. Feldman. 1982. *Reconstructing Reality in the Courtroom*. New Brunswick, NJ: Rutgers University Press.

Berger, Peter and Thomas Luckmann. 1967. *The Social Construction of Reality*. New York: Anchor Books.

Best, Joel and J. Horiuchi. 1985. "The Razor Blade in the Apple: The Social Construction of Urban Legends." *Social Problems* 32(5):488–99.

Bittner, Egon. 1965. "The Concept of Organization." *Social research* 32:230–55.

Black, Donald (ed.). 1984. *Toward a General Theory of Social Control*. New York: Academic Press.

Blumer, Herbert. 1969. *Symbolic Interactionism*. Englewood Cliffs, NJ: Prentice-Hall.

Blumler, Jay and Elihu Katz (eds.). 1974. *The Uses of Mass Communications: Current Perspectives on Gratifications Research*. Beverly Hills, CA: Sage.

Bodenseher, H. 1970. "A Console Keyboard for Improved Man-Machine Interaction." *Man-Computer Interaction Conference*. Publication No 68 (September), pp. 196–200.

Bonanate, L. 1979. "Some Unanticipated Consequences of Terrorism." *Journal of Peace Research* 16:197–213.

Bortner, M. G. 1984. "Media Images and Public Attitudes toward Crime and Justice." Pp. 15–30 in *Justice and the Media*, edited by Ray Surette. Springfield, IL: Charles C. Thomas.

Braestrup, Peter. 1978. *Big Story: How the American Press and Television Reported and Interpreted the Crisis of Tet in 1968 in Vietnam and Washington*. Garden City, NY: Anchor.

Buxbaum, David C. 1971. "Some Aspects of Civil Procedure and Practice at the Trial Level in Tanshue and Hsinchu from 1789 to 1895." *Journal of Asian Studies* 30:331–54.

Cantor, Muriel G. 1980. *Prime-Time Television: Content and Control*. Beverly Hills, CA: Sage.

Carey, James (ed). 1987. *Media, Myths, and Narratives*. Beverly Hills, CA: Sage.

Carey, James. 1989. *Communication as Culture: Essays on the Media and Society*. Boston: Unwin Hyman.

Cavender, Gray. 1984. "'Scared Straight': Ideology and the Media." Pp. 246–69 in *Justice and the Media*, edited by Ray Surette. Springfield, IL: Charles C. Thomas.

Chibnall, S. 1977. *Law-and-Order News*. London: Tavistock.

Clift, Eleanor. 1987. "The Legacy of Larry Speakes." *Columbia Journalism Review* (March):40–44.

Cohen, Akiba A., Hanna Adoni, and Charles R. Bantz. 1990. *Social Conflict and Television News*. Newbury Park, CA: Sage.

Collins, Randall. 1971. "Functional and Conflict Theories of Educational Stratification." *American Sociological Review* 36:1002–19.

Combs, James. 1984. *Polpop: Politics and Popular Culture in America*. Bowling Green, OH: Bowling Green University Press.

Comstock, George. 1980. *Television in America*. Beverly Hills, CA: Sage.

Couch, Carl J. 1984. *Constructing Civilization*, Greenwich, CT: JAI.

Couch, Carl J. 1990. "Mass Communications and State Structures." *Social Science Journal* 27:111–28.

Danzig, Richard and Michael Lowy. 1975. "Everyday Disputes and Mediation in the U.S.: A Reply to Professor Felstiner." *Law and Society Review* 9:675.

Dayan, Daniel and Elihu Katz. 1992. *Media Events: The Live Broadcasting of History.* Cambridge, MA: Harvard University Press.

de Certeau, Michel. 1984. *The Practice of Everyday Life* (translated by Steven F. Rendell). Berkeley: University of California Press.

DeFleur, Melvin L. and Sandra J. Ball-Rokeach. 1975. *Theories of Mass Communication* (3rd ed.). New York: David McKay.

Dennis, Dion. 1992. "Under the Sign of Saturn: An Exemplar of Political Economy." Unpublished paper, Arizona State University, Tempe.

Denzin, Norman K. and Yvonna Lincoln (eds.). 1994. *Handbook of Qualitative Research.* Newbury Park, CA: Sage.

Der Derian, James. 1990. "The Space of International Relations: Simulation, Surveillance, and Speed." *International Studies Quarterly* 34:295–310.

DiMaggio, P. 1982. "Cultural, Capital and School Success." *American Sociological Review* 47(2, April):189–201.

Dobash, R. Emerson and Dobash, Russell P. 1992. *Women, Violence and Social Change.* London: Routledge.

Dougherty, Richard A. 1989. "Research Library Networks: Leveraging the Benefits." *Academe* 75:22–25.

Douglas, Jack D. 1971. *American Social Order.* New York: Free Press.

Durance, Joan C. 1989. "Information Needs: Old Song, New Tune." *School Library Media Quarterly* 17:126–30.

Edelman, Murray. 1971. *Politics as Symbolic Action.* Chicago: Markham.

Edelman, Murray. 1988. *Constructing the Political Spectacle.* Chicago: University of Chicago Press.

Eisenstein, James, Roy B. Flemming, and Peter F. Nardulli. 1988. *The Contours of Justice: Communities and Their Courts.* Boston: Little, Brown.

Epstein, Edward J. 1973. *News from Nowhere.* New York: Random House.

Ericson, Richard V., Patricia M. Baranek, and Janet B. L. Chan. 1987. *Visualizing Deviance: A Study of News Organization.* Toronto: University of Toronto Press.

Ericson, Richard V., Patricia M. Baranek, and Janet B. L. Chan. 1989. *Negotiating Control: A Study of News Sources.* Toronto: University of Toronto Press.

Ericson, Richard V., Patricia M. Baranek, and Janet B. L. Chan. 1991. *Representing Order: Crime, Law, and Justice in the News Media.* Toronto: University of Toronto Press.

Ferrarotti, Franco. 1988. *The End of Conversation: The Impact of Mass Media on Modern Society.* Westport, CT: Greenwood.

Finkelhor, David, Gerald Hotaling, and Andrew Sellak. 1990. *Missing, Abducted, Runaway, and Throwaway Children in America: Executive Summary.* Washington, DC: United States Department of Justice.

Fishman, Mark. 1980. *Manufacturing the News.* Austin, TX: University of Texas Press.

Fiske, John and John Hartley. 1978. *Reading Television.* London: Methuen.

Fisse, Brent and John Braithwaite. 1983. *The Impact of Publicity on Corporate Offenders.* Albany, NY: SUNY Press.

Foucault, M. 1977. *Discipline and Punish: The Birth of the Prison*. New York: Pantheon.

Fritz, Noah and David L. Altheide. 1987. "The Mass Media and the Social Construction of the Missing Children Problem." *Sociological Quarterly* 28:473–92.

Galanter, Marc. 1988. "Adjudication, Litigation, and Related Phenomena." Pp. 151–257 in *Law and the Social Sciences*, edited by Leon Lipson and Stanton Wheeler. Beverly Hills, CA: Sage.

Gans, Herbert J. 1979. *Deciding What's News*. New York: Pantheon.

Gentry, Cynthia. 1986. "The Social Construction of a Spurious Social Problem: Abducted Children." Paper presented at the annual meeting of the Southwestern Sociological Association.

Gerbner, George and Larry Gross. 1976. "The Scary World of TV's Heavy Viewer." *Psychology Today* 9(11):41–45, 89.

Gerbner, George, Larry Gross, Michael Morgan, and Nancy Signorielli. 1982. "Charting the Mainstream: Television's Contributions to Political Orientations." *Journal of Communication* 32:2:100–27.

Gerth, Hans and C. Wright Mills. 1953. *Character and Social Structure: The Psychology of Social Institutions*. New York: Harcourt, Brace & World.

Gibbs, J. (ed.). 1982. *Social Control: Views from the Social Sciences*. Beverly Hills, CA: Sage.

Giddens, Anthony. 1984. *The Constitution of Society*. Cambridge: Polity.

Gitlin, Todd. 1980. *The Whole World Is Watching*. Berkeley,: University of California Press.

Glasgow University Media Group. 1976. *Bad News*. London: Routledge and Kegan Paul.

Glasgow University Media Group. 1985. *War and Peace News*. Milton Keynes, UK: Open University Press.

Glass, Andrew J. 1994. "The Key to PC Links." *Quill* (January/February):49.

Goffman, Erving. 1961. *Asylums*. New York: Anchor.

Goffman, Erving. 1974. *Frame Analysis: An Essay on the Organization of Experience*. New York: Harper and Row.

Goodman, Ellen. 1985. "Missing Children: Facts and Fears." *Washington Post*, 10 July.

Graber, Doris A. 1984a. *Processing the News: How People Tame the Information Tide*. New York: Longmans.

Graber, Doris A. 1984b. *Media Power in Politics*. Washington, DC: Congressional Quarterly Press.

Greenberg, Bradley S. and Walter Grant (eds.). 1993. *Desert Story and the Mass Media*. Cresskill, NJ: Hampton.

Griego, Diana and Louis Kilzer. 1985. "Missing Children Is 'Unfounded Fear'." *Arizona Republic*, August 5.

Gronbeck, Bruce E., Thomas Farrell, and Paul A. Soukup (eds.). 1991. *Media, Consciousness and Culture: Explorations of Walter Ong's Thought*. Newbury Park: Sage.

Gulliver, R. H. 1979. *Dispute and Negotiations*. New York: Academic Press.

Gunter, Barrie and Mallory Wober. 1983. "Television Viewing and Public Perceptions of Hazards to Life." *Journal of Environmental Psychology* 3:325–35.

Hagan, John. 1982. *Quantitative Criminology.* Beverly Hills, CA: Sage.

Hall, Peter M. 1988. "Asymmetry, Information Control and Information Technology." Pp. 341–56 in *Communication and Social Structure,* edited by David R. Maines and Carl J. Couch. Springfield, IL: Charles C. Thomas.

Hall, Stuart. 1980. "Cultural Studies and the Centre: Some Problematics and Problems." Pp. 15–47 in *Culture, Media, Language: Working Papers in Cultural Studies, 1972–79,* edited by S. Hall et al. London: Hutchinson.

Halloran, James D. 1986. "The Social Implications of Technological Innovations in Communication." Pp. 46–63 in *The Myth of the Information Revolution,* edited by Michael Traber. London: Sage.

Hanson, F. Allan. 1993. *Testing Testing: Social Consequences of the Examined Life.* Berkeley: University of California Press.

Harrington, Christine B. 1985. *Shadow Justice: The Ideology and Institutionalization of Alternatives to Court.* Westport, CT: Greenwood.

Heinz, A., H. Jacob, and R. L. Lineberry (eds.). 1983. *Crime in City Politics.* New York: Longman.

Henry, Stuart. 1983. *Private Justice. Toward Integrating Theorising in the Sociology of Law.* London: Routledge and Kegan Paul.

Hollnagel, E. 1983. "What We Do Not Know about Man-Machine Systems." *International Journal of Man-Machine Studies* 18:135–43.

Hughes, H. M. 1940. *News and the Human Interest Story.* Chicago: University of Chicago Press.

Innis, H. A. 1951. *The Bias of Communication.* Toronto: University of Toronto Press.

Johnson, Earl, Jr., Valerie Kantor, and Elizabeth Schwartz. 1977. *Outside the Courts: A Survey of Diversion Alternatives in Civil Cases.* Denver, CO: National Center for State Courts.

Johnson, John M. 1985 "Symbolic Salvation: The Changing Meaning of the Child Maltreatment Movement." *Studies in Symbolic Interaction* 6:289–305.

Johnson, John M. 1989. "Horror Stories and the Construction of Child Abuse." Pp. 4–19 in *Images and Issues,* edited by Joel Best. Chicago: Aldine.

Jones, R. 1989. "Time to Change the Culture of Information Systems Departments." *Information & Software Technology* 31:99–102.

Karlen, N., N. F. Greenberg, D.L. Gonzalez, and E. Williams. 1985. "How Many Missing Kids?" *Newsweek* (October 7):30, 35.

Kellner, Douglas. 1991. "The 'Crisis in the Gulf' and the Mainstream Media," *Electronic Journal of Communication* 2:1.

Koch, Klaus-Friedrich. 1984. "Liability and Social Structure." Pp. 95–130 in *Toward a General Theory of Social Control,* edited by Donald Black. New York: Academic Press.

Kuhlthau, Carol S. 1989. "The Information Search Process of High-, Middle-, and Low-Achieving High School Seniors." *School Library Media Quarterly* 17:224–26.

Ladinsky, Jack and Charles Susmilch. 1985. "Community Factors in the Brokerage of Consumer Products and Services Problems." Pp. 193–217 in *The Challenge of Social Control: Citizenship and Institution Building in Modern Society,* edited by G. Suttles and M. Zald. Norwood, NJ: Ablex.

Lang, Kurt and Gladys Engel Lang. 1968. *Politics and Television.* Chicago: Quandrangle.

Lang, Kurt and Gladys Engel Lang. 1981. "Mass Communications and Public Opinion: Strategies for Research." Pp. 653–81 in *Social Psychology: Sociological Perspectives*, edited by M. Rosenberg and R. H. Turner. New York: Basic Books.

Lang, Kurt and Gladys Engel Lang. 1984. *Politics and Television Reviewed*. Beverly Hills, CA: Sage.

Lefebvre, H. 1968. *Everyday Life in the Modern World*. New York: Harper and Row.

Levin, Jayne. 1993. "CIA, U.S. Government Intelligence Agencies Develop Internet." *Internet (The Well)*, September 22.

Levy, Mark R. 1979. "Watching TV as Para-Social Interaction." *Journal of Broadcasting* 23:69–80.

Lind, Joan Dyste. 1988. "Toward a Theory of Cultural Continuity and Change: The Innovation, Retention, Loss and Dissemination of Information." Pp. 173–94 in *Communication and Social Structure*, edited by David R. Maines and Carl J. Couch. Springfield, IL: Charles C. Thomas.

Maines, David R. and Carl J. Couch (eds.). 1988. *Communication and Social Structure*. Springfield, IL: Charles C. Thomas.

Maines, David R. and Joel O. Powell. 1986. "Thoughts on Mediated Disputes and Their Moral Orders." Pp. 33–45 in *Mediation: Contexts and Challenges*, edited by Joe Palenski and Harold Lanner. Springfield, IL: Charles C. Thomas.

Marx, G. T. 1988. *Undercover: Police Surveillance in America*. Berkeley: University of California Press.

Mather, Lynn and Barbara Yngvesson. 1981. "Language, Audience, and the Transformation of Disputes." *Law and Society Review* 15:775–821.

Mattice, Michael C. 1980. "Media in the Middle: A Study of the Mass Media Complaint Managers." Pp. 485–522 in *No Access to Law, Alternatives to the American Judicial System*, edited by Laura Nader. New York: Academic Press.

McEwen, Craig A. and Richard J. Maiman. 1981. "Small Claims Mediation in Maine: An Empirical Assessment." *Maine Law Review* 33:237–68.

McIntosh, D. 1983. "Max Weber as a Critical Theorist." *Theory and Society* 12(1, January):69–109.

McLuhan, Marshall. 1960. *Explorations in Communication*. Boston: Beacon.

McLuhan, Marshall. 1962. *The Gutenberg Galaxy: The Making of Typographic Man*. Toronto: University of Toronto Press.

McLuhan, Marshall. 1967. *The Medium Is the Massage: An Inventory of Effects*. New York: Random House.

McQuail, Denis. 1983. *Mass Communication Theory*. Beverly Hills, CA: Sage.

Mercer, Derek. 1987. "The Media on the Battlefield." Pp. 1–16 in *The Fog of War*, edited by Derek Mercer, Geoff Mungham, and Kevin Williams. London: Heinemann.

Mergen, Bernard. 1982. *Play and Play Things*. Westport, CT: Greenwood.

Meyrowitz, Joshua. 1985. *No Sense of Place*. New York: Oxford University Press.

Meyrowitz, Joshua. 1991. "First the Word . . . Now the Image." *Human Concerns* (Fall).

Mills, C. Wright. 1959. *The Sociological Imagination*. New York: Oxford University Press.

Mnookin, Robert H. and Lewis Kornhauser. 1975. "Bargaining in the Shadow of the Law: The Case of Divorce." *Yale Law Journal* 88:950–97.

Molotch, H. and M. Lester. 1974. "News as a Purposive Behavior." *American Socio-logical Review* 39:101–12.

Moriarity, William F., Jr., Thomas L. Norris, and Luis Salas. 1977. *Evaluation: Dade County Citizen Dispute Settlement Center*. Dade County Criminal Justice Planning Unit, Florida.

Morrison, David E. 1992. *Television and the Gulf War*. London: John Libbey.

Morrison, David E. and Howard Tumber. 1988. *Journalists at War: The Dynamics of News Reporting During the Falklands Conflict*. Newbury Park, CA: Sage.

Mungham, Geoff. 1987. "Grenada: News Blackout in the Caribbean." Pp. 291–310 in *The Fog of War*, edited by Derek Mercer, Geoff Mungham, and Kevin Williams. London: Heinemann.

Nader, Laura (ed.). 1980. *No Access to Law, Alternatives to the American Judicial System*. New York: Academic Press.

Nader, Laura (ed.). 1984. "From Disputing to Complaining." Pp. 71–94 in *Toward a General Theory of Social Control*, edited by Donald Black. New York: Academic Press.

Nardulli, Peter F., Roy B. Fleming, and James Eisenstein. 1988. *The Tenor of Justice: Criminal Courts and the Guilty Plea Process*. Urbana: University of Illinois Press.

Nelson, Barbara J. 1984. *Making an Issue of Child Abuse: Political Agenda Setting for Social Problems*. Chicago: University of Chicago Press.

O'Barr, William M. 1982. *Linguistic Evidence: Language, Power and Strategy in the Courtroom*. New York: Academic Press.

Odom, Ernie. 1986. "The Mediation Hearing: A Primer." Pp. 5–14 in *Mediation, Contexts, and Challenges*, edited by Joseph E. Palenski and Harold Lauder. Springfield, IL: C. C. Thomas.

Ong, Walter J. 1982. *Orality and Literacy*. London and New York: Methuen.

Oudes, Bruce. 1989. *From the President: President Nixon's Secret Files*. New York: Harper and Row.

Orne, Martin T. 1962. "On the Social Psychology of the Psychological Experiment: With Particular Reference to Demand Characteristics and Their Implications." *American Psychologist* 17:776–83.

Palen, Frank S. 1979. "Media Ombudsmen: A Critical Overview." *Law and Society Review* 13:799–850.

Palenski, Joe and Harold Launer (eds.). 1986. *Mediation: Contexts and Challenges*, Springfield, IL: Charles C. Thomas.

Paletz, David, John Z. Ayanian, and Peter A. Fozzard. 1982. "Terrorism on Television News: The IRA, the FALN, and the Red Brigades." Pp. 143–65 in *Television Coverage of International Affairs*, edited by William Adams. Norwood, NJ: Ablex.

Paletz, David L. and Alex P. Schmid (eds). 1992. *Terrorism and the Media*. Newbury Park, CA: Sage.

Park, R. E. 1940. "News as a Form of Knowledge." *American Journal of Sociology* 45:669–86.

Pearson, Jessica. 1983. "An Evaluation of Alternatives to Court Adjudication." *Justice System Journal* 7:420–44.

Peterson, Richard A. (ed.). 1976. *The Production of Culture*. Beverly Hills, CA: Sage.

Pfohl, Steven J. 1977. "The 'Discovery' of Child Abuse." *Social Problems* 24:310–323.

Pfuhl, Erdwin H., Jr., and Stuart Henry. 1993. *The Deviance Process* (3rd ed.). Hawthorne, NY: Aldine de Gruyter.

Pfuhl, Erdwin H., Jr., and David. L. Altheide. 1985. "TV Mediation of Disputes and Injustice." *Justice Quarterly* 4:99–118.

Poster, Mark. 1990. *The Mode of Information*. Cambridge: Basil Blackwell.

Randall, Colin. 1993. "Barcode Game in Battle at the Tills." *Daily Telegraph*, January 30.

Ritter, Lawrence S. 1992. *Lost Ballparks: A Celebration of Baseball's Legendary Fields*. New York: Penguin.

Roe, Keith. 1983. "Swedish Adolescents and Their Relation to Video." Media Panel Report No. 28, pp. 1–16.

Rosengren, Karl E., P. Arvidsson, and D. Sturesson. 1978. "The Barseback "Panic"—A Case of Media Deviance." Pp. 131–49 in *Deviance and Mass Media*, edited by Charles Winick. Beverly Hills, CA: Sage.

Rothschild, Donald P. and Bruce C. Throne. 1976. "Criminal Consumer Fraud: A Victim-Oriented Analysis." *Michigan Law Review* 74:661.

Rowland, Willard D., Jr., and Bruce Watkins (eds.). 1984. *Interpreting Television: Current Research Perspectives*. Newbury Park, CA: Sage.

Rubin, D. M. and A. M. Cunningham (ed.). 1983. *War, Peace & the News Media*. New York: New York University Press.

Samuelson, Robert J. 1986. "The True Tax Burden." *Newsweek*, April 21, p. 68.

Sapir, E. 1949. "Time Perspective in Aboriginal American Culture: A Study in Method." Pp. 389–462 in *Selected Writings in Language, Culture, and Personality*, edited by D. G. Mandelbaum. Berkeley, CA: University of California Press.

Scardino, Albert. 1985. "Experts Question Data About Missing Children." *New York Times*, 18 August.

Schechter, Danny. 1992. "The Gulf War and the Death of TV News." *Independent* (January/February):28–31.

Schiller, Herbert. 1971. *Mass Communications and American Empire*. Boston: Beacon.

Schiller, Herbert. 1989. *Culture, Inc*. New York: Oxford University Press.

Schlesinger, Philip. 1978. *Putting "Reality" Together*. London: Constable.

Schlesinger, Philip. 1991. *Media State and Nation: Political Violence and Collective Identities*. Newbury Park, CA: Sage.

Schlesinger, Philip, P. G. Murdock, and P. Elliott. 1983. *Televising "Terrorism": Political Violence in Popular Culture*. London: Comedia.

Schmid, A. P. and J. de Graaf. 1982. *Violence as Communication: Insurgent Terrorism and the Western News Media*. Beverly Hills, CA: Sage.

Schorr, Daniel. 1993. "The Theodore H. White Lecture." The Joan Shorenstein Barone Center, Harvard University, Cambridge, MA.

Schudson, Michael. 1978. *Discovering the News: A Social History of American Newspapers*. New York: Basic Books.

Schutz, Alfred. 1967. *The Phenomenology of the Social World*, translated by G. Walsh and F. Lenhert. Evanston, IL: Northwestern University Press.

Schwartz, Tony. 1974. *The Responsive Chord.* New York: Anchor.

Seckman, Mark A. and Carl J. Couch. 1989. "Jocularity, Sarcasm, and Relationships: An Empirical Study." *Journal of Contemporary Ethnography* 18:327–45.

Shapiro, Amy. 1983. "Action Lines." Pp. 509–21 in *Consumer Dispute Resolution: Exploring the Alternatives,* edited by Larry Ray, Deborah Smolover and Prudence Kestner. Washington, DC: American Bar Association.

Shaw, D. L. and M. E. McCombs. 1977. *The Emergence of American Political Issues: The Agenda-Setting Function of the Press.* St. Paul, MN: West.

Simmel, Georg. 1968. *The Conflict in Modern Culture* (translated by K. Peter Etzkorn). New York: Teachers College Press.

Singer, Linda R. 1983. "Nonjudicial Dispute Resolution Mechanisms: The Effects on Justice for the Poor." Pp. 353–67 in *Consumer Dispute Resolution: Exploring the Alternatives,* edited by Larry Ray, Deborah Smolover and Prudence Kestner. Washington, DC: American Bar Association.

Snow, R. P.1983. *Creating Media Culture.* Newbury Park, CA: Sage.

Spector, Malcolm and John I. Kitsuse. 1973. "Social Problems." *Social Problems* 21:145–59.

Spector, Malcolm and John I. Kitsuse. 1977. *Constructing Social Problems.* Menlo Park CA: Cummings.

Spykman, Nicholas J. 1966. *The Social Theory of Georg Simmel.* New York: Atherton.

Stacey, Frank. 1978. *Ombudsmen Compared.* Oxford: Oxford University Press.

Stone, G. P. 1971. "American Sports: Play and Display." Pp. 46–65 in *The Sociology of Sports,* edited by E. Dunning. London: Frank Cass.

Streeter, Thomas. 1984. "An Alternative Approach to Television Research: Developments in British Cultural Studies at Birmingham." Pp. 74–97 in *Interpreting Television: Current Research Perspectives,* edited by Willard S. Rowland, Jr., Willard D., and Bruce Watkins. Beverly Hills, CA: Sage.

Sutton-Smith, Brian. 1986. *Toys and Culture.* New York: Gardner.

Surette, R. 1992. *Media, Crime and Criminal Justice: Images and Realities.* Pacific Grove, CA: Brooks/Cole.

Sutherland, Edwin H. 1950. "The Diffusion of Sexual Psychopath Laws." *American Journal of Sociology* 56:142–48.

Taylor, Philip M. 1992. *War and the Media: Propaganda and Persuasion in the Gulf War.* Manchester: Manchester University Press.

Thompson, Hunter S. 1971. *Fear and Loathing in Las Vegas: A Savage Journey to the Heart of the American Dream.* New York: Vintage.

Toffler, Alvin. 1990. *Powershift.* New York: Bantam.

Traber, Michael. 1986. *The Myth of the Information Revolution.* London: Sage.

Tuchman, G. 1978. *Making News: A Study in the Construction of Reality.* New York: Free Press.

U.S. Senate. 1982. "Exploited and Missing Children." Hearings before the Subcommittee on Juvenile Justice. 97th Congress, 2nd session, April 1.

U.S. Senate. 1986. *America's Missing Children.* Washington, DC: U.S. Department of Justice.

von Hoffman, Nicholas. 1985. "The Press: Pack of Fools. Killer Bees, Missing Kids, and Other Phoney Stories." *New Republic* 3681:9–11.

Weber, Max. 1963. *The Sociology of Religion* (translated by Ephraim Fischoff). Boston: Beacon.

Weeks, Kent M. 1978. *Ombudsmen Around the World: A Comparative Chart*, 2nd ed. Berkeley: University of California Press.

Wieland, Lawrence. 1988. "Justice Through Troubleshooting." Unpublished Master's Thesis, Arizona State University, Tempe.

Williams, Raymond. 1982. *The Sociology of Culture*. New York: Shocken.

Wolff, Kurt (ed.). 1950. *The Sociology of Georg Simmel*. New York: Free Press.

Woolgar, Steve and Dorothy Pawluch. 1985. "Ontological Gerrymandering: The Anatomy of Social Problems Explanations." *Social Problems* 32:214–27.

Zerubavel, Eviatar. 1981. *Hidden Rhythms*. Chicago, IL: University of Chicago Press.

Author Index

Subject Index _____